Franklin

From an engraving by J. Thomson from the
original picture by J. A. Duplessis

EDITED BY FRANK WOODWORTH PINE

THE AUTOBIOGRAPHY OF BENJAMIN FRANKLIN

THE STAR
GCP Co
SERIES

GARDEN CITY PUBLISHING CO., INC.
GARDEN CITY, NEW YORK

PRINTED IN THE UNITED STATES OF AMERICA

CONTENTS

INTRODUCTION

E Americans devour eagerly any piece of writing that purports to tell us the secret of success in life; yet how often we are disappointed to find nothing but commonplace statements, or receipts that we know by heart but never follow. Most of the life stories of our famous and successful men fail to inspire because they lack the human element that makes the record real and brings the story within our grasp. While we are searching far and near for some Aladdin's Lamp to give coveted fortune, there is ready at our hand if we will only reach out and take it, like the charm in Milton's *Comus,*

> "Unknown, and like esteemed, and the dull swain
> Treads on it daily with his clouted shoon;"

the interesting, human, and vividly told story of one of the wisest and most useful lives in our own history, and perhaps in any history. In Franklin's *Autobiography* is offered not so much a ready-made formula for success, as the companionship of a real flesh and blood man of extraordinary mind and quality, whose daily walk and conversation will help us to meet our own difficulties, much as does the example of a wise and strong friend. While we are fascinated by the story, we absorb the human experience through which a strong and helpful character is building.

The thing that makes Franklin's *Autobiography* different from every other life story of a great and successful man is just this human aspect of the account. Franklin told the story of his life, as he himself says, for the benefit of his posterity. He wanted to help them by the relation of his own rise from obscurity and poverty to eminence and wealth. He is not unmindful of the importance of his public services and their recognition, yet his accounts of these achievements are given only as a part of the story, and the vanity displayed is incidental and in keeping with the honesty of the recital. There is nothing of the impossible in the method and practice of Franklin as he sets them forth. The youth who reads the fascinating story is astonished to find that Franklin in his early years struggled with the same everyday passions and difficulties that he himself experiences, and he loses the sense of discouragement that comes from a realization of his own shortcomings and inability to attain.

There are other reasons why the *Autobiography* should be an intimate friend of American young people. Here they may establish a close relationship with one of the foremost Americans as well as one of the wisest men of his age.

The life of Benjamin Franklin is of importance to every American primarily because of the part he played in securing the independence of the United States and in establishing it as a nation. Franklin shares with Washington the honors of the Revolution, and of the events leading to the birth of the new nation. While Washington was the animating spirit of the struggle in the colonies, Franklin was its ablest champion abroad. To Franklin's cogent reasoning and keen satire, we owe the clear and forcible presentation of the American case in England and France; while to his personality and diplomacy as well as to his facile pen, we are indebted for the foreign alliance and the funds without which Washington's work must have failed. His patience, fortitude, and practical wisdom, coupled with self-sacrificing devotion to the cause of his country, are hardly less noticeable than similar qualities displayed by Washington. In fact, Franklin as a public man was much like Washington, especially in the entire disinterestedness of his public service.

Franklin is also interesting to us because by his life and teachings he has done more than any other American to advance the material prosperity of his countrymen. It is said that his widely and faithfully read maxims made Philadelphia and Pennsylvania wealthy, while Poor Richard's pithy sayings, translated into many languages, have had a world-wide influence.

Franklin is a good type of our American manhood. Although not the wealthiest or the most powerful, he is undoubtedly, in the versatility of his genius and achievements, the greatest of our self-made men. The simple yet graphic story in the *Autobiography* of his steady rise from humble boyhood in a tallow-chandler shop, by industry, economy, and perseverance in self-improvement, to eminence, is the most remarkable of all the remarkable histories of our self-made men. It is in itself a wonderful illustration of the results possible to be attained in a land of unequaled opportunity by following Franklin's maxims.

Franklin's fame, however, was not confined to his own country. Although he lived in a century notable for the rapid evolution of scientific and political thought and activity, yet no less a keen judge and critic than Lord Jeffrey, the famous editor of the *Edinburgh Review,* a century ago said that "in one point of view the name of Franklin must be considered as standing higher than any of the others which illustrated the eighteenth century. Distinguished as a statesman, he was equally great as a philosopher, thus uniting in himself a rare degree of excellence in both these pursuits, to excel in either of which is deemed the highest praise."

Franklin has indeed been aptly called "many-sided." He was eminent in science and public service, in diplomacy and in literature. He was the Edison of his day, turning his scientific discoveries to the benefit of his fellow-men. He perceived the identity of lightning and electricity and set up the lightning rod. He invented the Franklin stove, still widely used, and refused to patent it. He possessed a masterly shrewdness in business and practical affairs. Carlyle called him the father of all the Yankees. He founded a fire company, assisted in founding a hospital, and improved the cleaning and lighting of streets. He developed journalism, established the American Philosophical Society, the public library in Philadelphia, and the University of Pennsylvania. He organized a postal system for the colonies, which was the basis of the present United States Post Office. Bancroft, the eminent historian, called him " the greatest diplomatist of his century." He perfected the Albany Plan of Union for the colonies. He is the only statesman who signed the Declaration of Independence, the Treaty of Alliance with France, the Treaty of Peace with England, and the Constitution. As a writer, he has produced, in his *Autobiography* and in *Poor Richard's Almanac,* two works that are not surpassed by similar writing. He received honorary degrees from Harvard and Yale, from Oxford and St. Andrews, and was made a fellow of the Royal Society, which awarded him the Copley gold medal for improving natural knowledge. He was one of the eight foreign associates of the French Academy of Science.

The careful study of the *Autobiography* is also valuable because of the style in which it is written. If Robert Louis Stevenson is right in believing that his remarkable style was acquired by imitation then the youth who would gain the power to express his ideas clearly, forcibly, and interestingly cannot do better than to study Franklin's method. Franklin's fame in the scientific world was due almost as much to his modest, simple, and sincere manner of presenting his discoveries and to the precision and clearness of the style in which he described his experiments, as to the results he was able to announce. Sir Humphry Davy, the celebrated English chemist, himself an excellent literary critic as well as a great scientist, said: "A singular felicity guided all Franklin's researches, and by very small means he established very grand truths. The style and manner of his publication on electricity are almost as worthy of admiration as the doctrine it contains."

Franklin's place in literature is hard to determine because he was not primarily a literary man. His aim in his writings as in his life work was to be helpful to his fellow-men. For him writing was never an end in itself, but always a means to an end. Yet his success as a scientist, a statesman, and a diplomat, as well as socially, was in no little part due to his ability as a writer. "His letters charmed all, and made his correspondence eagerly sought. His political arguments were the joy of his party and the dread of his opponents. His scientific discoveries were explained in language at once so simple and so clear that plow-boy and exquisite could follow his thought or his experiment to its conclusion." [1]

As far as American literature is concerned, Franklin has no contemporaries. Before the *Autobiography* only one literary work of impor-

[1] *The Many-Sided Franklin.* Paul L. Ford.

tance had been produced in this country—Cotton Mather's *Magnalia,* a church history of New England in a ponderous, stiff style. Franklin was the first American author to gain a wide and permanent reputation in Europe. The *Autobiography, Poor Richard, Father Abraham's Speech* or *The Way to Wealth,* as well as some of the *Bagatelles,* are as widely known abroad as any American writings. Franklin must also be classed as the first American humorist.

English literature of the eighteenth century was characterized by the development of prose. Periodical literature reached its perfection early in the century in *The Tatler* and *The Spectator* of Addison and Steele. Pamphleteers flourished throughout the period. The homelier prose of Bunyan and Defoe gradually gave place to the more elegant and artificial language of Samuel Johnson, who set the standard for prose writing from 1745 onward. This century saw the beginnings of the modern novel, in Fielding's *Tom Jones,* Richardson's *Clarissa Harlowe,* Sterne's *Tristram Shandy,* and Goldsmith's *Vicar of Wakefield.* Gibbon wrote *The Decline and Fall of the Roman Empire,* Hume his *History of England,* and Adam Smith the *Wealth of Nations.*

In the simplicity and vigor of his style Franklin more nearly resembles the earlier group of

writers. In his first essays he was not an inferior imitator of Addison. In his numerous
parables, moral allegories, and apologues he
showed Bunyan's influence. But Franklin was
essentially a journalist. In his swift, terse style,
he is most like Defoe, who was the first great
English journalist and master of the newspaper
narrative. The style of both writers is marked
by homely, vigorous expression, satire, burlesque,
repartee. Here the comparison must end.
Defoe and his contemporaries were authors.
Their vocation was writing and their success
rests on the imaginative or creative power they
displayed. To authorship Franklin laid no
claim. He wrote no work of the imagination.
He developed only incidentally a style in many
respects as remarkable as that of his English
contemporaries. He wrote the best autobiography in existence, one of the most widely known
collections of maxims, and an unsurpassed
series of political and social satires, because he
was a man of unusual scope of power and usefulness, who knew how to tell his fellow-men the
secrets of that power and that usefulness.

The Story of the Autobiography

The account of how Franklin's *Autobiography*
came to be written and of the adventures of the

original manuscript forms in itself an interesting
story. The *Autobiography* is Franklin's longest
work, and yet it is only a fragment. The first
part, written as a letter to his son, William
Franklin, was not intended for publication; and
the composition is more informal and the narrative more personal than in the second part, from
1730 on, which was written with a view to publication. The entire manuscript shows little
evidence of revision. In fact, the expression is
so homely and natural that his grandson,
William Temple Franklin, in editing the work
changed some of the phrases because he thought
them inelegant and vulgar.

Franklin began the story of his life while on
a visit to his friend, Bishop Shipley, at Twyford,
in Hampshire, southern England, in 1771. He
took the manuscript, completed to 1731, with
him when he returned to Philadelphia in 1775.
It was left there with his other papers when he
went to France in the following year, and dis-
appeared during the confusion incident to the
Revolution. Twenty-three pages of closely
written manuscript fell into the hands of Abel
James, an old friend, who sent a copy to Franklin at Passy, near Paris, urging him to complete
the story. Franklin took up the work at Passy
in 1784 and carried the narrative forward a few

months. He changed the plan to meet his new purpose of writing to benefit the young reader. His work was soon interrupted and was not resumed until 1788, when he was at home in Philadelphia. He was now old, infirm, and suffering, and was still engaged in public service. Under these discouraging conditions the work progressed slowly. It finally stopped when the narrative reached the year 1757. Copies of the manuscript were sent to friends of Franklin in England and France, among others to Monsieur Le Veillard at Paris.

The first edition of the *Autobiography* was published in French at Paris in 1791. It was clumsily and carelessly translated, and was imperfect and unfinished. Where the translator got the manuscript is not known. Le Veillard disclaimed any knowledge of the publication. From this faulty French edition many others were printed, some in Germany, two in England, and another in France, so great was the demand for the work.

In the meantime the original manuscript of the *Autobiography* had started on a varied and adventurous career. It was left by Franklin with his other works to his grandson, William Temple Franklin, whom Franklin designated as his literary executor. When Temple Franklin came to publish his grandfather's works in 1817, he sent the original manuscript of the *Autobiography* to the daughter of Le Veillard in exchange for her father's copy, probably thinking the clearer transcript would make better printer's copy. The original manuscript thus found its way to the Le Veillard family and connections, where it remained until sold in 1867 to Mr. John Bigelow, United States Minister to France. By him it was later sold to Mr. E. Dwight Church of New York, and passed with the rest of Mr. Church's library into the possession of Mr. Henry E. Huntington. The original manuscript of Franklin's *Autobiography* now rests in the vault in Mr. Huntington's residence at Fifth Avenue and Fifty-seventh Street, New York City.

When Mr. Bigelow came to examine his purchase, he was astonished to find that what people had been reading for years as the authentic *Life of Benjamin Franklin by Himself,* was only a garbled and incomplete version of the real *Autobiography*. Temple Franklin had taken unwarranted liberties with the original. Mr. Bigelow says he found more than twelve hundred changes in the text. In 1868, therefore, Mr. Bigelow published the standard edition of Franklin's *Autobiography*. It corrected errors in the previous editions and was the first English edition to contain the short fourth part, comprising the last few pages of the manuscript, written during the last year of Franklin's life. Mr. Bigelow republished the *Autobiography,* with additional interesting matter, in three volumes in 1875, in 1905, and in 1910. The text in this volume is that of Mr. Bigelow's editions.[1]

The *Autobiography* has been reprinted in the United States many scores of times and translated into all the languages of Europe. It has never lost its popularity and is still in constant demand at circulating libraries. The reason for this popularity is not far to seek. For in this work Franklin told in a remarkable manner the story of a remarkable life. He displayed hard common sense and a practical knowledge of the art of living. He selected and arranged his material, perhaps unconsciously, with the unerring instinct of the journalist for the best effects. His success is not a little due to his plain, clear, vigorous English. He used short sentences and words, homely expressions, apt illustrations, and pointed allusions. Franklin had a most interesting, varied, and unusual life. He was one of the greatest conversationalists of his time.

[1] For the division into chapters and the chapter titles, however, the present editor is responsible.

His book is the record of that unusual life told in Franklin's own unexcelled conversational style. It is said that the best parts of Boswell's famous biography of Samuel Johnson are those parts where Boswell permits Johnson to tell his own story. In the *Autobiography* a no less remarkable man and talker than Samuel Johnson is telling his own story throughout.

F. W. P.

The Gilman Country School,
  Baltimore, September, 1916.

THE
Pennſylvania *GAZETTE*.

Containing the freſheſt Advices Foreign and Domeſtick.

From Thurſday, September 25. to Thurſday, October 2. 1729.

THE Pennſylvania Gazette *being now to be carry'd on by other Hands, the Reader may expect ſome Account of the Method we deſign to proceed in.*

Upon a View of Chambers's great Dictionaries, from whence were taken the Materials of the Univerſal Inſtructor *in all Arts and Sciences, which uſually made the Firſt Part of this Paper, we find that beſides their containing many Things abſtruſe or inſignificant to us, it will probably be fifty Years before the Whole can be gone thro' in this Manner of Publication. There are likewiſe in thoſe Books continual References from Things under one Letter of the Alphabet to thoſe under another, which relate to the ſame Subject, and are neceſſary to explain and compleat it ; theſe taken in their Turn may perhaps be Ten Years* ——— *deſire to acquaint themſelves with any particular Art or Science, would gladly have the whole before them in a much leſs Time, we believe our Readers will not think ſuch a Method of communicating Knowledge to be a proper One.*

However, tho' we do not intend to continue the Publication of thoſe Dictionaries in a regular Alphabetical Method, as has hitherto been done ; yet as ſeveral Things exhibited from them in the Courſe of theſe Papers, have been entertaining to ſuch of the Curious, who never had and cannot have the Advantage of good Libraries ; and as there are many Things ſtill behind, which being in this Manner made generally known, may perhaps become of conſiderable Uſe, by giving ſuch Hints to the excellent natural Genius's of our Country, as may contribute either to the Improvement of our preſent Manufactures, or towards the Invention of new Ones ; we propoſe from Time to Time to communicate ſuch particular Parts as appear to be of the moſt general Conſequence.

As to the Religious Courtſhip, Part of which has been retail'd to the Publick in theſe Papers, the Reader may be inform'd, that the whole Book will probably in a little Time be printed and bound up by it ſelf ; and thoſe who approve of it, will doubtleſs be better pleas'd to have it entire, than in this broken interrupted Manner.

There are many who have long deſired to ſee a good News-Paper in Pennſylvania ; and we hope thoſe Gentlemen who are able, will contribute towards the making This ſuch. We ask Aſſiſtance, becauſe we are fully ſenſible, that to publiſh a good News-Paper is not ſo eaſy an Undertaking as many People imagine it to be. The Author of a Gazette (in the Opinion of the Learned) ought to be qualified with an extenſive Acquaintance with Languages, a great Eaſineſs and Command of Writing and Relating Things cleanly and intelligibly, and in few Words ; he ſhould be able to ſpeak of War both by Land and Sea ; be well acquainted with Geography, with the Hiſtory of the Time, with the ſeveral Intereſts of Princes and States, the Secrets of Courts, and the Manners and Cuſtoms of all Nations. Men thus accompliſh'd are very rare in this remote Part of the World ; and it would be well if the Writer of theſe Papers could make up among his Friends what is wanting in himſelf.

Upon the Whole, we may aſſure the Publick, that as far as the Encouragement we meet with will enable us, no Care and Pains ſhall be omitted, that may make the Pennſylvania Gazette *as agreeable and uſeful an Entertainment as the Nature of the Thing will allow.*

The Following is the laſt Meſſage ſent by his Excellency Governour *Burnet,* to the Houſe of Repreſentatives in *Boſton.*

Gentlemen of the Houſe of Repreſentatives,

IT is not with ſo vain a Hope as to convince you, that I take the Trouble to anſwer your Meſſages, but, if poſſible, to open the Eyes of the deluded People whom you repreſent, and whom you are at ſo much Pains to keep in Ignorance of the true State of their Affairs. I need not go further for an undeniable Proof of this Endeavour to blind them, than your ordering the Letter of Meſſieurs *Wilks* and *Belcher* of the 7th of *June* laſt to your Speaker to be publiſhed. This Letter is ſaid (in *Page* 1. of your Votes) *to incloſe a Copy of the Report of the Lords of the Committee of His Majeſty's Privy Council, with his Majeſty's Approbation and Order thereon in Council* ; Yet theſe Gentlemen had at the ſame time the unparallell'd Preſumption to write to the Speaker in this Manner ; *You'll obſerve by the Concluſion, what is propoſed to be the Conſequence of your not complying with His Majeſty's Inſtruction (the whole Matter to be laid*

---

terfeited but those of 18 d. And it is remarkable that all Attempts of this Kind upon the Paper Money of this and the neighbouring Provinces, have been detected and met with ill Success.

Custom-House, Philadelphia, Entred Inwards.

Sloop Hope, Elias Naudain, from Boston.
Sloop Dove, John Howel, from Antigua.
Brigt Pennswood, Thomas Braly, from Madera.

Entred Outwards.

Scooner John, Thomas Wright, to Boston.
Brigt. Richard and William, W. Mayle, for Lisbon.
Ship Diligence, James Bayley, for Maryland

Cleared for Departure.

Ship London Hope, Thomas Annis, for London.
Ship John and Anna, James Sherley, for Plymouth.

Advertisements.

TO be Sold by *Edward Shippen*, choice Hard Soap, very Reasonable.

RUN away on the 25th of *September* past, from *Rice Prichard* of *Whiteland* in *Chester* County, a Servant Man named *John Cresswel*, of a middle Stature and ruddy Countenance, his Hair inclining to Red: He had on when he went away, a little white short Wig, an old Hat, Drugget Waftcoat, the Body lined with Linnen; coarse Linnen Breeches, grey woollen Stockings, and round toe'd Shoes
Whoever shall secure the said Servant so that his Master may have him again, shall have *Three Pounds* Reward, and reasonable Charges paid, by
Rice Prichard.

RUN away on the 10th of *September* past, from *William Dewees* of *Germantown* Township, in *Philadelphia* County, a Servant Man named *Mechtizedes Arnold*, of a middle Stature, and reddish curled Hair: He had on when he went away, a good Felt Hat, and dark Cinnamon-colour'd Coat, black Drugget Jacket, mouse-colour'd drugget Breeches, grey Stockings, and new Shoes.
Whoever secures the said Runaway, so that his Master may have him again, shall have *Twenty Shillings* Reward, and reasonable Charges paid, by me
William Dewees.

Lately Re-printed and Sold at the New Print-ing-Office near the Market.

THE *Psalms* of *David*, Imita-ted in the Language of the *New Testament*, and ap-ply'd to the Christian State and Worship. By I. *Watts*, V D M The Seventh Edition.

N. B. *This Work has met with such a general good Reception and Esteem among the Protestant Dissenters in Great Britain, &c. whether Presbyterians, Independents, or Baptists, that Six large Impressions before This have been sold off in a very short Time*
The chief Design of this excellent Performance (as the Author
" *acquaints us in his Advertisement to the Reader) is* " *to im-*
" *prove Psalmody or Religious Singing, and to encourage and*
" *assist the frequent Practice of it in publick Assemblies and pri-*
" *vate Families with more Honour and Delight ; yet the*
" *Reading of it may also entertain the Parlour and the Closet*
" *with devout Pleasure and holy Meditations Therefore he would*
" *request his Readers, at proper Seasons, to peruse it thro', and*
" *among* 340 *sacred Hymns they may find out several that suit*
" *their own Case and Temper, or the Circumstances of their Fa-*
" *milies or Friends, they may teach their Children such as are*
" *proper for their Age, and by treasuring them in their Memory*
" *they may be furnish'd for pious Retirement, or may entertain*
" *their Friends with holy Melody.*

AUTOBIOGRAPHY
OF
BENJAMIN FRANKLIN

I

ANCESTRY AND EARLY YOUTH IN BOSTON

TWYFORD,[1] *at the Bishop of St. Asaph's,* 1771.

DEAR SON: I have ever had pleasure in obtaining any little anecdotes of my ancestors. You may remember the inquiries I made among the remains of my relations when you were with me in England, and the journey I undertook for that purpose. Imagining it may be equally agreeable to you to know the circumstances of my life, many of which you are yet unacquainted with, and expecting the enjoyment of a week's uninterrupted leisure in my present country retirement, I sit down to write them for you. To which I have besides some other inducements. Having emerged from the pov-

---

[1] A small village not far from Winchester in Hampshire, southern England. Here was the country seat of the Bishop of St. Asaph, Dr. Jonathan Shipley, the "good Bishop," as Dr. Franklin used to style him. Their relations were intimate and confidential. In his pulpit, and in the House of Lords, as well as in society, the bishop always opposed the harsh measures of the Crown toward the Colonies.—Bigelow.

erty and obscurity in which I was born and bred, to a state of affluence and some degree of reputation in the world, and having gone so far through life with a considerable share of felicity, the conducing means I made use of, which with the blessing of God so well succeeded, my posterity may like to know, as they may find some of them suitable to their own situations, and therefore fit to be imitated.

That felicity, when I reflected on it, has induced me sometimes to say, that were it offered to my choice, I should have no objection to a repetition of the same life from its beginning, only asking the advantages authors have in a second edition to correct some faults of the first. So I might, besides correcting the faults, change some sinister accidents and events of it for others more favourable. But though this were denied, I should still accept the offer. Since such a repetition is not to be expected, the next thing most like living one's life over again seems to be a recollection of that life, and to make that recollection as durable as possible by putting it down in writing.

Hereby, too, I shall indulge the inclination so natural in old men, to be talking of themselves and their own past actions; and I shall indulge it without being tiresome to others,

who, through respect to age, might conceive
themselves obliged to give me a hearing, since
this may be read or not as anyone pleases. And,
lastly (I may as well confess it, since my denial
of it will be believed by nobody), perhaps I
shall a good deal gratify my own *vanity*.[1] Indeed, I scarce ever heard or saw the introduc-
tory words, "*Without vanity I may say*," etc.,
but some vain thing immediately followed.
Most people dislike vanity in others, whatever
share they have of it themselves; but I give it
fair quarter wherever I meet with it, being persuaded that it is often productive of good to the
possessor, and to others that are within his
sphere of action; and therefore, in many cases,
it would not be altogether absurd if a man were
to thank God for his vanity among the other
comforts of life.

And now I speak of thanking God, I desire
with all humility to acknowledge that I owe the
mentioned happiness of my past life to IIis kind
providence, which lead me to the means I used

[1] In this connection Woodrow Wilson says, "And yet the surprising and delightful thing about this book (the *Autobiography*)
is that, take it all in all, it has not the low tone of conceit,
but is a staunch man's sober and unaffected assessment of himself and the circumstances of his career."

Gibbon and Hume, the great British historians, who were
contemporaries of Franklin, express in their autobiographies the
same feeling about the propriety of just self-praise.

and gave them success. My belief of this in-
duces me to *hope,* though I must not *presume,*
that the same goodness will still be exercised
toward me, in continuing that happiness, or
enabling me to bear a fatal reverse, which I may
experience as others have done; the complexion
of my future fortune being known to Him only
in whose power it is to bless to us even our
afflictions.

The notes one of my uncles (who had the
same kind of curiosity in collecting family anecdotes) once put into my hands, furnished me
with several particulars relating to our ancestors. From these notes I learned that the family had lived in the same village, Ecton, in
Northamptonshire,[1] for three hundred years, and
how much longer he knew not (perhaps from the
time when the name of Franklin, that before
was the name of an order of people,[2] was assumed by them as a surname when others took
surnames all over the kingdom), on a freehold
of about thirty acres, aided by the smith's business, which had continued in the family till his
time, the eldest son being always bred to that
business; a custom which he and my father
followed as to their eldest sons. When I
searched the registers at Ecton, I found an ac-

---

[1] See *Introduction.*   [2] A small landowner.

count of their births, marriages and burials from
the year 1555 only, there being no registers kept
in that parish at any time preceding. By that
register I perceived that I was the youngest son
of the youngest son for five generations back.
My grandfather Thomas, who was born in 1598,
lived at Ecton till he grew too old to follow
business longer, when he went to live with his
son John, a dyer at Banbury, in Oxfordshire,
with whom my father served an apprenticeship.
There my grandfather died and lies buried. We
saw his gravestone in 1758. His eldest son
Thomas lived in the house at Ecton, and left it
with the land to his only child, a daughter, who,
with her husband, one Fisher, of Welling-
borough, sold it to Mr. Isted, now lord of the
manor there. My grandfather had four sons
that grew up, viz.: Thomas, John, Benjamin and
Josiah. I will give you what account I can of
them at this distance from my papers, and if
these are not lost in my absence, you will among
them find many more particulars.

Thomas was bred a smith under his father;
but, being ingenious, and encouraged in learning (as all my brothers were) by an Esquire
Palmer, then the principal gentleman in that
parish, he qualified himself for the business of
scrivener; became a considerable man in the

county; was a chief mover of all public-spirited
undertakings for the county or town of North-
ampton, and his own village, of which many
instances were related of him; and much taken
notice of and patronized by the then Lord Halifax. He died in 1702, January 6, old style,[1] just
four years to a day before I was born. The
account we received of his life and character
from some old people at Ecton, I remember,
struck you as something extraordinary, from
its similarity to what you knew of mine. "Had
he died on the same day," you said, "one might
have supposed a transmigration."

John was bred a dyer, I believe of woollens,
Benjamin was bred a silk dyer, serving an apprenticeship at London. He was an ingenious
man. I remember him well, for when I was a
boy he came over to my father in Boston, and
lived in the house with us some years. He lived

---

[1] January 17, new style. This change in the calendar was
made in 1582 by Pope Gregory XIII, and adopted in England in
1752. Every year whose number in the common reckoning since
Christ is not divisible by 4, as well as every year whose number is divisible by 100 but not by 400, shall have 365 days, and
all other years shall have 366 days. In the eighteenth century
there was a difference of eleven days between the old and the
new style of reckoning, which the English Parliament canceled
by making the 3rd of September, 1752, the 14th. The Julian
calendar, or "old style," is still retained in Russia and Greece,
whose dates consequently are now 13 days behind those of other
Christian countries.

to a great age. His grandson, Samuel Franklin, now lives in Boston. He left behind him two quarto volumes, MS., of his own poetry, consisting of little occasional pieces addressed to his friends and relations, of which the following, sent to me, is a specimen.[1] He had formed a short-hand of his own, which he taught me, but, never practising it, I have now forgot it. I was named after this uncle, there being a particular affection between him and my father. He was very pious, a great attender of sermons of the best preachers, which he took down in his short-hand, and had with him many volumes of them. He was also much of a politician; too much, perhaps, for his station. There fell lately into my hands, in London, a collection he had made of all the principal pamphlets relating to public affairs, from 1641 to 1717; many of the volumes are wanting as appears by the numbering, but there still remain eight volumes in folio, and twenty-four in quarto and in octavo. A dealer in old books met with them, and knowing me by my sometimes buying of him, he brought them to me. It seems my uncle must have left them here when he went to America, which was about fifty years since. There are many of his notes in the margins.

[1] The specimen is not in the manuscript of the *Autobiography*.

This obscure family of ours was early in the Reformation, and continued Protestants through the reign of Queen Mary, when they were sometimes in danger of trouble on account of their zeal against popery. They had got an English Bible, and to conceal and secure it, it was fastened open with tapes under and within the cover of a joint-stool. When my great-great-grandfather read it to his family, he turned up the joint-stool upon his knees, turning over the leaves then under the tapes. One of the children stood at the door to give notice if he saw the apparitor coming, who was an officer of the spiritual court. In that case the stool was turned down again upon its feet, when the Bible remained concealed under it as before. This anecdote I had from my uncle Benjamin. The family continued all of the Church of England till about the end of Charles the Second's reign, when some of the ministers that had been outed for non-conformity, holding conventicles [1] in Northamptonshire, Benjamin and Josiah adhered to them, and so continued all their lives: the rest of the family remained with the Episcopal Church.

Josiah, my father, married young, and carried his wife with three children into New England,

[1] Secret gatherings of dissenters from the established Church.

about 1682. The conventicles having been forbidden by law, and frequently disturbed, induced some considerable men of his acquaintance to remove to that country, and he was prevailed with to accompany them thither, where they expected to enjoy their mode of religion with freedom. By the same wife he had four children more born there, and by a second

Birthplace of Franklin, Milk Street, Boston

wife ten more, in all seventeen; of which I remember thirteen sitting at one time at his table, who all grew up to be men and women, and married; I was the youngest son, and the youngest child but two, and was born in Boston, New England.[1] My mother, the second

[1] Franklin was born on Sunday, January 6, old style, 1706, in a house on Milk Street, opposite the Old South Meeting House, where he was baptized on the day of his birth, during a snowstorm. The house where he was born was burned in 1810.—Griffin.

wife, was Abiah Folger, daughter of Peter Folger, one of the first settlers of New England,
of whom honorable mention is made by Cotton Mather,[1] in his church history of that
country, entitled *Magnalia Christi Americana,*
as *"a godly, learned Englishman,"* if I remember the words rightly.   I have heard that he
wrote sundry small occasional pieces, but only
one of them was printed, which I saw now many
years since.   It was written in 1675, in the
home-spun verse of that time and people, and
addressed to those then concerned in the government there.   It was in favour of liberty of
conscience, and in behalf of the Baptists, Quakers, and other sectaries that had been under
persecution, ascribing the Indian wars, and
other distresses that had befallen the country,
to that persecution, as so many judgments of
God to punish so heinous an offense, and ex-
horting a repeal of those uncharitable laws.
The whole appeared to me as written with a good
deal of decent plainness and manly freedom.   The
six concluding lines I remember, though I have
forgotten the two first of the stanza; but the
purport of them was, that his censures pro-

---

[1] Cotton Mather (1663-1728), clergyman, author, and scholar.
Pastor of the North Church, Boston.   He took an active part
in the persecution of witchcraft.

ceeded from good-will, and, therefore, he would
be known to be the author.

> " Because to be a libeller (says he)
>   I hate it with my heart;
> From Sherburne town,[1] where now I dwell
>   My name I do put here;
> Without offense your real friend,
>   It is Peter Folgier."

My elder brothers were all put apprentices
to different trades. I was put to the grammar-
school at eight years of age, my father intending to devote me, as the tithe[2] of his sons, to
the service of the Church. My early readiness
in learning to read (which must have been very
early, as I do not remember when I could not
read), and the opinion of all his friends, that
I should certainly make a good scholar, encouraged him in this purpose of his. My uncle
Benjamin, too, approved of it, and proposed to
give me all his short-hand volumes of sermons,
I suppose as a stock to set up with, if I would
learn his character.[3] I continued, however, at
the grammar-school not quite one year, though
in that time I had risen gradually from the
middle of the class of that year to be the head
of it, and farther was removed into the next
class above it, in order to go with that into

[1] Nantucket.   [2] Tenth.   [3] System of shorthand.

the third at the end of the year. But my father, in the meantime, from a view of the expense of a college education, which having so large a family he could not well afford, and the mean living many so educated were afterwards able to obtain—reasons that he gave to his friends in my hearing—altered his first intention, took me from the grammar-school, and sent me to a school for writing and arithmetic, kept by a then famous man, Mr. George Brownell, very successful in his profession generally, and that by mild, encouraging methods. Under him I acquired fair writing pretty soon, but I failed in the arithmetic, and made no progress in it. At ten years old I was taken home to assist my father in his business, which was that of a tallow-chandler and sope-boiler; a business he was not bred to, but had assumed on his arrival in New England, and on finding his dyeing trade would not maintain his family, being in little request. Accordingly, I was employed in cutting wick for the candles, filling the dipping mould and the moulds for cast candles, attending the shop, going of errands, etc.

I disliked the trade, and had a strong inclination for the sea, but my father declared against it; however, living near the water, I was much in and about it, learnt early to swim well, and to manage boats; and when in a boat or canoe with other boys, I was commonly allowed to govern, especially in any case of difficulty; and upon other occasions I was generally a leader among the boys, and sometimes led them into scrapes, of which I will mention one instance, as it shows an early projecting public spirit, tho' not then justly conducted.

There was a salt-marsh that bounded part of the mill-pond, on the edge of which, at high water, we used to stand to fish for minnows. By much trampling, we had made it a mere quagmire. My proposal was to build a wharf there fit for us to stand upon, and I showed my comrades a large heap of stones, which were intended for a new house near the marsh, and which would very well suit our purpose. Accordingly, in the evening, when the workmen were gone, I assembled a number of my play-fellows, and working with them diligently like so many emmets, sometimes two or three to a stone, we brought them all away and built our little wharf. The next morning the workmen were surprised at missing the stones, which were found in our wharf. Inquiry was made after the removers; we were discovered and complained of; several of us were corrected by our fathers; and, though I pleaded the usefulness of the work, mine convinced me that nothing was useful which was not honest.

I think you may like to know something of his person and character. He had an excellent constitution of body, was of middle stature, but well set, and very strong; he was ingenious, could draw prettily, was skilled a little in music, and had a clear, pleasing voice, so that when he played psalm tunes on his violin and sung withal, as he sometimes did in an evening after the business of the day was over, it was extremely agreeable to hear. He had a mechanical genius too, and, on occasion, was very handy in the use of other tradesmen's tools; but his great excellence lay in a sound understanding and solid judgment in prudential matters, both in private and publick affairs. In the latter, indeed, he was never employed, the numerous family he had to educate and the straitness of his circumstances keeping him close to his trade; but I remember well his being frequently visited by leading people, who consulted him for his opinion in affairs of the town or of the church he belonged to, and showed a good deal of respect for his judgment and advice: he was also much consulted by private persons about their affairs when any difficulty occurred, and frequently chosen an arbitrator between contending parties. At his table he liked to have, as often as he could, some sensible friend or neighbor to converse with, and always took care to start some ingenious or useful topic for discourse, which might tend to improve the minds of his children. By this means he turned our attention to what was good, just, and prudent in the conduct of life; and little or no notice was ever taken of what related to the victuals on the table, whether it was well or ill dressed, in or out of season, of good or bad flavor, preferable or inferior to this or that other thing of the kind, so that I was bro't up in such a perfect inattention to those matters as to be quite indifferent what kind of food was set before me, and so unobservant of it, that to this day if I am asked I can scarce tell a few hours after dinner what I dined upon. This has been a convenience to me in traveling, where my companions have been sometimes very unhappy for want of a suitable gratification of their more delicate, because better instructed, tastes and appetites.

My mother had likewise an excellent constitution: she suckled all her ten children. I never knew either my father or mother to have any sickness but that of which they dy'd, he at 89, and she at 85 years of age. They lie buried together at Boston, where I some years since placed a marble over their grave,[1] with this inscription:

JOSIAH FRANKLIN,
and
ABIAH his wife,
lie here interred.
They lived lovingly together in wedlock
fifty-five years.
Without an estate, or any gainful employment,
By constant labor and industry,
with God's blessing,
They maintained a large family
comfortably,
and brought up thirteen children
and seven grandchildren
reputably.
From this instance, reader,
Be encouraged to diligence in thy calling,
And distrust not Providence.
He was a pious and prudent man;
She, a discreet and virtuous woman.
Their youngest son,
In filial regard to their memory,
Places this stone.
J. F. born 1655, died 1744, Ætat 89.
A. F. born 1667, died 1752, —— 85.

By my rambling digressions I perceive myself to be grown old. I us'd to write more me-

[1] This marble having decayed, the citizens of Boston in 1827, erected in its place a granite obelisk, twenty-one feet high, bearing the original inscription quoted in the text and another explaining the erection of the monument.

thodically. But one does not dress for private company as for a publick ball. 'Tis perhaps only negligence.

To return: I continued thus employed in my father's business for two years, that is, till I was twelve years old; and my brother John, who was bred to that business, having left my father, married, and set up for himself at Rhode Island, there was all appearance that I was destined to supply his place, and become a tallow-chandler. But my dislike to the trade continuing, my father was under apprehensions that if he did not find one for me more agreeable, I should break away and get to sea, as his son Josiah had done, to his great vexation. He therefore sometimes took me to walk with him, and see joiners, bricklayers, turners, braziers, etc., at their work, that he might observe my inclination, and endeavor to fix it on some trade or other on land. It has ever since been a pleasure to me to see good workmen handle their tools; and it has been useful to me, having learnt so much by it as to be able to do little jobs myself in my house when a workman could not readily be got, and to construct little machines for my experiments, while the intention of making the experiment was fresh and warm in my mind. My father at last fixed upon the cutler's trade, and my uncle Benjamin's son Samuel, who was bred to that business in London, being about that time established in Boston, I was sent to be with him some time on liking. But his expectations of a fee with me displeasing my father, I was taken home again.

II

BEGINNING LIFE AS A PRINTER

ROM a child I was fond of reading, and all the little money that came into my hands was ever laid out in books. Pleased with the *Pilgrim's Progress,* my first collection was of John Bunyan's works in separate little volumes. I afterward sold them to enable me to buy R. Burton's *Historical Collections;* they were small chapmen's books,[1] and cheap, 40 or 50 in all. My father's little library consisted chiefly of books in polemic divinity, most of which I read, and have since often regretted that, at a time when I had such a thirst for knowledge, more proper books had not fallen in my way, since it was now resolved I should not be a clergyman. Plutarch's *Lives* there was in which I read abundantly, and I still think that time spent to great advantage. There was also a book of DeFoe's, called an *Essay on Projects,* and another of Dr. Mather's, called *Essays to do Good,* which perhaps gave me

[1] Small books, sold by chapmen or peddlers.

a turn of thinking that had an influence on some
of the principal future events of my life.

This bookish inclination at length determined
my father to make me a printer, though he had
already one son (James) of that profession. In
1717 my brother James returned from England
with a press and letters to set up his business in
Boston. I liked it much better than that of my
father, but still had a hankering for the sea. To
prevent the apprehended effect of such an inclination, my father was impatient to have me
bound to my brother. I stood out some time, but
at last was persuaded, and signed the indentures
when I was yet but twelve years old. I was to
serve as an apprentice till I was twenty-one
years of age, only I was to be allowed journeyman's wages during the last year. In a little time
I made great proficiency in the business, and
became a useful hand to my brother. I now had
access to better books. An acquaintance with
the apprentices of booksellers enabled me sometimes to borrow a small one, which I was careful to return soon and clean. Often I sat up in
my room reading the greatest part of the night,
when the book was borrowed in the evening and
to be returned early in the morning, lest it should
be missed or wanted.

And after some time an ingenious tradesman,

Mr. Matthew Adams, who had a pretty collection of books, and who frequented our printing-house, took notice of me, invited me to his library, and very kindly lent me such books as I chose to read. I now took a fancy to poetry, and made some little pieces; my brother, thinking it might turn to account, encouraged me, and put me on composing occasional ballads. One was called *The Lighthouse Tragedy,* and contained an account of the drowning of Captain Worthilake, with his two daughters: the other was a sailor's song, on the taking of *Teach* (or Blackbeard) the pirate. They were wretched stuff, in the Grub-street-ballad style;[1] and when they were printed he sent me about the town to sell them. The first sold wonderfully, the event being recent, having made a great noise. This flattered my vanity; but my father discouraged me by ridiculing my performances, and telling me verse-makers were generally beggars. So I escaped being a poet, most probably a very bad one; but as prose writing has been of great use to me in the course of my life, and was a principal means of my advancement, I shall tell you how, in such a situation, I acquired what little ability I have in that way.

[1] Grub-street: famous in English literature as the home of poor writers.

There was another bookish lad in the town, John Collins by name, with whom I was intimately acquainted. We sometimes disputed, and very fond we were of argument, and very desirous of confuting one another, which disputatious turn, by the way, is apt to become a very bad habit, making people often extremely disagreeable in company by the contradiction that is necessary to bring it into practice; and thence, besides souring and spoiling the conversation, is productive of disgusts and, perhaps enmities where you may have occasion for friendship. I had caught it by reading my father's books of dispute about religion. Persons of good sense, I have since observed, seldom fall into it, except lawyers, university men, and men of all sorts that have been bred at Edinborough.

A question was once, somehow or other, started between Collins and me, of the propriety of educating the female sex in learning, and their abilities for study. He was of opinion that it was improper, and that they were naturally unequal to it. I took the contrary side, perhaps a little for dispute's sake. He was naturally more eloquent, had a ready plenty of words, and sometimes, as I thought, bore me down more by his fluency than by the strength of his reasons. As we parted without settling the point, and were not to see one another again for some time, I sat down to put my arguments in writing, which I copied fair and sent to him. He answered, and I replied. Three or four letters of a side had passed, when my father happened to find my papers and read them. Without entering into the discussion, he took occasion to talk to me about the manner of my writing; observed that, though I had the advantage of my antagonist in correct spelling and pointing (which I ow'd to the printing-house), I fell far short in elegance of expression, in method and in perspicuity, of which he convinced me by several instances. I saw the justice of his remarks, and thence grew more attentive to the manner in writing, and determined to endeavor at improvement.

About this time I met with an odd volume of the *Spectator*.[1] It was the third. I had never before seen any of them. I bought it, read it over and over, and was much delighted with it. I thought the writing excellent, and wished, if possible, to imitate it. With this view I took some of the papers, and, making short hints

[1] A daily London journal, comprising satirical essays on social subjects, published by Addison and Steele in 1711-1712. The *Spectator* and its predecessor, the *Tatler* (1709), marked the beginning of periodical literature.

of the sentiment in each sentence, laid them by a few days, and then, without looking at the book, try'd to compleat the papers again, by expressing each hinted sentiment at length, and as fully as it had been expressed before, in any suitable words that should come to hand. Then I compared my *Spectator* with the original, discovered some of my faults, and corrected them. But I found I wanted a stock of words, or a readiness in recollecting and using them, which I thought I should have acquired before that time if I had gone on making verses; since the continual occasion for words of the same import, but of different length, to suit the measure, or of different sound for the rhyme, would have laid me under a constant necessity of searching for variety, and also have tended to fix that variety in my mind, and make me master of it. Therefore I took some of the tales and turned them into verse; and, after a time, when I had pretty well forgotten the prose, turned them back again. I also sometimes jumbled my collections of hints into confusion, and after some weeks endeavored to reduce them into the best order, before I began to form the full sentences and compleat the paper. This was to teach me method in the arrangement of thoughts. By comparing my work afterwards with the original, I discovered many faults and amended them; but I some. times had the pleasure of fancying that, in certain particulars of small import, I had been lucky enough to improve the method of the language, and this encouraged me to think I might possibly in time come to be a tolerable English writer, of which I was extremely ambitious. My time for these exercises and for reading was at night, after work or before it began in the morning, or on Sundays, when I contrived to be in the printing-house alone, evading as much as I could the common attendance on public worship which my father used to exact of me when I was under his care, and which indeed I still thought a duty, thought I could not, as it seemed to me, afford time to practise it.

When about 16 years of age I happened to meet with a book, written by one Tryon, recommending a vegetable diet. I determined to go into it. My brother, being yet unmarried, did not keep house, but boarded himself and his apprentices in another family. My refusing to eat flesh occasioned an inconveniency, and I was frequently chid for my singularity. I made myself acquainted with Tryon's manner of preparing some of his dishes, such as boiling potatoes or rice, making hasty pudding, and a few others, and then proposed to my brother, that if he would give me, weekly, half the money he paid for my board, I would board myself. He instantly agreed to it, and I presently found that I could save half what he paid me. This was an additional fund for buying books. But I had another advantage in it. My brother and the rest going from the printing-house to their meals, I remained there alone, and, dispatching presently my light repast, which often was no more than a bisket or a slice of bread, a handful of raisins or a tart from the pastry-cook's, and a glass of water, had the rest of the time till their return for study, in which I made the greater progress, from that greater clearness of head and quicker apprehension which usually attend temperance in eating and drinking.

And now it was that, being on some occasion made asham'd of my ignorance in figures, which I had twice failed in learning when at school, I took Cocker's book of Arithmetick, and went through the whole by myself with great ease. I also read Seller's and Shermy's books of Navigation, and became acquainted with the little geometry they contain; but never proceeded far in that science. And I read about this time Locke *On Human Understanding*,[1] and the *Art of Thinking*, by Messrs. du Port Royal.[2]

While I was intent on improving my language, I met with an English grammar (I think it was Greenwood's), at the end of which there were two little sketches of the arts of rhetoric and logic, the latter finishing with a specimen of a dispute in the Socratic[3] method; and soon after I procur'd Xenophon's Memorable Things of Socrates, wherein there are many instances of the same method. I was charm'd with it, adopted it, dropt my abrupt contradiction and positive argumentation, and put on the humble inquirer and doubter. And being then, from reading Shaftesbury and Collins, become a real doubter in many points of our religious doctrine, I found this method safest for myself and very embarrassing to those against whom I used it; therefore I took a delight in it, practis'd it continually, and grew

[1] John Locke (1632-1704), a celebrated English philosopher, founder of the so-called "common-sense" school of philosophers. He drew up a constitution for the colonists of Carolina.

[2] A noted society of scholarly and devout men occupying the abbey of Port Royal near Paris, who published learned works, among them the one here referred to, better known as the *Port Royal Logic*.

[3] Socrates confuted his opponents in argument by asking questions so skillfully devised that the answers would confirm the questioner's position or show the error of the opponent.

very artful and expert in drawing people, even
of superior knowledge, into concessions, the
consequences of which they did not foresee,
entangling them in difficulties out of which they
could not extricate themselves, and so obtaining victories that neither myself nor my cause
always deserved. I continu'd this method some
few years, but gradually left it, retaining only
the habit of expressing myself in terms of
modest diffidence; never using, when I advanced anything that may possibly be disputed,
the words *certainly, undoubtedly,* or any others
that give the air of positiveness to an opinion;
but rather say, I conceive or apprehend a thing
to be so and so; it appears to me, or *I should
think it so or so,* for such and such reasons;
or *I imagine it to be so;* or *it is so, if I am not
mistaken.* This habit, I believe, has been of
great advantage to me when I have had occasion to inculcate my opinions, and persuade
men into measures that I have been from time
to time engaged in promoting; and, as the chief
ends of conversation are to *inform* or to be
informed, to *please* or to *persuade,* I wish well-
meaning, sensible men would not lessen their
power of doing good by a positive, assuming
manner, that seldom fails to disgust, tends to
create opposition, and to defeat everyone of

those purposes for which speech was given to us, to wit, giving or receiving information or pleasure. For, if you would inform, a positive and dogmatical manner in advancing your sentiments may provoke contradiction and prevent a candid attention. If you wish information and improvement from the knowledge of others, and yet at the same time express yourself as firmly fix'd in your present opinions, modest, sensible men, who do not love disputation, will probably leave you undisturbed in the possession of your error. And by such a manner, you can seldom hope to recommend yourself in *pleasing* your hearers, or to persuade those whose concurrence you desire. Pope [1] says, judiciously:

> "*Men should be taught as if you taught them not,*
> *And things unknown propos'd as things forgot;*"

farther recommending to us

> "To speak, tho' sure, with seeming diffidence."

And he might have coupled with this line that which he has coupled with another, I think, less properly,

> "For want of modesty is want of sense."

If you ask, Why less properly? I must repeat the lines,

[1] Alexander Pope (1688-1744). the greatest English poet of the first half of the eighteenth century.

"Immodest words admit of no defense,
For want of modesty is want of sense."

Now, is not *want of sense* (where a man is so
unfortunate as to want it) some apology for his
want of modesty? and would not the lines stand
more justly thus?

"Immodest words admit *but* this defense,
That want of modesty is want of sense."

This, however, I should submit to better judgments.

My brother had, in 1720 or 1721, begun to
print a newspaper. It was the second that
appeared in America,[1] and was called the New
England Courant. The only one before it was
the Boston News-Letter. I remember his being dissuaded by some of his friends from the
undertaking, as not likely to succeed, one newspaper being, in their judgment, enough for
America. At this time (1771) there are not less
than five-and-twenty. He went on, however,
with the undertaking, and after having worked
in composing the types and printing off the

[1] Franklin's memory does not serve him correctly here. The
Courant was really the fifth newspaper established in America,
although generally called the fourth, because the first, *Public Oc-
currences,* published in Boston in 1690, was suppressed after the
first issue. Following is the order in which the other four
papers were published: *Boston News Letter,* 1704; *Boston Gazette,* December 21, 1719; *The American Weekly Mercury,* Philadelphia, December 22, 1719; *The New England Courant,* 1721.

THE
New-England Courant.

From M O N D A Y December 4. to M O N D A Y December 11. 1 7 2 1.

On SYLVIA *the Fair.* A Jingle.

A Swarm of Sparks, young, gay, and bold,
  Lov'd *Sylvia* long. but she was cold ;
In'treit and Pride the Nymph control'd,
So they in vain their Paſſion told.
At laſt came Dalman, he was old,
Nay, he was ugly, but had Gold.
He came, and ſaw, and took the Hold,
While t'other Beaux their Loſs Condol'd.
Some ſay, ſhe's Wed ; I ſay, ſhe's ſold.

The Letter againſt Inoculating the Small Pox, (Sign'd
Abſinthium) giving an Account of the Number of
Perſons who have dy'd under that Operation, will be
Inſerted in our next.

FOREIGN AFFAIRS.

Iſpahan, March 6. The Conſpiracy form'd by the
Grand Vizir laſt January was Twelvemonth, with deſign to make himſelf King of Perſia, was ſeaſonably
diſcover'd, and himſelf and Accomplices ſecured ; ſince
which the State hath enjoy'd its former Tranquility,
and a new Vizir is appointed in his room, The old
one's Eyes being both put out, he is kept alive (but
in Priſon) to make him diſcover all his Riches ;
which muſt be immenſely great, ſince they found in
one of his Cheſts four hundred thouſand Perſian Du-
cats, beſide Foreign Coin, and in another Place abun-
dance of Jewels, Gold and Silver ; and ſo in proportion among ſeveral of his Accomplices ; by the help of
which Treaſure they hoped to compaſs their Ends.
Tripoli, July 12. As ſoon as our Squadron fitted out
againſt the famous Baſſaw Gianur. Cogia, appear'd off
Darna and Bengan, with two thouſand five hundred
Mooriſh Horſe, and a thouſand Foot, and skirmiſh'p
a little with his Squadron, he abandon'd both thoſe
Places, and fled to the Iſland of Serby in the Territo-
ries of Tunis : But the Bey of that Place having deny'd him Shelter, he ſail'd farther away, in a French
Barque, we know not whether ; and his own Galleys
and Barques, are gone after him, ſo that we are now
entirely rid of that troubleſome Gueſt. Our Rovers
keep all in Port, for fear of the Malteze.
Cadiz, Aug. 12. The Flota is expected Home from
the Weſt-Indies before the End of this Month.
Thirteen Pieces of Cannon and two Mortars were lately ſent from hence to Ceuta. The three Spaniſh Men
of War of 50 to 60 Guns each, which carried the Spaniſh Cardinals to Italy, are now at Alicant : It is ſaid
they are to join the Dutch Vice-Admiral, who is now
in this Bay with four Ships of his Squadron of 50
Guns each, and cruize againſt the Algerines. Wheat
and Parley being very cheap in theſe Parts, great
Quantities have been ſent lately to the Canaries,
where for ſome Time paſt the Inhabitants have been
in great Want of Corn. On the 9th Inſtant died Mr.
Charles, His Britannick Majeſty's Conſul at St.
Lucar.
Ferne, Aug. 20. The Deputies of this Canton who
went to the Diet at Frawenfeldt, are now aſſembled
at Baden with thoſe of Zurich and Glaris, to regulate
certain Affairs relating to the Town and Country of
Baden, which formerly belonged to the Eight Eldeſt

Cantons, but in the laſt Swiſs War was given up to
Zurich and Berne in Propriety, with a Reſervation to
the Canton of Glaris (which is moſtly Proteſtant) of
the Share it had berore in the Sovereignty of that
Diſtrict. The three Deputies of Zurich, Lucern &
Ury, who were commiſſioned by the late General Dyet
to go to Wilchingen, to try to compoſe the Differences which have been long ſtanding between the Inhabitants of that Place and the Canton of Schafhuy-
ſen whoſe Subjects they are, have offered thoſe Inhabitants a full Pardon for all paſt Miſbehaviour, and
the Maintenance of their Priviledges for the future,
provided they forthwith return to their Duty ; but
it is adviſed that thoſe of Wilchingen perſiſt hitherto
in their Diſobedience.
Schaffhauſen Sept. 1. They write from Italy, that
the Plague is no longer obſerv'd at Marſeilles, Aix, &
ſeveral other Places ; and that at Toulon it is very
much decreas'd : But alas ! how ſhould it be other-
wiſe, when the Diſtemper hath hardly any Objects
left to work upon ? At Arles it is likewiſe abated,
we fear for the ſame Reaſon. Mean while, it ſpreads
in the Gevaudan ; and two large Villages in the
Neighbourhood of Frejus were attack'd the beginning of this Month. The French Court hath prohibited all communication with the Gevaudan upon ſe-
vere Penalties. The Plague is certainly got into the
ſmall Town of Marvegue in that Diſtrict, which
Town is ſhut in by eight hundred Men. Letters from
Geneva ſay, the two Battalions employ'd in ſurroun-
ding La Canourgue, are infected ; and that Maages is
very much ſuſpected. The Marquis de Quelus had
retired to a Caſtle near Avignon ; but the Sickneſs
being got among his Domeſticks, he was fled farther
away.
Paris, Sept. 5. The Diſtrict over which the Duke
of Berwick is to have the Command, extends to the
Borders of the Bourbonnois ; and the Court puts a
great Confidence in the Care of that General to hinder
the Infection from ſpreading. The Marquis de
Verceil is actually drawing Lines to ſhut in the Gevaudan ; and twelve Regiments of Foot, and as many
of Dragoons, are marching to reinforce the Troops
already poſted on that ſide. The Plague ſeems to
have almoſt ſpent itſelf in Provence. Tho' it is yet
a great way off of us, Men talk nevertheleſs of laying
up Magazines of all ſort of Proviſions here, and of making twenty thouſand Beds, to be ſet up in the Hoſpi-
tals and Tennis-Courts.
Hague, Sept. 9. The Deputies of our Admiralties
had, laſt Saturday, an extraordinary Conference with
thoſe of the States General, upon the ſpreading of a
Report, that ten or twelve Perſons died daily at a certain Place in Normandy, which was therefore ſuſpected to have received the Contagion ; But upon the
matter, it doth not appear there was the leaſt Foun-
dation for ſuch a Report ; tho' it is too plain the
Diſtemper gains ground ſpace in the Southern Parts
of France.
We can by no means penetrate into the Deſigns of
the Czar ; who, notwithſtanding 'tis confidently
written that the Peace between him and Sweden is as
good as concluded, hath a Fleet of thirty Men of War
and two hundred Galleys at Sea near Aland. However, an Expreſs gone by from Stockholm, doth not
                                confirm

sheets, I was employed to carry the papers thro' the streets to the customers.

He had some ingenious men among his friends, who amus'd themselves by writing little pieces for this paper, which gain'd it credit and made it more in demand, and these gentlemen often visited us. Hearing their conversations, and their accounts of the approbation their papers were received with, I was excited to try my hand among them; but, being still a boy, and suspecting that my brother would object to printing anything of mine in his paper if he knew it to be mine, I contrived to disguise my hand, and, writing an anonymous paper, I put it in at night under the door of the printing-house. It was found in the morning, and communicated to his writing friends when they call'd in as usual. They read it, commented on it in my hearing, and I had the exquisite pleasure of finding it met with their approbation, and that, in their different guesses at the author, none were named but men of some character among us for learning and ingenuity. I suppose now that I was rather lucky in my judges, and that perhaps they were not really so very good ones as I then esteem'd them.

Encourag'd, however, by this, I wrote and

conveyed in the same way to the press several
more papers which were equally approv'd; and
I kept my secret till my small fund of sense
for such performances was pretty well ex-
hausted, and then I discovered[1] it, when I
began to be considered a little more by my
brother's acquaintance, and in a manner that
did not quite please him, as he thought, probably with reason, that it tended to make me
too vain. And, perhaps, this might be one occasion of the differences that we began to have
about this time. Though a brother, he considered himself as my master, and me as his
apprentice, and, accordingly, expected the same
services from me as he would from another,
while I thought he demean'd me too much in
some he requir'd of me, who from a brother
expected more indulgence. Our disputes were
often brought before our father, and I fancy
I was either generally in the right, or else a
better pleader, because the judgment was generally in my favor. But my brother was pas-
sionate, and had often beaten me, which I took
extreamly amiss; and, thinking my apprenticeship very tedious, I was continually wishing
for some opportunity of shortening it, which
at length offered in a manner unexpected.

[1] Disclosed.

One of the pieces in our newspaper on some political point, which I have now forgotten, gave offense to the Assembly. He was taken up, censur'd, and imprison'd for a month, by the speaker's warrant, I suppose, because he would not discover his author. I too was taken up and examin'd before the council; but, tho' I did not give them any satisfaction, they contented themselves with admonishing me, and dismissed me, considering me, perhaps, as an apprentice, who was bound to keep his master's secrets.

During my brother's confinement, which I resented a good deal, notwithstanding our private differences, I had the management of the paper; and I made bold to give our rulers some rubs in it, which my brother took very kindly, while others began to consider me in an unfavorable light, as a young genius that had a turn for libeling and satyr. My brother's discharge was accompany'd with an order of the House (a very odd one), that *"James Franklin should no longer print the paper called the New England Courant."*

There was a consultation held in our printing-house among his friends, what he should do in this case. Some proposed to evade the order by changing the name of the paper; but

my brother, seeing inconveniences in that, it
was finally concluded on as a better way, to
let it be printed for the future under the name
of BENJAMIN FRANKLIN; and to avoid the censure of the Assembly, that might fall on him as
still printing it by his apprentice, the contrivance was that my old indenture should be return'd to me, with a full discharge on the back
of it, to be shown on occasion, but to secure to
him the benefit of my service, I was to sign
new indentures for the remainder of the term,
which were to be kept private. A very flimsy
scheme it was; however, it was immediately
executed, and the paper went on accordingly,
under my name for several months.

At length, a fresh difference arising between
my brother and me, I took upon me to assert
my freedom, presuming that he would not venture to produce the new indentures. It was
not fair in me to take this advantage, and this
I therefore reckon one of the first errata of
my life; but the unfairness of it weighed little
with me, when under the impressions of resentment for the blows his passion too often
urged him to bestow upon me, though he was
otherwise not an ill-natur'd man: perhaps I
was too saucy and provoking.

When he found I would leave him, he took care to prevent my getting employment in any other printing-house of the town, by going round and speaking to every master, who accordingly refus'd to give me work. I then thought of going to New York, as the nearest place where there was a printer; and I was rather inclin'd to leave Boston when I reflected that I had already made myself a little obnoxious to the governing party, and, from the arbitrary proceedings of the Assembly in my brother's case, it was likely I might, if I stay'd, soon bring myself into scrapes; and farther, that my indiscreet disputations about religion began to make me pointed at with horror by good people as an infidel or atheist. I determin'd on the point, but my father now siding with my brother, I was sensible that, if I attempted to go openly, means would be used to prevent me. My friend Collins, therefore, undertook to manage a little for me. He agreed with the captain of a New York sloop for my passage, under the notion of my being a young acquaintance of his. So I sold some of my books to raise a little money, was taken on board privately, and as we had a fair wind, in three days I found myself in New York, near 300 miles from home, a boy of but 17, without the least recommendation to, or knowledge of, any person in the place, and with very little money in my pocket.

III

ARRIVAL IN PHILADELPHIA

Y inclinations for the sea were by this time worne out, or I might now have gratify'd them. But, having a trade, and supposing myself a pretty good workman, I offer'd my service to the printer in the place, old Mr. William Bradford, who had been the first printer in Pennsylvania, but removed from thence upon the quarrel of George Keith. He could give me no employment, having little to do, and help enough already; but says he, "My son at Philadelphia has lately lost his principal hand, Aquilla Rose, by death; if you go thither, I believe he may employ you." Philadelphia was a hundred miles further; I set out, however, in a boat for Amboy, leaving my chest and things to follow me round by sea.

In crossing the bay, we met with a squall that tore our rotten sails to pieces, prevented our getting into the Kill,[1] and drove us upon

[1] Kill van Kull, the channel separating Staten Island from New Jersey on the north.

Long Island. In our way, a drunken Dutchman, who was a passenger too, fell overboard;
when he was sinking, I reached through the
water to his shock pate, and drew him up, so
that we got him in again. His ducking sobered
him a little, and he went to sleep, taking first
out of his pocket a book, which he desir'd I
would dry for him. It proved to be my old
favorite author, Bunyan's Pilgrim's Progress,
in Dutch, finely printed on good paper, with
copper cuts, a dress better than I had ever
seen it wear in its own language. I have since
found that it has been translated into most
of the languages of Europe, and suppose it
has been more generally read than any other
book, except perhaps the Bible. Honest John
was the first that I know of who mix'd narra-
tion and dialogue; a method of writing very
engaging to the reader, who in the most interesting parts finds himself, as it were, brought
into the company and present at the discourse.
De Foe in his Cruso, his Moll Flanders, Religious Courtship, Family Instructor, and other
pieces, has imitated it with success; and Richardson [1] has done the same in his Pamela, etc.

---

[1] Samuel Richardson, the father of the English novel, wrote
Pamela, Clarissa Harlowe, and the *History of Sir Charles Grandi-
son,* novels published in the form of letters.

When we drew near the island, we found it was at a place where there could be no landing, there being a great surff on the stony beach. So we dropt anchor, and swung round towards the shore. Some people came down to the water edge and hallow'd to us, as we did to them; but the wind was so high, and the surff so loud, that we could not hear so as to understand each other. There were canoes on the shore, and we made signs, and hallow'd that they should fetch us; but they either did not understand us, or thought it impracticable, so they went away, and night coming on, we had no remedy but to wait till the wind should abate; and, in the meantime, the boatman and I concluded to sleep, if we could; and so crowded into the scuttle, with the Dutchman, who was still wet, and the spray beating over the head of our boat, leak'd thro' to us, so that we were soon almost as wet as he. In this manner we lay all night, with very little rest; but, the wind abating the next day, we made a shift to reach Amboy before night, having been thirty hours on the water, without victuals, or any drink but a bottle of filthy rum, and the water we sail'd on being salt.

In the evening I found myself very feverish, and went in to bed; but, having read some-

where that cold water drank plentifully was
good for a fever, I follow'd the prescription,
sweat plentifully most of the night, my fever
left me, and in the morning, crossing the ferry,
I proceeded on my journey on foot, having
fifty miles to Burlington, where I was told I

should find boats that would carry me the rest
of the way to Philadelphia.

It rained very hard all the day; I was
thoroughly soak'd, and by noon a good deal
tired; so I stopt at a poor inn, where I staid
all night, beginning now to wish that I had
never left home. I cut so miserable a figure,
too, that I found, by the questions ask'd me,
I was suspected to be some runaway servant,
and in danger of being taken up on that suspicion. However, I proceeded the next day,

and got in the evening to an inn, within eight
or ten miles of Burlington, kept by one Dr.
Brown. He entered into conversation with
me while I took some refreshment, and, finding I had read a little, became very sociable
and friendly. Our acquaintance continu'd as
long as he liv'd. He had been, I imagine, an
itinerant doctor, for there was no town in
England, or country in Europe, of which he
could not give a very particular account. He
had some letters, and was ingenious, but much
of an unbeliever, and wickedly undertook, some
years after, to travesty the Bible in doggrel
verse, as Cotton had done Virgil. By this
means he set many of the facts in a very
ridiculous light, and might have hurt weak
minds if his work had been published; but it
never was.

At his house I lay that night, and the next
morning reach'd Burlington, but had the mortification to find that the regular boats were
gone a little before my coming, and no other
expected to go before Tuesday, this being Saturday; wherefore I returned to an old woman
in the town, of whom I had bought ginger-
bread to eat on the water, and ask'd her advice.
She invited me to lodge at her house till a
passage by water should offer; and being tired

with my foot traveling, I accepted the invita-
tion. She understanding I was a printer, would
have had me stay at that town and follow my
business, being ignorant of the stock necessary
to begin with. She was very hospitable, gave
me a dinner of ox-cheek with great good will,
accepting only of a pot of ale in return; and I
thought myself fixed till Tuesday should come.
However, walking in the evening by the side
of the river, a boat came by, which I found was
going towards Philadelphia, with several people
in her. They took me in, and, as there was no
wind, we row'd all the way; and about midnight, not having yet seen the city, some of the
company were confident we must have passed
it, and would row no farther; the others knew
not where we were; so we put toward the
shore, got into a creek, landed near an old
fence, with the rails of which we made a fire,
the night being cold, in October, and there we
remained till daylight. Then one of the company knew the place to be Cooper's Creek, a
little above Philadelphia, which we saw as soon
as we got out of the creek, and arriv'd there
about eight or nine o'clock on the Sunday
morning, and landed at the Market-street
wharf.

   I have been the more particular in this description of my journey, and shall be so of my first entry into that city, that you may in your mind compare such unlikely beginnings with the figure I have since made there. I was in my working dress, my best clothes being to come round by sea. I was dirty from my journey; my pockets were stuff'd out with shirts and stockings, and I knew no soul nor where to look for lodging. I was fatigued with traveling, rowing, and want of rest, I was very hungry; and my whole stock of cash consisted of a Dutch dollar, and about a shilling in copper. The latter I gave the people of the boat for my passage, who at first refus'd it, on account of my rowing; but I insisted on their taking it. A man being sometimes more generous when he has but a little money than when he has plenty, perhaps thro' fear of being thought to have but little.

Then I walked up the street, gazing about till near the market house I met a boy with bread. I had made many a meal on bread, and, inquiring where he got it, I went immediately to the baker's he directed me to, in Second-street, and ask'd for bisket, intending such as we had in Boston; but they, it seems, were not made in Philadelphia. Then I asked for a three-penny loaf, and was told they had

none such. So not considering or knowing
the difference of money, and the greater cheapness nor the names of his bread, I bade him
give me three-penny worth of any sort. He
gave me, accordingly, three great puffy rolls.
I was surpriz'd at the quantity, but took it,
and, having no room in my pockets, walk'd
off with a roll under each arm, and eating
the other. Thus I went up Market-street as
far as Fourth-street, passing by the door of
Mr. Read, my future wife's father; when she,
standing at the door, saw me, and thought I
made, as I certainly did, a most awkward,
ridiculous appearance. Then I turned and went
down Chestnut-street and part of Walnut-
street, eating my roll all the way, and, coming round, found myself again at Market-street
wharf, near the boat I came in, to which I
went for a draught of the river water; and,
being filled with one of my rolls, gave the other
two to a woman and her child that came down
the river in the boat with us, and were waiting
to go farther.

Thus refreshed, I walked again up the street,
which by this time had many clean-dressed
people in it, who were all walking the same
way. I joined them, and thereby was led into
the great meeting-house of the Quakers near

the market. I sat down among them, and, after looking round awhile and hearing nothing said, being very drowsy thro' labour and want of rest the preceding night, I fell fast asleep, and continu'd so till the meeting broke up, when one was kind enough to rouse me. This was, therefore, the first house I was in, or slept in, in Philadelphia.

Walking down again toward the river, and, looking in the faces of people, I met a young Quaker man, whose countenance I lik'd, and, accosting him, requested he would tell me where a stranger could get lodging. We were then near the sign of the Three Mariners. "Here," says he, "is one place that entertains strangers, but it is not a reputable house; if thee wilt walk with me, I'll show thee a better." He brought me to the Crooked Billet in Water-street. Here I got a dinner; and, while I was eating it, several sly questions were asked me, as it seemed to be suspected from my youth and appearance, that I might be some runaway.

After dinner, my sleepiness return'd, and being shown to a bed, I lay down without undressing, and slept till six in the evening, was call'd to supper, went to bed again very early, and slept soundly till next morning.

Then I made myself as tidy as I could, and
went to Andrew Bradford the printer's. I
found in the shop the old man his father,
whom I had seen at New York, and who,
traveling on horseback, had got to Philadelphia before me. He introduc'd me to his son,
who receiv'd me civilly, gave me a breakfast,
but told me he did not at present want a hand,
being lately suppli'd with one; but there was
another printer in town, lately set up, one
Keimer, who, perhaps, might employ me; if
not, I should be welcome to lodge at his house,
and he would give me a little work to do now
and then till fuller business should offer.

The old gentleman said he would go with
me to the new printer; and when we found
him, "Neighbour," says Bradford, "I have
brought to see you a young man of your business; perhaps you may want such a one." He
ask'd me a few questions, put a composing
stick in my hand to see how I work'd, and then
said he would employ me soon, though he
had just then nothing for me to do; and, taking old Bradford, whom he had never seen
before, to be one of the town's people that had
a good will for him, enter'd into a conversation on his present undertaking and prospects;
while Bradford, not discovering that he was

the other printer's father, on Keimer's saying
he expected soon to get the greatest part of
the business into his own hands, drew him
on by artful questions, and starting little
doubts, to explain all his views, what interest
he reli'd on, and in what manner he intended
to proceed. I, who stood by and heard all,
saw immediately that one of them was a crafty
old sophister, and the other a mere novice.
Bradford left me with Keimer, who was greatly
surpris'd when I told him who the old man
was.

Keimer's printing-house, I found, consisted
of an old shatter'd press, and one small, worn-
out font of English, which he was then using
himself, composing an Elegy on Aquilla Rose,
before mentioned, an ingenious young man,
of excellent character, much respected in the
town, clerk of the Assembly, and a pretty
poet. Keimer made verses too, but very indif-
ferently. He could not be said to write them,
for his manner was to compose them in the
types directly out of his head. So there being
no copy,[1] but one pair of cases, and the Elegy
likely to require all the letter, no one could
help him. I endeavour'd to put his press (which
he had not yet us'd, and of which he under-

[1] Manuscript.

stood nothing) into order fit to be work'd with; and, promising to come and print off his Elegy as soon as he should have got it ready, I return'd to Bradford's, who gave me a little job to do for the present, and there I lodged and dieted. A few days after, Keimer sent for me to print off the Elegy. And now he had got another pair of cases,[1] and a pamphlet to reprint, on which he set me to work.

These two printers I found poorly qualified for their business. Bradford had not been bred to it, and was very illiterate; and Keimer, tho' something of a scholar, was a mere compositor, knowing nothing of presswork. He had been one of the French prophets,[2] and could act their enthusiastic agitations. At this time he did not profess any particular religion, but something of all on occasion; was very ignorant of the world, and had, as I afterward found, a good deal of the knave in his composition. He did not like my lodging at Bradford's while I work'd with him. He had a house, indeed, but without furniture, so he could not lodge

---

[1] The frames for holding type are in two sections, the upper for capitals and the lower for small letters.

[2] Protestants of the South of France, who became fanatical under the persecutions of Louis XIV, and thought they had the gift of prophecy. They had as mottoes "No Taxes" and "Liberty of Conscience."

me; but he got me a lodging at Mr. Read's before mentioned, who was the owner of his house; and, my chest and clothes being come by this time, I made rather a more respectable appearance in the eyes of Miss Read than I had done when she first happen'd to see me eating my roll in the street.

I began now to have some acquaintance among the young people of the town, that were lovers of reading, with whom I spent my evenings very pleasantly; and gaining money by my industry and frugality, I lived very agreeably, forgetting Boston as much as I could, and not desiring that any there should know where I resided, except my friend Collins, who was in my secret, and kept it when I wrote to him. At length, an incident happened that sent me back again much sooner than I had intended. I had a brother-in-law, Robert Holmes, master of a sloop that traded between Boston and Delaware. He being at Newcastle, forty miles below Philadelphia, heard there of me, and wrote me a letter mentioning the concern of my friends in Boston at my abrupt departure, assuring me of their good will to me, and that everything would be accommodated to my mind if I would return, to which he exhorted me very earnestly. I wrote an answer to his letter, thank'd him for his advice, but stated my reasons for quitting Boston fully and in such a light as to convince him I was not so wrong as he had apprehended.

IV

FIRST VISIT TO BOSTON

SIR WILLIAM KEITH, governor of the province, was then at Newcastle, and Captain Holmes, happening to be in company with him when my letter came to hand, spoke to him of me, and show'd him the letter. The governor read it, and seem'd surpris'd when he was told my age. He said I appear'd a young man of promising parts, and therefore should be encouraged; the printers at Philadelphia were wretched ones; and, if I would set up there, he made no doubt I should succeed; for his part, he would procure me the public business, and do me every other service in his power. This my brother-in-law afterwards told me in Boston, but I knew as yet nothing of it; when, one day, Keimer and I being at work together near the window, we saw the governor and another gentleman (which proved to be Colonel French, of Newcastle), finely dress'd, come directly across the street to our house, and heard them at the door.

Keimer ran down immediately, thinking it
a visit to him; but the governor inquir'd for me,
came up, and with a condescension and polite-
ness I had been quite unus'd to, made me many
compliments, desired to be acquainted with me,
blam'd me kindly for not having made myself known to him when I first came to the
place, and would have me away with him to
the tavern, where he was going with Colonel
French to taste, as he said, some excellent
Madeira. I was not a little surprised, and
Keimer star'd like a pig poison'd.[1] I went,
however, with the governor and Colonel French
to a tavern, at the corner of Third-street, and
over the Madeira he propos'd my setting up
my business, laid before me the probabilities
of success, and both he and Colonel French
assur'd me I should have their interest and
influence in procuring the public business of
both governments.[2] On my doubting whether
my father would assist me in it, Sir William
said he would give me a letter to him, in
which he would state the advantages, and he
did not doubt of prevailing with him. So it
was concluded I should return to Boston in

[1] Temple Franklin considered this specific figure vulgar and
changed it to " stared with astonishment."
[2] Pennsylvania and Delaware.

the first vessel, with the governor's letter recommending me to my father. In the meantime the intention was to be kept a secret, and I went on working with Keimer as usual, the governor sending for me now and then to dine with him, a very great honour I thought it, and conversing with me in the most affable, familiar, and friendly manner imaginable.

About the end of April, 1724, a little vessel offer'd for Boston. I took leave of Keimer as going to see my friends. The governor gave me an ample letter, saying many flattering things of me to my father, and strongly recommending the project of my setting up at Philadelphia as a thing that must make my fortune. We struck on a shoal in going down the bay, and sprung a leak; we had a blustering time at sea, and were oblig'd to pump almost continually, at which I took my turn. We arriv'd safe, however, at Boston in about a fortnight. I had been absent seven months, and my friends had heard nothing of me; for my br. Holmes was not yet return'd, and had not written about me. My unexpected appearance surpriz'd the family; all were, however, very glad to see me, and made me welcome, except my brother. I went to see him at his printing-house. I was better dress'd than ever while in his service, having a genteel new suit from head to foot, a watch, and my pockets lin'd with near five pounds sterling in silver. He receiv'd me not very frankly, look'd me all over, and turn'd to his work again.

The journeymen were inquisitive where I had been, what sort of a country it was, and

how I lik'd it. I prais'd it much, and the happy life I led in it, expressing strongly my intention of returning to it; and, one of them asking what kind of money we had there, I produc'd a handful of silver, and spread it before them, which was a kind of raree-show [1] they had not been us'd to, paper being the money of Boston.[2] Then I took an opportunity

---

[1] A peep-show in a box.

[2] There were no mints in the colonies, so the metal money was of foreign coinage and not nearly so common as paper money,

of letting them see my watch; and, lastly (my brother still grum and sullen), I gave them a piece of eight [1] to drink, and took my leave. This visit of mine offended him extreamly; for, when my mother some time after spoke to him of a reconciliation, and of her wishes to see us on good terms together, and that we might live for the future as brothers, he said I had insulted him in such a manner before his people that he could never forget or forgive it. In this, however, he was mistaken.

My father received the governor's letter with some apparent surprise, but said little of it to me for some days, when Capt. Holmes returning he show'd it to him, asked him if he knew Keith, and what kind of man he was; adding his opinion that he must be of small discretion to think of setting a boy up in business who wanted yet three years of being at man's estate. Holmes said what he could in favour of the project, but my father was clear in the impropriety of it, and at last, gave a flat denial to it. Then he wrote a civil letter to Sir William, thanking him for the patronage he had so kindly offered me, but declining to assist

which was printed in large quantities in America, even in small denominations.

[1] Spanish dollar about equivalent to our dollar.

me as yet in setting up, I being, in his opinion, too young to be trusted with the management of a business so important, and for which the preparation must be so expensive.

My friend and companion Collins, who was a clerk in the post-office, pleas'd with the account I gave him of my new country, determined to go thither also; and, while I waited for my father's determination, he set out before me by land to Rhode Island, leaving his books, which were a pretty collection of mathematicks and natural philosophy, to come with mine and me to New York, where he propos'd to wait for me.

My father, tho' he did not approve Sir William's proposition, was yet pleas'd that I had been able to obtain so advantageous a character from a person of such note where I had resided, and that I had been so industrious and careful as to equip myself so handsomely in so short a time; therefore, seeing no prospect of an accommodation between my brother and me, he gave his consent to my returning again to Philadelphia, advis'd me to behave respectfully to the people there, endeavour to obtain the general esteem, and avoid lampooning and libeling, to which he thought I had too much inclination; telling me, that by steady industry and a prudent parsimony I might save enough by the time I was one-and-twenty to set me up; and that, if I came near the matter, he would help me out with the rest. This was all I could obtain, except some small gifts as tokens of his and my mother's love, when I embark'd again for New York, now with their approbation and their blessing.

The sloop putting in at Newport, Rhode Island, I visited my brother John, who had been married and settled there some years. He received me very affectionately, for he always lov'd me. A friend of his, one Vernon, having some money due to him in Pensilvania, about thirty-five pounds currency, desired I would receive it for him, and keep it till I had his directions what to remit it in. Accordingly, he gave me an order. This afterwards occasion'd me a good deal of uneasiness.

At Newport we took in a number of passengers for New York, among which were two young women, companions, and a grave, sensible, matronlike Quaker woman, with her attendants. I had shown an obliging readiness to do her some little services, which impress'd her I suppose with a degree of good will toward me; therefore, when she saw a daily growing familiarity between me and the two young women, which they appear'd to encourage, she took me aside, and said, " Young man, I am concern'd for thee, as thou hast no friend with thee, and seems not to know much of the world, or of the snares youth is expos'd to; depend upon it, those are very bad women; I can see it in all their actions; and if thee art not upon thy guard, they will draw thee into some danger; they are strangers to thee, and I advise thee, in a friendly concern for thy welfare, to have no acquaintance with them." As I seem'd at first not to think so ill of them as she did, she mentioned some things she had observ'd and heard that had escap'd my notice, but now convinc'd me she was right. I thank'd her for her kind advice, and promis'd to follow it. When we arriv'd at New York, they told me where they liv'd, and invited me to come and see them; but I avoided it, and it was well I did; for the next day the captain miss'd a silver spoon and some other things, that had been taken out of his cabbin, and, knowing that these were a couple of strumpets, he got a warrant to scarch their lodgings, found the stolen goods, and had the thieves punish'd. So, tho' we had escap'd a sunken rock, which we scrap'd upon in the passage, I thought this escape of rather more importance to me.

At New York I found my friend Collins, who had arriv'd there some time before me. We had been intimate from children, and had read the same books together; but he had the advantage of more time for reading and studying, and a wonderful genius for mathematical learning, in which he far outstript me. While I liv'd in Boston, most of my hours of leisure for conversation were spent with him, and he continu'd a sober as well as an industrious lad; was much respected for his learning by several of the clergy and other gentlemen, and seemed to promise making a good figure in life. But, during my absence, he had acquir'd a habit of sotting with brandy; and I found by his own account, and what I heard from others, that he had been drunk every day since his arrival at New York, and behav'd very oddly. He had gam'd, too, and lost his money, so that I was oblig'd to discharge his lodgings, and defray his expenses to and at Philadelphia, which prov'd extremely inconvenient to me.

The then governor of New York, Burnet (son of Bishop Burnet), hearing from the captain that a young man, one of his passengers, had a great many books, desir'd he would bring

me to see him. I waited upon him accordingly,
and should have taken Collins with me but
that he was not sober. The gov'r. treated me
with great civility, show'd me his library, which
was a very large one, and we had a good deal
of conversation about books and authors. This
was the second governor who had done me the
honour to take notice of me; which, to a poor
boy like me, was very pleasing.

We proceeded to Philadelphia. I received
on the way Vernon's money, without which
we could hardly have finish'd our journey.
Collins wished to be employ'd in some count-
ing-house; but, whether they discover'd his
dramming by his breath, or by his behaviour,
tho' he had some recommendations, he met with
no success in any application, and continu'd
lodging and boarding at the same house with
me, and at my expense. Knowing I had that
money of Vernon's, he was continually borrowing of me, still promising repayment as
soon as he should be in business. At length
he had got so much of it that I was distress'd
to think what I should do in case of being
call'd on to remit it.

His drinking continu'd, about which we sometimes quarrel'd; for, when a little intoxicated,
he was very fractious. Once, in a boat on the

Delaware with some other young men, he refused to row in his turn. "I will be row'd home," says he. "We will not row you," says I. "You must, or stay all night on the water," says he, "just as you please." The others said, "Let us row; what signifies it?" But, my mind being soured with his other conduct, I continu'd to refuse. So he swore he would make me row, or throw me overboard; and coming along, stepping on the thwarts, toward me, when he came up and struck at me, I clapped my hand under his crutch, and, rising, pitched him head-foremost into the river. I knew he was a good swimmer, and so was under little concern about him; but before he could get round to lay hold of the boat, we had with a few strokes pull'd her out of his reach; and ever when he drew near the boat, we ask'd if he would row, striking a few strokes to slide her away from him. He was ready to die with vexation, and obstinately would not promise to row. However, seeing him at last beginning to tire, we lifted him in and brought him home dripping wet in the evening. We hardly exchang'd a civil word afterwards, and a West India captain, who had a commission to procure a tutor for the sons of a gentleman at Barbados, happening to meet with him, agreed

to carry him thither. He left me then, promising to remit me the first money he should
receive in order to discharge the debt; but I
never heard of him after.

The breaking into this money of Vernon's
was one of the first great errata of my life;
and this affair show'd that my father was not
much out in his judgment when he suppos'd
me too young to manage business of importance. But Sir William, on reading his letter,
said he was too prudent. There was great difference in persons; and discretion did not always
accompany years, nor was youth always
without it. "And since he will not set you up,"
says he, "I will do it myself. Give me an
inventory of the things necessary to be had
from England, and I will send for them. You
shall repay me when you are able; I am resolv'd
to have a good printer here, and I am sure you
must succeed." This was spoken with such
an appearance of cordiality, that I had not the
least doubt of his meaning what he said. I
had hitherto kept the proposition of my setting
up, a secret in Philadelphia, and I still kept
it. Had it been known that I depended on the
governor, probably some friend, that knew him
better, would have advis'd me not to rely on
him, as I afterwards heard it as his known

character to be liberal of promises which he never meant to keep. Yet, unsolicited as he was by me, how could I think his generous offers insincere? I believ'd him one of the best men in the world.

I presented him an inventory of a little print'-house, amounting by my computation to about one hundred pounds sterling. He lik'd it, but ask'd me if my being on the spot in England to chuse the types, and see that everything was good of the kind, might not be of some advantage. "Then," says he, "when there, you may make acquaintances, and establish correspondences in the bookselling and stationery way." I agreed that this might be advantageous. "Then," says he, "get yourself ready to go with Annis;" which was the annual ship, and the only one at that time usually passing between London and Philadelphia. But it would be some months before Annis sail'd, so I continu'd working with Keimer, fretting about the money Collins had got from me, and in daily apprehensions of being call'd upon by Vernon, which, however, did not happen for some years after.

I believe I have omitted mentioning that, in my first voyage from Boston, being becalm'd off Block Island, our people set about catching cod, and hauled up a great many. Hitherto I had stuck to my resolution of not eating animal food, and on this occasion I consider'd, with my master Tryon, the taking every fish as a kind of unprovoked murder, since none of them had, or ever could do us any injury that might justify the slaughter. All this seemed very reasonable. But I had formerly been a great lover of fish, and, when this came hot out of the frying-pan, it smelt admirably well. I balanc'd some time between principle and inclination, till I recollected that, when the fish were opened, I saw smaller fish taken out of their stomachs; then thought I, "If you eat one another, I don't see why we mayn't eat you." So I din'd upon cod very heartily, and continued to eat with other people, returning only now and then occasionally to a vegetable diet. So convenient a thing is it to be a *reasonable creature,* since it enables one to find or make a reason for everything one has a mind to do.

V

EARLY FRIENDS IN PHILADELPHIA

KEIMER and I liv'd on a pretty good familiar footing, and agreed tolerably well, for he suspected nothing of my setting up. He retained a great deal of his old enthusiasms and lov'd argumentation. We therefore had many disputations. I used to work him so with my Socratic method, and had trepann'd him so often by questions apparently so distant from any point we had in hand, and yet by degrees led to the point, and brought him into difficulties and contradictions, that at last he grew ridiculously cautious, and would hardly answer me the most common question, without asking first, *"What do you intend to infer from that?"* However, it gave him so high an opinion of my abilities in the confuting way, that he seriously proposed my being his colleague in a project he had of setting up a new sect. He was to preach the doctrines, and I was to confound all opponents. When he came to explain with me upon the doctrines, I found several conun-

drums which I objected to, unless I might have
my way a little too, and introduce some of
mine.

Keimer wore his beard at full length, because
somewhere in the Mosaic law it is said, *" Thou
shalt not mar the corners of thy beard."* He
likewise kept the Seventh day, Sabbath; and
these two points were essentials with him.
I dislik'd both; but agreed to admit them upon
condition of his adopting the doctrine of using
no animal food.   " I doubt," said he, " my constitution will not bear that."   I assur'd him it
would, and that he would be the better for it.
He was usually a great glutton, and I promised myself some diversion in half starving him.
He agreed to try the practice, if I would keep
him company.   I did so, and we held it for
three months.   We had our victuals dress'd,
and brought to us regularly by a woman in the
neighborhood, who had from me a list of forty
dishes, to be prepar'd for us at different times,
in all which there was neither fish, flesh, nor
fowl, and the whim suited me the better at this
time from the cheapness of it, not costing us
above eighteenpence sterling each per week.   I
have since kept several Lents most strictly,
leaving the common diet for that, and that for
the common, abruptly, without the least incon-

venience, so that I think there is little in the advice of making those changes by easy gradations. I went on pleasantly, but poor Keimer suffered grievously, tired of the project, long'd for the flesh-pots of Egypt, and order'd a roast pig. He invited me and two women friends to dine with him; but, it being brought too soon upon table, he could not resist the temptation, and ate the whole before we came.

I had made some courtship during this time to Miss Read. I had a great respect and affection for her, and had some reason to believe she had the same for me; but, as I was about to take a long voyage, and we were both very young, only a little above eighteen, it was thought most prudent by her mother to prevent our going too far at present, as a marriage, if it was to take place, would be more convenient after my return, when I should be, as I expected, set up in my business. Perhaps, too, she thought my expectations not so well founded as I imagined them to be.

My chief acquaintances at this time were Charles Osborne, Joseph Watson, and James Ralph, all lovers of reading. The two first were clerks to an eminent scrivener or conveyancer in the town, Charles Brogden; the other was clerk to a merchant. Watson was a pious, sensible young man, of great integrity; the others rather more lax in their principles of religion, particularly Ralph, who, as well as Collins, had been unsettled by me, for which they both made me suffer. Osborne was sensible,

candid, frank; sincere and affectionate to his friends; but, in literary matters, too fond of criticizing. Ralph was ingenious, genteel in his manners, and extremely eloquent; I think I never knew a prettier talker. Both of them were great admirers of poetry, and began to try their hands in little pieces. Many pleasant walks we four had together on Sundays into the woods, near Schuylkill, where we read to one another, and conferr'd on what we read.

Ralph was inclin'd to pursue the study of poetry, not doubting but he might become emi-

nent in it, and make his fortune by it, alleging
that the best poets must, when they first began
to write, make as many faults as he did. Osborne dissuaded him, assur'd him he had no
genius for poetry, and advis'd him to think of
nothing beyond the business he was bred to;
that, in the mercantile way, tho' he had no
stock, he might, by his diligence and punctuality, recommend himself to employment as a
factor, and in time acquire wherewith to trade
on his own account. I approv'd the amusing
one's self with poetry now and then, so far
as to improve one's language, but no farther.

On this it was propos'd that we should each
of us, at our next meeting, produce a piece of
our own composing, in order to improve by our
mutual observations, criticisms, and corrections.
As language and expression were what we had
in view, we excluded all considerations of invention by agreeing that the task should be a
version of the eighteenth Psalm, which de-
scribes the descent of a Deity. When the time
of our meeting drew nigh, Ralph called on me
first, and let me know his piece was ready. I
told him I had been busy, and, having little
inclination, had done nothing. He then show'd
me his piece for my opinion, and I much approv'd it, as it appear'd to me to have great

merit. " Now," says he, " Osborne never will allow the least merit in anything of mine, but makes 1000 criticisms out of mere envy. He is not so jealous of you; I wish, therefore, you would take this piece, and produce it as yours; I will pretend not to have had time, and so produce nothing. We shall then see what he will say to it." It was agreed, and I immediately transcrib'd it, that it might appear in my own hand.

We met; Watson's performance was read; there were some beauties in it, but many defects. Osborne's was read; it was much better; Ralph did it justice; remarked some faults, but applauded the beauties. He himself had nothing to produce. I was backward; seemed desirous of being excused; had not had sufficient time to correct, etc.; but no excuse could be admitted; produce I must. It was read and repeated; Watson and Osborne gave up the contest, and join'd in applauding it. Ralph only made some criticisms, and propos'd some amendments; but I defended my text. Osborne was against Ralph, and told him he was no better a critic than poet, so he dropt the argument. As they two went home together, Osborne expressed himself still more strongly in favor of what he thought my production; having restrain'd himself before, as he said, lest I should think it flattery. "But who would have imagin'd," said he, "that Franklin had been capable of such a performance; such painting, such force, such fire! He has even improv'd the original. In his common conversation he seems to have no choice of words; he hesitates and blunders; and yet, good God! how he writes!" When we next met, Ralph discovered the trick we had plaid him, and Osborne was a little laughed at.

This transaction fixed Ralph in his resolution of becoming a poet. I did all I could to dissuade him from it, but he continued scribbling verses till *Pope* cured him.[1] He became, however, a pretty good prose writer. More of him hereafter. But, as I may not have occasion again to mention the other two, I shall just remark here, that Watson died in my arms a few years after, much lamented, being the best of our set. Osborne went to the West Indies, where he became an eminent lawyer and

---

[1] "In one of the later editions of the *Dunciad* occur the following lines:

'Silence, ye wolves! while Ralph to Cynthia howls,
And makes night hideous—answer him, ye owls.'

To this the poet adds the following note:

'James Ralph, a name inserted after the first editions, not known till he writ a swearing-piece called *Sawney,* very abusive of Dr. Swift, Mr. Gay, and myself.'"

made money, but died young. He and I had made a serious agreement, that the one who happen'd first to die should, if possible, make a friendly visit to the other, and acquaint him how he found things in that separate state. But he never fulfill'd his promise.

VI

FIRST VISIT TO LONDON

THE governor, seeming to like my company, had me frequently to his house, and his setting me up was always mention'd as a fixed thing. I was to take with me letters recommendatory to a number of his friends, besides the letter of credit to furnish me with the necessary money for purchasing the press and types, paper, etc. For these letters I was appointed to call at different times, when they were to be ready; but a future time was still named. Thus he went on till the ship, whose departure too had been several times postponed, was on the point of sailing. Then, when I call'd to take my leave and receive the letters, his secretary, Dr. Bard, came out to me and said the governor was extremely busy in writing, but would be down at Newcastle, before the ship, and there the letters would be delivered to me.

Ralph, though married, and having one child, had determined to accompany me in this voyage. It was thought he intended to establish

a correspondence, and obtain goods to sell on
commission; but I found afterwards, that, thro'
some discontent with his wife's relations, he
purposed to leave her on their hands, and never
return again. Having taken leave of my friends,
and interchang'd some promises with Miss
Read, I left Philadelphia in the ship, which
anchor'd at Newcastle. The governor was
there; but when I went to his lodging, the secretary came to me from him with the civillest
message in the world, that he could not then
see me, being engaged in business of the utmost importance, but should send the letters
to me on board, wished me heartily a good
voyage and a speedy return, etc. I returned on
board a little puzzled, but still not doubting.

Mr. Andrew Hamilton, a famous lawyer of
Philadelphia, had taken passage in the same
ship for himself and son, and with Mr. Denham,
a Quaker merchant, and Messrs. Onion and
Russel, masters of an iron work in Maryland,
had engaged the great cabin; so that Ralph and
I were forced to take up with a berth in the
steerage, and none on board knowing us, were
considered as ordinary persons. But Mr. Hamilton and his son (it was James, since governor) return'd from Newcastle to Philadelphia, the father being recall'd by a great fee

to plead for a seized ship; and, just before we sail'd, Colonel French coming on board, and showing me great respect, I was more taken notice of, and, with my friend Ralph, invited by the other gentlemen to come into the cabin, there being now room. Accordingly, we remov'd thither.

Understanding that Colonel French had brought on board the governor's despatches, I ask'd the captain for those letters that were to be under my care. He said all were put into the bag together and he could not then come at them; but, before we landed in England, I should have an opportunity of picking them out; so I was satisfied for the present, and we proceeded on our voyage. We had a sociable company in the cabin, and lived uncommonly well, having the addition of all Mr. Hamilton's stores, who had laid in plentifully. In this passage Mr. Denham contracted a friendship for me that continued during his life. The voyage was otherwise not a pleasant one, as we had a great deal of bad weather.

When we came into the Channel, the captain kept his word with me, and gave me an opportunity of examining the bag for the governor's letters. I found none upon which my name was put as under my care. I picked out

six or seven, that, by the handwriting, I thought
might be the promised letters, especially as one
of them was directed to Basket, the king's
printer, and another to some stationer. We
arriv'd in London the 24th of December, 1724.
I waited upon the stationer, who came first
in my way, delivering the letter as from Governor Keith. "I don't know such a person,"

says he; but, opening the letter, "O! this is
from Riddlesden. I have lately found him to
be a compleat rascal, and I will have nothing
to do with him, nor receive any letters from
him." So, putting the letter into my hand, he
turn'd on his heel and left me to serve some
customer. I was surprized to find these were
not the governor's letters; and, after recollecting and comparing circumstances, I began to

doubt his sincerity. I found my friend Denham, and opened the whole affair to him. He let me into Keith's character; told me there was not the least probability that he had written any letters for me; that no one, who knew him, had the smallest dependence on him; and he laught at the notion of the governor's giving me a letter of credit, having, as he said, no credit to give. On my expressing some concern about what I should do, he advised me to endeavour getting some employment in the way of my business. "Among the printers here," said he, "you will improve yourself, and when you return to America, you will set up to greater advantage."

We both of us happen'd to know, as well as the stationer, that Riddlesden, the attorney, was a very knave. He had half ruin'd Miss Read's father by persuading him to be bound for him. By this letter it appear'd there was a secret scheme on foot to the prejudice of Hamilton (suppos'd to be then coming over with us); and that Keith was concerned in it with Riddlesden. Denham, who was a friend of Hamilton's, thought he ought to be acquainted with it; so, when he arriv'd in England, which was soon after, partly from resentment and ill-will to Keith and Riddlesden, and

partly from good-will to him, I waited on
him, and gave him the letter. He thank'd
me cordially, the information being of importance to him; and from that time he became my friend, greatly to my advantage afterwards on many occasions.

But what shall we think of a governor's
playing such pitiful tricks, and imposing so
grossly on a poor ignorant boy! It was a
habit he had acquired. He wish'd to please
everybody; and, having little to give, he gave
expectations. He was otherwise an ingenious,
sensible man, a pretty good writer, and a good
governor for the people, tho' not for his con-
stituents, the proprietaries, whose instructions
he sometimes disregarded. Several of our best
laws were of his planning and passed during
his administration.

Ralph and I were inseparable companions.
We took lodgings together in Little Britain [1]
at three shillings and sixpence a week—as
much as we could then afford. He found some
relations, but they were poor, and unable to
assist him. He now let me know his intentions of remaining in London, and that he

[1] One of the oldest parts of London, north of St. Paul's Ca-
thedral, called "Little Britain" because the Dukes of Brittany
used to live there. See the essay entitled "Little Britain" in
Washington Irving's *Sketch Book*.

never meant to return to Philadelphia. He had brought no money with him, the whole he could muster having been expended in paying his passage. I had fifteen pistoles;[1] so he borrowed occasionally of me to subsist, while he was looking out for business. He first endeavoured to get into the play-house, believing himself qualify'd for an actor; but Wilkes,[2] to whom he apply'd, advis'd him candidly not to think of that employment, as it was impossible he should succeed in it. Then he propos'd to Roberts, a publisher in Paternoster Row,[3] to write for him a weekly paper like the Spectator, on certain conditions, which Roberts did not approve. Then he endeavoured to get employment as a hackney writer, to copy for the stationers and lawyers about the Temple,[4] but could find no vacancy.

I immediately got into work at Palmer's, then a famous printing-house in Bartholomew Close, and here I continu'd near a year. I was pretty diligent, but spent with Ralph a good deal of my earnings in going to plays and other places of amusement. We had together

---

[1] A gold coin worth about four dollars in our money.
[2] A popular comedian, manager of Drury Lane Theater.
[3] Street north of St. Paul's, occupied by publishing houses.
[4] Law schools and lawyers' residences situated southwest of St. Paul's, between Fleet Street and the Thames.

consumed all my pistoles, and now just rubbed
on from hand to mouth. He seem'd quite to
forget his wife and child, and I, by degrees,
my engagements with Miss Read, to whom I
never wrote more than one letter, and that
was to let her know I was not likely soon
to return. This was another of the great
errata of my life, which I should wish to correct if I were to live it over again. In fact, by
our expenses, I was constantly kept unable to
pay my passage.

At Palmer's I was employed in composing
for the second edition of Wollaston's "Religion of Nature." Some of his reasonings not
appearing to me well founded, I wrote a little
metaphysical piece in which I made remarks
on them. It was entitled "A Dissertation on
Liberty and Necessity, Pleasure and Pain."
I inscribed it to my friend Ralph; I printed a
small number. It occasion'd my being more
consider'd by Mr. Palmer as a young man of
some ingenuity, tho' he seriously expostulated
with me upon the principles of my pamphlet,
which to him appear'd abominable. My printing this pamphlet was another erratum.

While I lodg'd in Little Britain, I made an
acquaintance with one Wilcox, a bookseller,
whose shop was at the next door. He had an

immense collection of second-hand books. Circulating libraries were not then in use; but we agreed that, on certain reasonable terms, which I have now forgotten, I might take, read, and return any of his books. This I esteem'd a great advantage, and I made as much use of it as I could.

My pamphlet by some means falling into the hands of one Lyons, a surgeon, author of a book entitled " The Infallibility of Human Judgment," it occasioned an acquaintance between us. He took great notice of me, called on me often to converse on those subjects, carried me to the Horns, a pale alehouse in —— Lane, Cheapside, and introduced me to Dr. Mandeville, author of the " Fable of the Bees," who had a club there, of which he was the soul, being a most facetious, entertaining companion. Lyons, too, introduced me to Dr. Pemberton, at Batson's Coffee-house, who promis'd to give me an opportunity, sometime or other, of seeing Sir Isaac Newton, of which I was extreamly desirous; but this never happened.

I had brought over a few curiosities, among which the principal was a purse made of the asbestos, which purifies by fire. Sir Hans Sloane heard of it, came to see me, and invited me to his house in Bloomsbury Square, where he show'd me all his curiosities, and persuaded me to let him add that to the number, for which he paid me handsomely.

In our house there lodg'd a young woman, a milliner, who, I think, had a shop in the Cloisters. She had been genteelly bred, was sensible and lively, and of most pleasing conversation. Ralph read plays to her in the evenings, they grew intimate, she took another lodging, and he followed her. They liv'd together some time; but, he being still out of business, and her income not sufficient to maintain them with her child, he took a resolution of going from London, to try for a country school, which he thought himself well qualified to undertake, as he wrote an excellent hand, and was a master of arithmetic and accounts. This, however, he deemed a business below him, and confident of future better fortune, when he should be unwilling to have it known that he once was so meanly employed, he changed his name, and did me the honour to assume mine; for I soon after had a letter from him, acquainting me that he was settled in a small village (in Berkshire, I think it was, where he taught reading and writing to ten or a dozen boys, at sixpence each per week), recommending Mrs. T—— to my care, and desiring me to write to him, directing for Mr. Franklin, schoolmaster, at such a place.

He continued to write frequently, sending me large specimens of an epic poem which he was then composing, and desiring my remarks and corrections. These I gave him from time to time, but endeavour'd rather to discourage his proceeding. One of Young's Satires [1] was then just published. I copy'd and sent him a great part of it, which set in a strong light the folly of pursuing the Muses with any hope of advancement by them. All was in vain; sheets of the poem continued to come by every post. In the meantime, Mrs. T——, having on his account lost her friends and business, was often in distresses, and us'd to send for me and borrow what I could spare to help her out of them. I grew fond of her company, and, being at that time under no religious restraint, and presuming upon my importance to her, I attempted familiarities (another erratum) which she repuls'd with a proper resentment, and acquainted him with my behaviour. This made a breach between us; and, when he returned again to London, he let

---

[1] Edward Young (1681-1765), an English poet. See his satires, Vol. III, Epist. ii, page 70.

me know he thought I had cancell'd all the
obligations he had been under to me. So I
found I was never to expect his repaying me
what I lent to him or advanc'd for him. This,
however, was not then of much consequence,
as he was totally unable; and in the loss of his
friendship I found myself relieved from a
burthen. I now began to think of getting
a little money beforehand, and, expecting better work, I left Palmer's to work at Watts's,
near Lincoln's Inn Fields, a still greater printing-house.[1] Here I continued all the rest of
my stay in London.

At my first admission into this printing-
house I took to working at press, imagining
I felt a want of the bodily exercise I had been
us'd to in America, where presswork is mix'd
with composing. I drank only water; the other
workmen, near fifty in number, were great
guzzlers of beer. On occasion, I carried up
and down stairs a large form of types in each
hand, when others carried but one in both
hands. They wondered to see, from this and
several instances, that the *Water-American,* as
they called me, was *stronger* than themselves,
who drank *strong* beer! We had an alehouse boy

[1] The printing press at which Franklin worked is preserved in
the Patent Office at Washington.

who attended always in the house to supply the workmen. My companion at the press drank every day a pint before breakfast, a pint at breakfast with his bread and cheese, a pint between breakfast and dinner, a pint at dinner, a pint in the afternoon about six o'clock, and another when he had done his day's work. I thought it a detestable custom; but it was necessary, he suppos'd, to drink *strong* beer, that he might be *strong* to labour. I endeavoured to convince him that the bodily strength afforded by beer could only be in proportion to the grain or flour of the barley dissolved in the water of which it was made; that there was more flour in a pennyworth of bread; and therefore, if he would eat that with a pint of water, it would give him more strength than a quart of beer. He drank on, however, and had four or five shillings to pay out of his wages every Saturday night for that muddling liquor; an expense I was free from. And thus these poor devils keep themselves always under.

Watts, after some weeks, desiring to have me in the composing-room,[1] I left the pressmen; a new bien venu or sum for drink, being

---

[1] Franklin now left the work of operating the printing presses, which was largely a matter of manual labor, and began setting type, which required more skill and intelligence.

five shillings, was demanded of me by the compositors. I thought it an imposition, as I had paid below; the master thought so too, and forbade my paying it. I stood out two or three weeks, was accordingly considered as an excommunicate, and had so many little pieces of private mischief done me, by mixing my sorts, transposing my pages, breaking my matter, etc., etc., if I were ever so little out of the room, and all ascribed to the chappel ghost, which they said ever haunted those not regularly admitted, that, notwithstanding the master's protection, I found myself oblig'd to comply and pay the money, convinc'd of the folly of being on ill terms with those one is to live with continually.

I was now on a fair footing with them, and soon acquir'd considerable influence. I pro-pos'd some reasonable alterations in their chap-pel laws,[1] and carried them against all opposi-tion. From my example, a great part of them left their muddling breakfast of beer, and bread, and cheese, finding they could with me be sup-ply'd from a neighbouring house with a large porringer of hot water-gruel, sprinkled with

[1] A printing house is called a chapel because Caxton, the first English printer, did his printing in a chapel connected with West-minster Abbey.

pepper, crumb'd with bread, and a bit of butter
in it, for the price of a pint of beer, viz., three
half-pence. This was a more comfortable as
well as cheaper breakfast, and keep their heads
clearer. Those who continued sotting with
beer all day, were often, by not paying, out
of credit at the alehouse, and us'd to make interest with me to get beer; their *light,* as they
phrased it, *being out.* I watch'd the pay-table
on Saturday night, and collected what I stood
engag'd for them, having to pay sometimes
near thirty shillings a week on their accounts.
This, and my being esteem'd a pretty good
riggite, that is, a jocular verbal satirist, supported my consequence in the society. My
constant attendance (I never making a St.
Monday)[1] recommended me to the master; and
my uncommon quickness at composing occasioned my being put upon all work of dispatch,
which was generally better paid. So I went on
now very agreeably.

My lodging in Little Britain being too remote, I found another in Duke-street, opposite to the Romish Chapel. It was two pair
of stairs backwards, at an Italian warehouse.
A widow lady kept the house; she had a daughter, and a maid servant, and a journeyman who

[1] A holiday taken to prolong the dissipation of Saturday's wages.

attended the warehouse, but lodg'd abroad.
After sending to inquire my character at
the house where I last lodg'd she agreed to
take me in at the same rate, 3s. 6d. per week:
cheaper, as she said, from the protection she
expected in having a man lodge in the house.
She was a widow, an elderly woman; had been
bred a Protestant, being a clergyman's daughter, but was converted to the Catholic religion
by her husband, whose memory she much re-
vered; had lived much among people of distinction, and knew a thousand anecdotes of
them as far back as the times of Charles the
Second. She was lame in her knees with the
gout, and, therefore, seldom stirred out of her
room, so sometimes wanted company; and hers
was so highly amusing to me, that I was sure
to spend an evening with her whenever she
desired it. Our supper was only half an
anchovy each, on a very little strip of bread
and butter, and half a pint of ale between us;
but the entertainment was in her conversation.
My always keeping good hours, and giving little
trouble in the family, made her unwilling to
part with me, so that, when I talk'd of a lodging I had heard of, nearer my business, for two
shillings a week, which, intent as I now was
on saving money, made some difference, she

bid me not think of it, for she would abate me
two shillings a week for the future; so I remained with her at one shilling and sixpence
as long as I staid in London.

In a garret of her house there lived a maiden
lady of seventy, in the most retired manner,
of whom my landlady gave me this account:
that she was a Roman Catholic, had been sent
abroad when young, and lodg'd in a nunnery
with an intent of becoming a nun; but, the
country not agreeing with her, she returned
to England, where, there being no nunnery, she
had vow'd to lead the life of a nun, as near as
might be done in those circumstances. Accordingly, she had given all her estate to
charitable uses, reserving only twelve pounds
a year to live on, and out of this sum she still
gave a great deal in charity, living herself on
water-gruel only, and using no fire but to boil
it. She had lived many years in that garret,
being permitted to remain there gratis by suc-
cessive Catholic tenants of the house below,
as they deemed it a blessing to have her there.
A priest visited her to confess her every day.
"I have ask'd her," says my landlady, "how
she, as she liv'd, could possibly find so much
employment for a confessor?" "Oh," said she,
"it is impossible to avoid *vain thoughts*." I

was permitted once to visit her. She was
cheerful and polite, and convers'd pleasantly.
The room was clean, but had no other furniture than a matras, a table with a crucifix and
book, a stool which she gave me to sit on, and
a picture over the chimney of Saint Veronica
displaying her handkerchief, with the mirac-
ulous figure of Christ's bleeding face on it,[1]
which she explained to me with great seriousness. She look'd pale, but was never sick;
and I give it as another instance on how small
an income, life and health may be supported.

At Watts's printing-house I contracted an
acquaintance with an ingenious young man,
one Wygate, who, having wealthy relations,
had been better educated than most printers;
was a tolerable Latinist, spoke French, and
lov'd reading. I taught him and a friend of
his to swim at twice going into the river, and
they soon became good swimmers. They introduc'd me to some gentlemen from the country, who went to Chelsea by water to see the
College and Don Saltero's curiosities.[2]   In our

---

[1] The story is that she met Christ on His way to crucifixion
and offered Him her handkerchief to wipe the blood from His
face, after which the handkerchief always bore the image of
Christ's bleeding face.

[2] James Salter, a former servant of Hans Sloane, lived in Cheyne
Walk, Chelsea. "His house, a barber-shop, was known as 'Don
Saltero's Coffee-House.' The curiosities were in glass cases and

return, at the request of the company, whose
curiosity Wygate had excited, I stripped and
leaped into the river, and swam from near
Chelsea to Blackfryar's,[1] performing on the
way many feats of activity, both upon and under water, that surpris'd and pleas'd those to
whom they were novelties.

I had from a child been ever delighted with
this exercise, had studied and practis'd all
Thevenot's motions and positions, added some
of my own, aiming at the graceful and easy
as well as the useful. All these I took this
occasion of exhibiting to the company, and
was much flatter'd by their admiration; and
Wygate, who was desirous of becoming a master, grew more and more attach'd to me on
that account, as well as from the similarity
of our studies. He at length proposed to me
traveling all over Europe together, supporting ourselves everywhere by working at our
business. I was once inclined to it; but, mentioning it to my good friend Mr. Denham, with
whom I often spent an hour when I had leisure,
he dissuaded me from it, advising me to think

constituted an amazing and motley collection—a petrified crab
from China, a 'lignified hog,' Job's tears, Madagascar lances, William the Conqueror's flaming sword, and Henry the Eighth's coat
of mail."—Smyth.
[1] About three miles.

only of returning to Pennsilvania, which he was now about to do.

I must record one trait of this good man's character. He had formerly been in business at Bristol, but failed in debt to a number of people, compounded and went to America. There, by a close application to business as a merchant, he acquir'd a plentiful fortune in a few years. Returning to England in the ship with me, he invited his old creditors to an entertainment, at which he thank'd them for the easy composition they had favoured him with, and, when they expected nothing but the treat, every man at the first remove found under his plate an order on a banker for the full amount of the unpaid remainder with interest.

He now told me he was about to return to Philadelphia, and should carry over a great quantity of goods in order to open a store there. He propos'd to take me over as his clerk, to keep his books, in which he would instruct me, copy his letters, and attend the store. He added, that, as soon as I should be acquainted with mercantile business, he would promote me by sending me with a cargo of flour and bread, etc., to the West Indies, and procure me commissions from others which would be profitable; and, if I manag'd well, would establish me handsomely. The thing pleas'd me; for I was grown tired of London, remembered with pleasure the happy months I had spent in Pennsylvania, and wish'd again to see it; therefore I immediately agreed on the terms of fifty pounds a year,[1] Pennsylvania money; less, indeed, than my present gettings as a compositor, but affording a better prospect.

I now took leave of printing, as I thought, forever, and was daily employed in my new business, going about with Mr. Denham among the tradesmen to purchase various articles, and seeing them pack'd up, doing errands, calling upon workmen to dispatch, etc.; and, when all was on board, I had a few days' leisure. On one of these days, I was, to my surprise, sent for by a great man I knew only by name, a Sir William Wyndham, and I waited upon him. He had heard by some means or other of my swimming from Chelsea to Blackfriars, and of my teaching Wygate and another young man to swim in a few hours. He had two sons, about to set out on their travels; he wish'd to have them first taught swimming, and proposed to gratify me handsomely if I would teach them. They were not yet come to town,

[1] About $167.

and my stay was uncertain, so I could not undertake it; but, from this incident, I thought it likely that, if I were to remain in England and open a swimming-school, I might get a good deal of money; and it struck me so strongly, that, had the overture been sooner made me, probably I should not so soon have returned to America. After many years, you and I had something of more importance to do with one of these sons of Sir William Wyndham, become Earl of Egremont, which I shall mention in its place.

Thus I spent about eighteen months in London; most part of the time I work'd hard at my business, and spent but little upon myself except in seeing plays and in books. My friend Ralph had kept me poor; he owed me about twenty-seven pounds, which I was now never likely to receive; a great sum out of my small earnings! I lov'd him, notwithstanding, for he had many amiable qualities. I had by no means improv'd my fortune; but I had picked up some very ingenious acquaintance, whose conversation was of great advantage to me; and I had read considerably.

VII

BEGINNING BUSINESS IN
PHILADELPHIA

E sail'd from Gravesend on the 23rd of July, 1726. For the incidents of the voyage, I refer you to my Journal, where you will find them all minutely related. Perhaps the most important part of that journal is the *plan* [1] to be found in it, which I formed at sea, for regulating my future conduct in life. It is the more remarkable, as being formed when I was so young, and yet being pretty faithfully adhered to quite thro' to old age.

We landed in Philadelphia on the 11th of October, where I found sundry alterations. Keith was no longer governor, being superseded by Major Gordon. I met him walking the streets as a common citizen. He seem'd a little asham'd at seeing me, but pass'd without saying anything. I should have been as much asham'd at seeing Miss Read, had not

[1] "Not found in the manuscript journal, which was left among Franklin's papers."—Bigelow.

her friends, despairing with reason of my return after the receipt of my letter, persuaded her to marry another, one Rogers, a potter, which was done in my absence. With him, however, she was never happy, and soon parted from him, refusing to cohabit with him or bear his name, it being now said that he had another wife. He was a worthless fellow, tho' an excellent workman, which was the temptation to her friends. He got into debt, ran away in 1727 or 1728, went to the West Indies, and died there. Keimer had got a better house, a shop well supply'd with stationery, plenty of new types, a number of hands, tho' none good, and seem'd to have a great deal of business.

Mr. Denham took a store in Water-street, where we open'd our goods; I attended the business diligently, studied accounts, and grew, in a little time, expert at selling. We lodg'd and boarded together; he counsell'd me as a father, having a sincere regard for me. I respected and loved him, and we might have gone on together very happy; but, in the beginning of February, 172$\frac{6}{7}$, when I had just pass'd my twenty-first year, we both were taken ill. My distemper was a pleurisy, which very nearly carried me off. I suffered a good

deal, gave up the point in my own mind, and
was rather disappointed when I found myself
recovering, regretting, in some degree, that I
must now, some time or other, have all that
disagreeable work to do over again. I forget
what his distemper was; it held him a long
time, and at length carried him off. He left

me a small legacy in a nuncupative will, as
a token of his kindness for me, and he left
me once more to the wide world; for the store
was taken into the care of his executors, and
my employment under him ended.

My brother-in-law, Holmes, being now at
Philadelphia, advised my return to my business; and Keimer tempted me, with an offer
of large wages by the year, to come and take
the management of his printing-house, that
he might better attend his stationer's shop.

I had heard a bad character of him in London from his wife and her friends, and was not fond of having any more to do with him. I tri'd for farther employment as a merchant's clerk; but, not readily meeting with any, I clos'd again with Keimer. I found in his house these hands: Hugh Meredith, a Welsh Pensilvanian, thirty years of age, bred to country work; honest, sensible, had a great deal of solid observation, was something of a reader, but given to drink. Stephen Potts, a young countryman of full age, bred to the same, of uncommon natural parts, and great wit and humor, but a little idle. These he had agreed with at extream low wages per week to be rais'd a shilling every three months, as they would deserve by improving in their business; and the expectation of these high wages, to come on hereafter, was what he had drawn them in with. Meredith was to work at press, Potts at book-binding, which he, by agreement, was to teach them, though he knew neither one nor t'other. John ——, a wild Irishman, brought up to no business, whose service, for four years, Keimer had purchased from the captain of a ship; he, too, was to be made a pressman. George Webb, an Oxford scholar, whose time for four years he had likewise bought, intending him for a compositor, of whom more presently; and David Harry, a country boy, whom he had taken apprentice.

I soon perceiv'd that the intention of engaging me at wages so much higher than he had been us'd to give, was, to have these raw, cheap hands form'd thro' me; and, as soon as I had instructed them, then they being all articled to him, he should be able to do without me. I went on, however, very chearfully, put his printing-house in order, which had been in great confusion, and brought his hands by degrees to mind their business and to do it better.

It was an odd thing to find an Oxford scholar in the situation of a bought servant. He was not more than eighteen years of age, and gave me this account of himself; that he was born in Gloucester, educated at a grammar-school there, had been distinguish'd among the scholars for some apparent superiority in performing his part, when they exhibited plays; belong'd to the Witty Club there, and had written some pieces in prose and verse, which were printed in the Gloucester newspapers; thence he was sent to Oxford; where he continued about a year, but not well satisfi'd, wishing of all things to see London, and become a player. At

length, receiving his quarterly allowance of
fifteen guineas, instead of discharging his debts
he walk'd out of town, hid his gown in a furze
bush, and footed it to London, where, having
no friend to advise him, he fell into bad company, soon spent his guineas, found no means
of being introduc'd among the players, grew
necessitous, pawn'd his cloaths, and wanted bread.
Walking the street very hungry, and not knowing what to do with himself, a crimp's bill [1]
was put into his hand, offering immediate entertainment and encouragement to such as would
bind themselves to serve in America. He went
directly, sign'd the indentures, was put into
the ship, and came over, never writing a line
to acquaint his friends what was become of
him. He was lively, witty, good-natur'd, and
a pleasant companion, but idle, thoughtless,
and imprudent to the last degree.

John, the Irishman, soon ran away; with
the rest I began to live very agreeably, for
they all respected me the more, as they found
Keimer incapable of instructing them, and that
from me they learned something daily. We
never worked on Saturday, that being Keimer's

[1] A crimp was the agent of a shipping company. Crimps were
sometimes employed to decoy men into such service as is here
mentioned.

Sabbath, so I had two days for reading. My acquaintance with ingenious people in the town increased. Keimer himself treated me with great civility and apparent regard, and nothing now made me uneasy but my debt to Vernon, which I was yet unable to pay, being hitherto but a poor æconomist. He, however, kindly made no demand of it.

Our printing-house often wanted sorts, and there was no letter-founder in America; I had seen types cast at James's in London, but without much attention to the manner; however, I now contrived a mould, made use of the letters we had as puncheons, struck the mattrices in lead, and thus supply'd in a pretty tolerable way all deficiencies. I also engrav'd several things on occasion; I made the ink; I was warehouseman, and everything, and, in short, quite a fac-totum.

But, however serviceable I might be, I found that my services became every day of less importance, as the other hands improv'd in the business; and, when Keimer paid my second quarter's wages, he let me know that he felt them too heavy, and thought I should make an abatement. He grew by degrees less civil, put on more of the master, frequently found fault, was captious, and seem'd ready for an outbreaking. I went on, nevertheless, with a good deal of patience, thinking that his encumber'd circumstances were partly the cause. At length a trifle snapt our connections; for, a great noise happening near the court-house, I put my head out of the window to see what was the matter. Keimer, being in the street, look'd up and saw me, call'd out to me in a loud voice and angry tone to mind my business, adding some reproachful words, that nettled me the more for their publicity, all the neighbours who were looking out on the same occasion being witnesses how I was treated. He came up immediately into the printing-house, continu'd the quarrel, high words pass'd on both sides, he gave me the quarter's warning we had stipulated, expressing a wish that he had not been oblig'd to so long a warning. I told him his wish was unnecessary, for I would leave him that instant; and so, taking my hat, walk'd out of doors, desiring Meredith, whom I saw below, to take care of some things I left, and bring them to my lodgings.

Meredith came accordingly in the evening, when we talked my affair over. He had conceiv'd a great regard for me, and was very unwilling that I should leave the house while he remain'd in it. He dissuaded me from returning to my native country, which I began to think of; he reminded me that Keimer was in debt for all he possess'd; that his creditors began to be uneasy; that he kept his shop miserably, sold often without profit for ready money, and often trusted without keeping accounts; that he must therefore fail, which would make a vacancy I might profit of. I objected my want of money. He then let me know that his father had a high opinion of me, and, from some discourse that had pass'd between them, he was sure would advance money to set us up, if I would enter into partnership with him. "My time," says he, "will be out with Keimer in the spring; by that time we may have our press and types in from London. I am sensible I am no workman; if you like it, your skill in the business shall be set against the stock I furnish, and we will share the profits equally."

The proposal was agreeable, and I consented; his father was in town and approv'd of it; the more as he saw I had great influence with his son, had prevail'd on him to abstain long from dram-drinking, and he hop'd might break him of that wretched habit entirely, when we came to be so closely connected. I gave an inventory

to the father, who carry'd it to a merchant; the
things were sent for, the secret was to be kept
till they should arrive, and in the meantime
I was to get work, if I could, at the other
printing-house. But I found no vacancy there,
and so remain'd idle a few days, when Keimer,
on a prospect of being employ'd to print some
paper money in New Jersey, which would require cuts and various types that I only could
supply, and apprehending Bradford might engage me and get the jobb from him, sent me
a very civil message, that old friends should
not part for a few words, the effect of sudden passion, and wishing me to return. Meredith persuaded me to comply, as it would give
more opportunity for his improvement under
my daily instructions; so I return'd, and we
went on more smoothly than for some time
before. The New Jersey jobb was obtained,
I contriv'd a copperplate press for it, the first
that had been seen in the country; I cut several ornaments and checks for the bills. We
went together to Burlington, where I executed
the whole to satisfaction; and he received so
large a sum for the work as to be enabled
thereby to keep his head much longer above
water.

At Burlington I made an acquaintance with

many principal people of the province. Several of them had been appointed by the Assembly a committee to attend the press, and take care that no more bills were printed than the law directed. They were therefore, by turns, constantly with us, and generally he who attended, brought with him a friend or two for company. My mind having been much more improv'd by reading than Keimer's, I suppose it was for that reason my conversation seem'd to be more valu'd. They had me to their houses, introduced me to their friends, and show'd me much civility; while he, tho' the master, was a little neglected. In truth, he was an odd fish; ignorant of common life, fond of rudely opposing receiv'd opinions, slovenly to extream dirtiness, enthusiastic in some points of religion, and a little knavish withal.

We continu'd there near three months; and by that time I could reckon among my acquired friends, Judge Allen, Samuel Bustill, the secretary of the Province, Isaac Pearson, Joseph Cooper, and several of the Smiths, members of Assembly, and Isaac Decow, the surveyor-general. The latter was a shrewd, sagacious old man, who told me that he began for himself, when young, by wheeling clay for brickmakers, learned to write after he was of age, carri'd the chain for surveyors, who taught him surveying, and he had now by his industry, acquir'd a good estate; and says he, "I foresee that you will soon work this man out of his business, and make a fortune in it at Philadelphia." He had not then the least intimation of my intention to set up there or anywhere. These friends were afterwards of great use to me, as I occasionally was to some of them. They all continued their regard for me as long as they lived.

Before I enter upon my public appearance in business, it may be well to let you know the then state of my mind with regard to my principles and morals, that you may see how far those influenc'd the future events of my life. My parents had early given me religious impressions, and brought me through my childhood piously in the Dissenting way. But I was scarce fifteen, when, after doubting by turns of several points, as I found them disputed in the different books I read, I began to doubt of Revelation itself. Some books against Deism [1] fell into my hands; they were

[1] The creed of an eighteenth century theological sect which, while believing in God, refused to credit the possibility of miracles and to acknowledge the validity of revelation.

said to be the substance of sermons preached at Boyle's Lectures. It happened that they wrought an effect on me quite contrary to what was intended by them; for the arguments of the Deists, which were quoted to be refuted, appeared to me much stronger than the refutations; in short, I soon became a thorough Deist. My arguments perverted some others, particularly Collins and Ralph; but, each of them having afterwards wrong'd me greatly without the least compunction, and recollecting Keith's conduct towards me (who was another free-thinker), and my own towards Vernon and Miss Read, which at times gave me great trouble, I began to suspect that this doctrine, tho' it might be true, was not very useful. My London pamphlet, which had for its motto these lines of Dryden: [1]

> "Whatever is, is right. Though purblind man
> Sees but a part o' the chain, the nearest link:
> His eyes not carrying to the equal beam,
> That poises all above;"

and from the attributes of God, his infinite wisdom, goodness and power, concluded that nothing could possibly be wrong in the world, and that vice and virtue were empty distinc-

[1] A great English poet, dramatist, and critic (1631-1700).
The lines are inaccurately quoted from Dryden's *Œdipus*, Act III, Scene I, line 293.

tions, no such things existing, appear'd now not so clever a performance as I once thought it; and I doubted whether some error had not insinuated itself unperceiv'd into my argument, so as to infect all that follow'd, as is common in metaphysical reasonings.

I grew convinc'd that *truth, sincerity* and *integrity* in dealings between man and man were of the utmost importance to the felicity of life; and I form'd written resolutions, which still remain in my journal book, to practice them ever while I lived. Revelation had indeed no weight with me, as such; but I entertain'd an opinion that, though certain actions might not be bad *because* they were forbidden by it, or good *because* it commanded them, yet probably these actions might be forbidden *because* they were bad for us, or commanded *because* they were beneficial to us, in their own natures, all the circumstances of things considered. And this persuasion, with the kind hand of Providence, or some guardian angel, or accidental favourable circumstances and situations, or all together, preserved me, thro' this dangerous time of youth, and the hazardous situations I was sometimes in among strangers, remote from the eye and advice of my father, without any willful gross immorality or injustice, that might

have been expected from my want of religion.
I say willful, because the instances I have mentioned had something of *necessity* in them, from
my youth, inexperience, and the knavery of
others. I had therefore a tolerable character
to begin the world with; I valued it properly,
and determin'd to preserve it.

We had not been long return'd to Philadelphia
before the new types arriv'd from London. We
settled with Keimer, and left him by his consent before he heard of it. We found a house
to hire near the market, and took it. To lessen
the rent, which was then but twenty-four
pounds a year, tho' I have since known it to
let for seventy, we took in Thomas Godfrey,
a glazier, and his family, who were to pay a
considerable part of it to us, and we to board
with them. We had scarce opened our letters
and put our press in order, before George
House, an acquaintance of mine, brought a countryman to us, whom he had met in the street
inquiring for a printer. All our cash was now
expended in the variety of particulars we had
been obliged to procure, and this countryman's
five shillings, being our first-fruits, and coming
so seasonably, gave me more pleasure than any
crown I have since earned; and the gratitude
I felt toward House has made me often more

ready than perhaps I should otherwise have been to assist young beginners.

There are croakers in every country, always boding its ruin. Such a one then lived in Philadelphia; a person of note, an elderly man, with a wise look and a very grave manner of speaking; his name was Samuel Mickle. This gentleman, a stranger to me, stopt one day at my door, and asked me if I was the young man who had lately opened a new printing-house. Being answered in the affirmative, he said he was sorry for me, because it was an expensive undertaking, and the expense would be lost; for Philadelphia was a sinking place, the people already half-bankrupts, or near being so; all appearances to the contrary, such as new buildings and the rise of rents, being to his certain knowledge fallacious; for they were, in fact, among the things that would soon ruin us. And he gave me such a detail of misfortunes now existing, or that were soon to exist, that he left me half melancholy. Had I known him before I engaged in this business, probably I never should have done it. This man continued to live in this decaying place, and to declaim in the same strain, refusing for many years to buy a house there, because all was going to destruction; and at last I had the pleasure of seeing him give five times as much for one as he might have bought it for when he first began his croaking.

I should have mentioned before, that, in the autumn of the preceding year, I had form'd most of my ingenious acquaintance into a club of mutual improvement, which was called the JUNTO;[1] we met on Friday evenings. The rules that I drew up required that every member, in his turn, should produce one or more queries on any point of Morals, Politics, or Natural Philosophy, to be discuss'd by the company; and once in three months produce and read an essay of his own writing, on any subject he pleased. Our debates were to be under the direction of a president, and to be conducted in the sincere spirit of inquiry after truth, without fondness for dispute, or desire of victory; and, to prevent warmth, all expressions of positiveness in opinions, or direct contradiction, were after some time made contraband, and prohibited under small pecuniary penalties.

The first members were Joseph Breintnal, a copyer of deeds for the scriveners, a good-natur'd, friendly middle-ag'd man, a great lover

---

[1] A Spanish term meaning a combination for political intrigue; here a club or society.

of poetry, reading all he could meet with, and writing some that was tolerable; very ingenious in many little Nicknackeries, and of sensible conversation.

Thomas Godfrey, a self-taught mathematician, great in his way, and afterward inventor of what is now called Hadley's Quadrant. But he knew little out of his way, and was not a pleasing companion; as, like most great mathematicians I have met with, he expected universal precision in everything said, or was forever denying or distinguishing upon trifles, to the disturbance of all conversation. He soon left us.

Nicholas Scull, a surveyor, afterwards surveyor-general, who lov'd books, and sometimes made a few verses.

William Parsons, bred a shoemaker, but, loving reading, had acquir'd a considerable share of mathematics, which he first studied with a view to astrology, that he afterwards laught at it. He also became surveyor-general.

William Maugridge, a joiner, a most exquisite mechanic, and a solid, sensible man.

Hugh Meredith, Stephen Potts, and George Webb I have characteriz'd before.

Robert Grace, a young gentleman of some

fortune, generous, lively, and witty; a lover of punning and of his friends.

And William Coleman, then a merchant's clerk, about my age, who had the coolest, clearest head, the best heart, and the exactest morals of almost any man I ever met with. He became afterwards a merchant of great note, and one of our provincial judges. Our friendship continued without interruption to his death, upwards of forty years; and the club continued almost as long, and was the best school of philosophy, morality, and politics that then existed in the province; for our queries, which were read the week preceding their discussion, put us upon reading with attention upon the several subjects, that we might speak more to the purpose; and here, too, we acquired better habits of conversation, everything being studied in our rules which might prevent our disgusting each other. From hence the long continuance of the club, which I shall have frequent occasion to speak further of hereafter.

But my giving this account of it here is to show something of the interest I had, everyone of these exerting themselves in recommending business to us. Breintnal particularly procur'd us from the Quakers the printing forty sheets of their history, the rest being to be done by Keimer; and upon this we work'd exceedingly hard, for the price was low. It was a folio, pro patria size, in pica, with long primer notes.[1] I compos'd of it a sheet a day, and Meredith worked it off at press; it was often eleven at night, and sometimes later, before I had finished my distribution for the next day's work, for the little jobbs sent in by our other friends now and then put us back. But so determin'd I was to continue doing a sheet a day of the folio, that one night, when, having impos'd[2] my forms, I thought my day's work over, one of them by accident was broken, and two pages reduced to pi,[3] I immediately distribut'd and composed it over again before I went to bed; and this industry, visible to our neighbors, began to give us character and credit; particularly, I was told, that mention being made of the new printing-office at the merchants' Every-night club, the general opinion was that it must fail, there being already two printers in the place, Keimer and

---

[1] A sheet 8½ by 13½ inches, having the words *pro patria* in translucent letters in the body of the paper. Pica—a size of type; as, A B C D: Long Primer—a smaller size of type; as, A B C D.

[2] To arrange and lock up pages or columns of type in a rec-tangular iron frame, ready for printing.

[3] Reduced to complete disorder.

Bradford; but Dr. Baird (whom you and I saw many years after at his native place, St. Andrew's in Scotland) gave a contrary opinion: "For the industry of that Franklin," says he, "is superior to anything I ever saw of the kind; I see him still at work when I go home from club, and he is at work again before his neighbors are out of bed." This struck the rest, and we soon after had offers from one of them to supply us with stationery; but as yet we did not chuse to engage in shop business.

I mention this industry the more particularly and the more freely, tho' it seems to be talking in my own praise, that those of my posterity, who shall read it, may know the use of that virtue, when they see its effects in my favour throughout this relation.

George Webb, who had found a female friend that lent him wherewith to purchase his time of Keimer, now came to offer himself as a journeyman to us. We could not then imploy him; but I foolishly let him know as a secret that I soon intended to begin a newspaper, and might then have work for him. My hopes of success, as I told him, were founded on this, that the then only newspaper, printed by Bradford, was a paltry thing, wretchedly manag'd, no way

entertaining, and yet was profitable to him; I
therefore thought a good paper would scarcely
fail of good encouragement. I requested Webb
not to mention it; but he told it to Keimer,
who immediately, to be beforehand with me,
published proposals for printing one himself,
on which Webb was to be employ'd. I resented this; and, to counteract them, as I
could not yet begin our paper, I wrote several
pieces of entertainment for Bradford's paper,
under the title of the BUSY BODY, which Breintnal continu'd some months. By this means
the attention of the publick was fixed on that
paper, and Keimer's proposals, which we bur-
lesqu'd and ridicul'd, were disregarded. He
began his paper, however, and, after carrying
it on three quarters of a year, with at most
only ninety subscribers, he offered it to me
for a trifle; and I, having been ready some
time to go on with it, took it in hand directly;
and it prov'd in a few years extremely profitable to me.

I perceive that I am apt to speak in the
singular number, though our partnership still
continu'd; the reason may be that, in fact, the
whole management of the business lay upon
me. Meredith was no compositor, a poor pressman, and seldom sober. My friends lamented

my connection with him, but I was to make the best of it.

Our first papers made a quite different appearance from any before in the province; a better type, and better printed; but some spirited remarks of my writing, on the dispute then going on between Governor Burnet and the Massachusets Assembly, struck the principal people, occasioned the paper and the manager of it to be much talk'd of, and in a few weeks brought them all to be our subscribers.

Their example was follow'd by many, and our number went on growing continually. This was one of the first good effects of my having learnt a little to scribble; another was, that the leading men, seeing a newspaper now in the hands of one who could also handle a pen, thought it convenient to oblige and encourage me. Bradford still printed the votes, and laws, and other publick business. He had printed an address of the House to the governor, in a coarse, blundering manner; we reprinted it elegantly and correctly, and sent one to every member. They were sensible of the difference: it strengthened the hands of our friends in the House, and they voted us their printers for the year ensuing.

Among my friends in the House I must not forget Mr. Hamilton, before mentioned, who was then returned from England, and had a seat in it. He interested himself for me strongly in that instance, as he did in many others afterward, continuing his patronage till his death.[1]

Mr. Vernon, about this time, put me in mind of the debt I ow'd him, but did not press me. I wrote him an ingenuous letter of acknowledgment, crav'd his forbearance a little longer, which he allow'd me, and as soon as I was able, I paid the principal with interest, and many thanks; so that erratum was in some degree corrected.

But now another difficulty came upon me which I had never the least reason to expect. Mr. Meredith's father, who was to have paid for our printing-house, according to the expectations given me, was able to advance only one hundred pounds currency, which had been paid; and a hundred more was due to the merchant, who grew impatient, and su'd us all. We gave bail, but saw that, if the money could not be rais'd in time, the suit must soon come to a judgment and execution, and our hopeful prospects must, with us, be ruined, as

[1] I got his son once £500.—*Marg. note.*

the press and letters must be sold for payment, perhaps at half price.

In this distress two true friends, whose kindness I have never forgotten, nor ever shall forget while I can remember any thing, came to me separately, unknown to each other, and, without any application from me, offering each of them to advance me all the money that should be necessary to enable me to take the whole business upon myself, if that should be practicable; but they did not like my continuing the partnership with Meredith, who, as they said, was often seen drunk in the streets, and playing at low games in alehouses, much to our discredit. These two friends were William Coleman and Robert Grace. I told them I could not propose a separation while any prospect remain'd of the Meredith's fulfilling their part of our agreement, because I thought myself under great obligations to them for what they had done, and would do if they could; but, if they finally fail'd in their performance, and our partnership must be dissolv'd, I should then think myself at liberty to accept the assistance of my friends.

Thus the matter rested for some time, when I said to my partner, "Perhaps your father is dissatisfied at the part you have undertaken in this affair of ours, and is unwilling to advance for you and me what he would for you alone. If that is the case, tell me, and I will resign the whole to you, and go about my business." " No," said he, " my father has really been disappointed, and is really unable; and I am unwilling to distress him farther. I see this is a business I am not fit for. I was bred a farmer, and it was a folly in me to come to town, and put myself, at thirty years of age, an apprentice to learn a new trade. Many of our Welsh people are going to settle in North Carolina, where land is cheap. I am inclin'd to go with them, and follow my old employment. You may find friends to assist you. If you will take the debts of the company upon you; return to my father the hundred pounds he has advanced; pay my little personal debts, and give me thirty pounds and a new saddle, I will relinquish the partnership, and leave the whole in your hands." I agreed to this proposal: it was drawn up in writing, sign'd, and seal'd immediately. I gave him what he demanded, and he went soon after to Carolina, from whence he sent me next year two long letters, containing the best account that had been given of that country, the climate, the soil, husbandry, etc., for in those matters he was very judicious. I printed them in the papers, and they gave great satisfaction to the publick.

As soon as he was gone, I recurr'd to my two friends; and because I would not give an unkind preference to either, I took half of what each had offered and I wanted of one, and half of the other; paid off the company's debts, and went on with the business in my own name, advertising that the partnership was dissolved. I think this was in or about the year 1729.

VIII

BUSINESS SUCCCESS AND FIRST
PUBLIC SERVICE

BOUT this time there was a cry among the people for more paper money, only fifteen thousand pounds being extant in the province, and that soon to be sunk.[1] The wealthy inhabitants oppos'd any addition, being against all paper currency, from an apprehension that it would depreciate, as it had done in New England, to the prejudice of all creditors. We had discuss'd this point in our Junto, where I was on the side of an addition, being persuaded that the first small sum struck in 1723 had done much good by increasing the trade, employment, and number of inhabitants in the province, since I now saw all the old houses inhabited, and many new ones building: whereas I remembered well, that when I first walk'd about the streets of Philadelphia, eating my roll, I saw most of the houses in Walnut Street, between Second and Front streets,[2]

[1] Recalled to be redeemed.
[2] This part of Philadelphia is now the center of the wholesale business district.

with bills on their doors, "To be let"; and many likewise in Chestnut-street and other streets, which made me then think the inhabitants of the city were deserting it one after another.

Our debates possess'd me so fully of the subject, that I wrote and printed an anonymous pamphlet on it, entitled *"The Nature and Necessity of a Paper Currency."* It was well receiv'd by the common people in general; but the rich men dislik'd it, for it increas'd and strengthen'd the clamor for more money, and they happening to have no writers among them that were able to answer it, their opposition slacken'd, and the point was carried by a majority in the House. My friends there, who conceiv'd I had been of some service, thought fit to reward me by employing me in printing the money; a very profitable jobb and a great help to me. This was another advantage gain'd by my being able to write.

The utility of this currency became by time and experience so evident as never afterwards to be much disputed; so that it grew soon to fifty-five thousand pounds, and in 1739 to eighty thousand pounds, since which it arose during war to upwards of three hundred and fifty thousand pounds, trade, building, and inhabi-

tants all the while increasing, tho' I now think
there are limits beyond which the quantity
may be hurtful.[1]

I soon after obtain'd, thro' my friend Hamilton, the printing of the Newcastle paper
money, another profitable jobb as I then
thought it; small things appearing great to
those in small circumstances; and these, to me,
were really great advantages, as they were
great encouragements. He procured for me,
also, the printing of the laws and votes of that
government, which continu'd in my hands as
long as I follow'd the business.

I now open'd a little stationer's shop. I
had in it blanks of all sorts, the correctest that
ever appear'd among us, being assisted in that
by my friend Breintnal. I had also paper,
parchment, chapmen's books, etc. One White-
mash, a compositor I had known in London,
an excellent workman, now came to me, and
work'd with me constantly and diligently; and
I took an apprentice, the son of Aquilla Rose.

I began now gradually to pay off the debt

---

[1] Paper money is a promise to pay its face value in gold or
silver. When a state or nation issues more such promises than
there is a likelihood of its being able to redeem, the paper representing the promises depreciates in value. Before the success of
the Colonies in the Revolution was assured, it took hundreds of
dollars of their paper money to buy a pair of boots.

I was under for the printing-house. In order
to secure my credit and character as a tradesman, I took care not only to be in *reality*
industrious and frugal, but to avoid all appearances to the contrary. I drest plainly; I was
seen at no places of idle diversion. I never
went out a fishing or shooting; a book, indeed,

sometimes debauch'd me from my work, but
that was seldom, snug, and gave no scandal;
and, to show that I was not above my business, I sometimes brought home the paper I
purchas'd at the stores thro' the streets on
a wheelbarrow. Thus being esteem'd an industrious, thriving young man, and paying duly
for what I bought, the merchants who imported stationery solicited my custom; others
proposed supplying me with books, and I went
on swimmingly. In the meantime, Keimer's
credit and business declining daily, he was at

last forc'd to sell his printing-house to satisfy his creditors. He went to Barbadoes, and there lived some years in very poor circumstances.

His apprentice, David Harry, whom I had instructed while I work'd with him, set up in his place at Philadelphia, having bought his materials. I was at first apprehensive of a powerful rival in Harry, as his friends were very able, and had a good deal of interest. I therefore propos'd a partnership to him, which he, fortunately for me, rejected with scorn. He was very proud, dress'd like a gentleman, liv'd expensively, took much diversion and pleasure abroad, ran in debt, and neglected his business; upon which, all business left him; and, finding nothing to do, he followed Keimer to Barbadoes, taking the printing-house with him. There this apprentice employ'd his former master as a journeyman; they quarrell'd often; Harry went continually behindhand, and at length was forc'd to sell his types and return to his country work in Pensilvania. The person that bought them employ'd Keimer to use them, but in a few years he died.

There remained now no competitor with me at Philadelphia but the old one, Bradford; who was rich and easy, did a little printing now and then by straggling hands, but was not very anxious about the business. However, as he kept the post-office, it was imagined he had better opportunities of obtaining news; his paper was thought a better distributer of advertisements than mine, and therefore had many more, which was a profitable thing to him, and a disadvantage to me; for, tho' I did indeed receive and send papers by the post, yet the publick opinion was otherwise, for what I did send was by bribing the riders, who took them privately, Bradford being unkind enough to forbid it, which occasion'd some resentment on my part; and I thought so meanly of him for it, that, when I afterward came into his situation, I took care never to imitate it.

I had hitherto continu'd to board with Godfrey, who lived in part of my house with his wife and children, and had one side of the shop for his glazier's business, tho' he worked little, being always absorbed in his mathematics. Mrs. Godfrey projected a match for me with a relation's daughter, took opportunities of bringing us often together, till a serious courtship on my part ensu'd, the girl being in herself very deserving. The old folks encourag'd me by continual invitations to supper, and by leaving us together, till at length it was time

to explain.   Mrs. Godfrey manag'd our little
treaty.   I let her know that I expected as
much money with their daughter as would pay
off my remaining debt for the printing-house,
which I believe was not then above a hundred
pounds.   She brought me word they had no
such sum to spare; I said they might mort-
gage their house in the loan-office.   The answer
to this, after some days, was, that they did
not approve the match; that, on inquiry of
Bradford, they had been informed the printing business was not a profitable one; the types
would soon be worn out, and more wanted;
that S. Keimer and D. Harry had failed one
after the other, and I should probably soon
follow them; and, therefore, I was forbidden
the house, and the daughter shut up.

Whether this was a real change of sentiment or only artifice, on a supposition of our
being too far engaged in affection to retract,
and therefore that we should steal a marriage, which would leave them at liberty to
give or withhold what they pleas'd, I know
not; but I suspected the latter, resented it, and
went no more.   Mrs. Godfrey brought me
afterward some more favorable accounts of
their disposition, and would have drawn me
on again; but I declared absolutely my reso-

lution to have nothing more to do with that family. This was resented by the Godfreys; we differ'd, and they removed, leaving me the whole house, and I resolved to take no more inmates.

But this affair having turned my thoughts to marriage, I look'd round me and made overtures of acquaintance in other places; but soon found that, the business of a printer being generally thought a poor one, I was not to expect money with a wife, unless with such a one as I should not otherwise think agreeable. A friendly correspondence as neighbours and old acquaintances had continued between me and Mrs. Read's family, who all had a regard for me from the time of my first lodging in their house. I was often invited there and consulted in their affairs, wherein I sometimes was of service. I piti'd poor Miss Read's unfortunate situation, who was generally dejected, seldom chearful, and avoided company. I considered my giddiness and inconstancy when in London as in a great degree the cause of her unhappiness, tho' the mother was good enough to think the fault more her own than mine, as she had prevented our marrying before I went thither, and persuaded the other match in my absence. Our mutual affection was revived, but there were now great objections to our union. The match was indeed looked upon as invalid, a preceding wife being said to be living in England; but this could not easily be prov'd, because of the distance; and, tho' there was a report of his death, it was not certain. Then, tho' it should be true, he had left many debts, which his successor might be call'd upon to pay. We ventured, however, over all these difficulties, and I took her to wife, September 1st, 1730. None of the inconveniences happened that we had apprehended; she proved a good and faithful helpmate,[1] assisted me much by attending the shop; we throve together, and have ever mutually endeavour'd to make each other happy. Thus I corrected that great *erratum* as well as I could.

About this time, our club meeting, not at a tavern, but in a little room of Mr. Grace's, set apart for that purpose, a proposition was made

---

[1] Mrs. Franklin survived her marriage over forty years. Franklin's correspondence abounds with evidence that their union was a happy one. "We are grown old together, and if she has any faults, I am so used to them that I don't perceive them." The following is a stanza from one of Franklin's own songs written for the Junto:

"Of their Chloes and Phyllises poets may prate,
　　I sing my plain country Joan,
These twelve years my wife, still the joy of my life,
　　Blest day that I made her my own."

by me, that, since our books were often re-
ferr'd to in our disquisitions upon the queries, it
might be convenient to us to have them altogether where we met, that upon occasion they
might be consulted; and by thus clubbing our
books to a common library, we should, while
we lik'd to keep them together, have each of
us the advantage of using the books of all
the other members, which would be nearly as
beneficial as if each owned the whole. It was
lik'd and agreed to, and we fill'd one end of
the room with such books as we could best
spare. The number was not so great as we
expected; and tho' they had been of great use,
yet some inconveniences occurring for want of
due care of them, the collection, after about a
year, was separated, and each took his books
home again.

And now I set on foot my first project of
a public nature, that for a subscription library.
I drew up the proposals, got them put into form
by our great scrivener, Brockden, and, by the
help of my friends in the Junto, procured fifty
subscribers of forty shillings each to begin
with, and ten shillings a year for fifty years,
the term our company was to continue. We
afterwards obtain'd a charter, the company
being increased to one hundred: this was the

mother of all the North American subscription
libraries, now so numerous. It is become a
great thing itself, and continually increasing.
These libraries have improved the general conversation of the Americans, made the common tradesmen and farmers as intelligent as
most gentlemen from other countries, and perhaps have contributed in some degree to the
stand so generally made throughout the colonies in defense of their privileges.[1]

Mem°. Thus far was written with the intention express'd in the beginning and therefore
contains several little family anecdotes of no
importance to others. What follows was written many years after in compliance with the
advice contain'd in these letters, and accordingly intended for the public. The affairs
of the Revolution occasion'd the interruption.[2]

[*Continuation of the Account of my Life, begun
at Passy, near Paris*, 1784.]

It is some time since I receiv'd the above
letters, but I have been too busy till now to

[1] Here the first part of the *Autobiography*, written at Twyford
in 1771, ends. The second part, which follows, was written at
Passy in 1784.

[2] After this memorandum, Franklin inserted letters from Abel
James and Benjamin Vaughan, urging him to continue his *Autobiography.*

think of complying with the request they contain. It might, too, be much better done if I were at home among my papers, which would aid my memory, and help to ascertain dates; but my return being uncertain, and having just now a little leisure, I will endeavour to recollect and write what I can; if I live to get home, it may there be corrected and improv'd.

Not having any copy here of what is already written, I know not whether an account is given of the means I used to establish the Philadelphia public library, which, from a small beginning, is now become so considerable, though I remember to have come down to near the time of that transaction (1730). I will therefore begin here with an account of it, which may be struck out if found to have been already given.

At the time I establish'd myself in Pennsylvania, there was not a good bookseller's shop in any of the colonies to the southward of Boston. In New York and Philad'a the printers were indeed stationers; they sold only paper, etc., almanacs, ballads, and a few common school-books. Those who lov'd reading were oblig'd to send for their books from England; the members of the Junto had each a few. We

had left the alehouse, where we first met, and
hired a room to hold our club in. I propos'd
that we should all of us bring our books to
that room, where they would not only be ready
to consult in our conferences, but become a
common benefit, each of us being at liberty
to borrow such as he wish'd to read at home.
This was accordingly done, and for some time
contented us.

Finding the advantage of this little collection, I propos'd to render the benefit from
books more common, by commencing a public
subscription library. I drew a sketch of the
plan and rules that would be necessary, and
got a skilful conveyancer, Mr. Charles Brockden, to put the whole in form of articles of
agreement to be subscribed, by which each sub-
scriber engag'd to pay a certain sum down
for the first purchase of books, and an annual
contribution for increasing them. So few were
the readers at that time in Philadelphia, and
the majority of us so poor, that I was not
able, with great industry, to find more than
fifty persons, mostly young tradesmen, willing
to pay down for this purpose forty shillings
each, and ten shillings per annum. On this
little fund we began. The books were imported;
the library was opened one day in the week

for lending to the subscribers, on their prom-
issory notes to pay double the value if not duly
returned.   The institution soon manifested its
utility, was imitated by other towns, and in
other provinces.   The libraries were augmented
by donations; reading became fashionable; and
our people, having no publick amusements to
divert their attention from study, became better acquainted with books, and in a few years
were observ'd by strangers to be better
instructed and more intelligent than people of
the same rank generally are in other countries.

When we were about to sign the above-
mentioned articles, which were to be binding
on us, our heirs, etc., for fifty years, Mr. Brockden, the scrivener, said to us, "You are young
men, but it is scarcely probable that any of
you will live to see the expiration of the term
fix'd in the instrument."   A number of us,
however, are yet living; but the instrument was
after a few years rendered null by a charter
that incorporated and gave perpetuity to the
company.

The objections and reluctances I met with
in soliciting the subscriptions, made me soon
feel the impropriety of presenting one's self
as the proposer of any useful project, that
might be suppos'd to raise one's reputation

in the smallest degree above that of one's neighbours, when one has need of their assistance to accomplish that project. I therefore put myself as much as I could out of sight, and stated it as a scheme of a *number of friends*, who had requested me to go about and propose it to such as they thought lovers of reading. In this way my affair went on more smoothly, and I ever after practis'd it on such occasions; and, from my frequent successes, can heartily recommend it. The present little sacrifice of your vanity will afterwards be amply repaid. If it remains a while uncertain to whom the merit belongs, someone more vain than yourself will be encouraged to claim it, and then even envy will be disposed to do you justice by plucking those assumed feathers, and restoring them to their right owner.

This library afforded me the means of improvement by constant study, for which I set apart an hour or two each day, and thus repair'd in some degree the loss of the learned education my father once intended for me. Reading was the only amusement I allow'd myself. I spent no time in taverns, games, or frolicks of any kind; and my industry in my business continu'd as indefatigable as it was necessary. I was indebted for my printing-house; I had a young family coming on to be educated, and I had to contend with for business two printers, who were established in the place before me. My circumstances, however, grew daily easier. My original habits of frugality continuing, and my father having, among his instructions to me when a boy, frequently repeated a proverb of Solomon, "Seest thou a man diligent in his calling, he shall stand before kings, he shall not stand before mean men," I from thence considered industry as a means of obtaining wealth and distinction, which encourag'd me, tho' I did not think that I should ever literally *stand before kings,* which, however, has since happened; for I have stood before *five,* and even had the honor of sitting down with one, the King of Denmark, to dinner.

We have an English proverb that says, *"He that would thrive, must ask his wife."* It was lucky for me that I had one as much dispos'd to industry and frugality as myself. She assisted me chearfully in my business, folding and stitching pamphlets, tending shop, purchasing old linen rags for the paper-makers, etc., etc. We kept no idle servants, our table was plain and simple, our furniture of the cheapest. For instance, my breakfast was a long time break and milk (no tea), and I ate it out of a twopenny earthen porringer, with a pewter spoon. But mark how luxury will enter families, and make a progress, in spite of principle: being call'd one morning to breakfast, I found it in a China bowl, with a spoon of silver! They had been bought for me without my knowledge by my wife, and had cost her the enormous sum of three-and-twenty shillings, for which she had no other excuse or apology to make, but that she thought *her* husband deserv'd a silver spoon and China bowl as well as any of his neighbors. This was the first appearance of plate and China in our house, which afterward, in a course of years, as our wealth increas'd, augmented gradually to several hundred pounds in value.

I had been religiously educated as a Presbyterian; and though some of the dogmas of that persuasion, such as *the eternal decrees of God, election, reprobation, etc.,* appeared to me unintelligible, others doubtful, and I early absented myself from the public assemblies of the sect, Sunday being my studying day, I never was without some religious principles. I never doubted, for instance, the existence of the Deity; that he made the world, and govern'd it by his Providence; that the most

acceptable service of God was the doing good
to man; that our souls are immortal; and that
all crime will be punished, and virtue rewarded,
either here or hereafter. These I esteem'd
the essentials of every religion; and, being to
be found in all the religions we had in our
country, I respected them all, tho' with different degrees of respect, as I found them more
or less mix'd with other articles, which, without any tendency to inspire, promote, or confirm morality, serv'd principally to divide us,
and make us unfriendly to one another. This
respect to all, with an opinion that the worst
had some good effects, induc'd me to avoid all
discourse that might tend to lessen the good
opinion another might have of his own religion;
and as our province increas'd in people, and
new places of worship were continually wanted,
and generally erected by voluntary contribution, my mite for such purpose, whatever might
be the sect, was never refused.

Tho' I seldom attended any public worship,
I had still an opinion of its propriety, and of
its utility when rightly conducted, and I regularly paid my annual subscription for the support of the only Presbyterian minister or meeting we had in Philadelphia. He us'd to visit
me sometimes as a friend, and admonished me

to attend his administrations, and I was now and then prevail'd on to do so, once for five Sundays successively. Had he been in my opinion a good preacher, perhaps I might have continued,[1] notwithstanding the occasion I had for the Sunday's leisure in my course of study; but his discourses were chiefly either polemic arguments, or explications of the peculiar doctrines of our sect, and were all to me very dry, uninteresting, and unedifying, since not a single moral principle was inculcated or enforc'd, their aim seeming to be rather to make us Presbyterians than good citizens.

At length he took for his text that verse of the fourth chapter of Philippians, "*Finally, brethren, whatsoever things are true, honest, just, pure, lovely, or of good report, if there be any virtue, or any praise, think on these things.*" And I imagin'd, in a sermon on such a text, we could not miss of having some morality. But he confin'd himself to five points only, as meant by the apostle, viz.: 1. Keeping holy the Sabbath day. 2. Being diligent in reading the holy Scriptures. 3. Attending duly the publick worship. 4. Partaking of the Sacrament. 5. Paying a due respect to God's min-

---

[1] Franklin expressed a different view about the duty of attending church later.

isters.   These might be all good things; but,
as they were not the kind of good things that
I expected from that text, I despaired of ever
meeting with them from any other, was dis-
gusted, and attended his preaching no more.
I had some years before compos'd a little
Liturgy, or form of prayer, for my own private
use (viz., in 1728), entitled, *Articles of Belief
and Acts of Religion.*   I return'd to the use
of this, and went no more to the public assemblies.   My conduct might be blameable, but
I leave it, without attempting further to excuse
it; my present purpose being to relate facts,
and not to make apologies for them.

IX

PLAN FOR ATTAINING MORAL PERFECTION

T was about this time I conceived the bold and arduous project of arriving at moral perfection. I wish'd to live without committing any fault at any time; I would conquer all that either natural inclination, custom, or company might lead me into. As I knew, or thought I knew, what was right and wrong, I did not see why I might not always do the one and avoid the other. But I soon found I had undertaken a task of more difficulty than I had imagined.[1] While my care was employ'd in guarding against one fault, I was often surprised by another; habit took the advantage of inattention; inclination was sometimes too strong for reason. I concluded, at length, that the mere speculative conviction that it was our interest to be completely virtuous, was not sufficient to prevent our slipping; and that the contrary habits must be broken, and good ones acquired and established, before we can have any de-

[1] Compare Philippians iv, 8.

pendence on a steady, uniform rectitude of conduct. For this purpose I therefore contrived the following method.

In the various enumerations of the moral virtues I had met with in my reading, I found the catalogue more or less numerous, as different writers included more or fewer ideas under the same name. Temperance, for example, was by some confined to eating and drinking, while by others it was extended to mean the moderating every other pleasure, appetite, inclination, or passion, bodily or mental, even to our avarice and ambition. I propos'd to myself, for the sake of clearness, to use rather more names, with fewer ideas annex'd to each, than a few names with more ideas; and I included under thirteen names of virtues all that at that time occurr'd to me as necessary or desirable, and annexed to each a short precept, which fully express'd the extent I gave to its meaning.

These names of virtues, with their precepts, were:

1. TEMPERANCE.

Eat not to dullness; drink not to elevation.

2. SILENCE.

Speak not but what may benefit others or yourself; avoid trifling conversation.

3. ORDER.

Let all your things have their places; let each part of your business have its time.

4. RESOLUTION.

Resolve to perform what you ought; perform without fail what you resolve.

5. FRUGALITY.

Make no expense but to do good to others or yourself; *i. e.,* waste nothing.

6. INDUSTRY.

Lose no time; be always employ'd in something useful; cut off all unnecessary actions.

7. SINCERITY.

Use no hurtful deceit; think innocently and justly; and, if you speak, speak accordingly.

8. JUSTICE.

Wrong none by doing injuries, or omitting the benefits that are your duty.

9. MODERATION.

Avoid extreams; forbear resenting injuries so much as you think they deserve.

10. CLEANLINESS.

Tolerate no uncleanliness in body, cloaths, or habitation.

11.   TRANQUILLITY.

Be not disturbed at trifles, or at accidents common or unavoidable.

12.   CHASTITY.

13.   HUMILITY.

Imitate Jesus and Socrates.

My intention being to acquire the *habitude* of all these virtues, I judg'd it would be well not to distract my attention by attempting the whole at once, but to fix it on one of them at a time; and, when I should be master of that, then to proceed to another, and so on, till I should have gone thro' the thirteen; and, as the previous acquisition of some might facilitate the acquisition of certain others, I arrang'd them with that view, as they stand above. Temperance first, as it tends to procure that coolness and clearness of head, which is so necessary where constant vigilance was to be kept up, and guard maintained against the unremitting attraction of ancient habits, and the force of perpetual temptations. This being acquir'd and establish'd, Silence would be more easy; and my desire being to gain knowledge at the same time that I improv'd in virtue, and considering that in conversation it was obtain'd rather by the use of the ears than of the tongue, and therefore wishing to break a habit I was getting into of prattling, punning, and joking, which only made me acceptable to trifling company, I gave *Silence* the second place. This and the next, *Order,* I expected would allow me more time for attending to my project and my studies. *Resolution,* once become habitual, would keep me firm in my endeavours to obtain all the subsequent virtues; *Frugality* and Industry freeing me from my remaining debt, and producing affluence and independence, would make more easy the practice of Sincerity and Justice, etc., etc. Conceiving then, that, agreeably to the advice of Pythagoras[1] in his Golden Verses, daily examination would be necessary, I contrived the following method for conducting that examination.

I made a little book, in which I allotted a page for each of the virtues.[2] I rul'd each page with red ink, so as to have seven columns. one for each day of the week, marking each column with a letter for the day. I cross'd

[1] A famous Greek philosopher, who lived about 582-500 B. C. The *Golden Verses* here ascribed to him are probably of later origin. "The time which he recommends for this work is about even or bed-time, that we may conclude the action of the day with the judgment of conscience, making the examination of our conversation an evening song to God.

[2] This "little book" is dated July 1, 1733.—W. T. F.

these columns with thirteen red lines, marking the beginning of each line with the first
letter of one of the virtues, on which line, and
in its proper column, I might mark, by a little
black spot, every fault I found upon examination to have been committed respecting that
virtue upon that day.

Form of the pages.

	S.	M.	T.	W.	T.	F.	S.
TEMPERANCE.							
EAT NOT TO DULLNESS. DRINK NOT TO ELEVATION.							
T.							
S.	*	*		*		*	
O.	* *	*	*		*	*	*
R.			*			*	
F.		*			*		
I.			*				
S.							
J.							
M.							
C.							
T.							
C.							
H.							

I determined to give a week's strict attention
to each of the virtues successively. Thus, in the

first week, my great guard was to avoid every the least offense against *Temperance,* leaving the other virtues to their ordinary chance, only marking every evening the faults of the day. Thus, if in the first week I could keep my first line, marked T, clear of spots, I suppos'd the habit of that virtue so much strengthen'd, and its opposite weaken'd, that I might venture extending my attention to include the next, and for the following week keep both lines clear of spots. Proceeding thus to the last, I could go thro' a course compleat in thirteen weeks, and four courses in a year. And like him who, having a garden to weed, does not attempt to eradicate all the bad herbs at once, which would exceed his reach and his strength, but works on one of the beds at a time, and, having accomplish'd the first, proceeds to a second, so I should have, I hoped, the encouraging pleasure of seeing on my pages the progress I made in virtue, by clearing successively my lines of their spots, till in the end, by a number of courses, I should be happy in viewing a clean book, after a thirteen weeks' daily examination.

This my little book had for its motto these lines from Addison's *Cato:*

"Here will I hold. If there's a power above us
(And that there is, all nature cries aloud
Thro' all her works), He must delight in virtue;
And that which he delights in must be happy."

Another from Cicero,

"O vitæ Philosophia dux! O virtutum indagatrix ex-
pultrixque vitiorum! Unus dies, bene et ex præceptis tuis
actus, peccanti immortalitati est anteponendus." [1]

Another from the Proverbs of Solomon, speaking of wisdom or virtue:

"Length of days is in her right hand, and in her left hand
riches and honour. Her ways are ways of pleasantness,
and all her paths are peace." iii. 16, 17.

And conceiving God to be the fountain of
wisdom, I thought it right and necessary to
solicit his assistance for obtaining it; to this
end I formed the following little prayer, which
was prefix'd to my tables of examination, for
daily use.

"*O powerful Goodness! bountiful Father! merciful
Guide! Increase in me that wisdom which discovers my
truest interest. Strengthen my resolutions to perform what
that wisdom dictates. Accept my kind offices to thy other
children as the only return in my power for thy continual
favours to me.*"

---

[1] "O philosophy, guide of life! O searcher out of virtue and
exterminator of vice! One day spent well and in accordance
with thy precepts is worth an immortality of sin."—*Tusculan Inquiries*, Book V.

I used also sometimes a little prayer which I took from Thomson's Poems, viz.:

"Father of light and life, thou Good Supreme!
O teach me what is good; teach me Thyself!
Save me from folly, vanity, and vice,
From every low pursuit; and fill my soul
With knowledge, conscious peace, and virtue pure;
Sacred, substantial, never-fading bliss!"

The precept of *Order* requiring that *every part of my business should have its allotted time,* one page in my little book contain'd the following scheme of employment for the twenty-four hours of a natural day.

THE MORNING. *Question.* What good shall I do this day?	5 6 7	Rise, wash, and address *Powerful Goodness!* Contrive day's business, and take the resolution of the day; prosecute the present study, and breakfast.
	8 9 10 11	Work.
NOON.	12 1	Read, or overlook my accounts, and dine.
	2 3 4 5	Work.

EVENING. *Question.* What good have I have done to-day?	$\left\{\begin{array}{c} 6 \\ 7 \\ 8 \\ 9 \end{array}\right\}$	Put things in their places. Supper. Music or diversion, or conversation. Examination of the day.
NIGHT.	$\left\{\begin{array}{c} 10 \\ 11 \\ 12 \\ 1 \\ 2 \\ 3 \\ 4 \end{array}\right\}$	Sleep.

I enter'd upon the execution of this plan for self-examination, and continu'd it with occasional intermissions for some time. I was suspris'd to find myself so much fuller of faults than I had imagined; but I had the satisfaction of seeing them diminish. To avoid the trouble of renewing now and then my little book, which, by scraping out the marks on the paper of old faults to make room for new ones in a new course, became full of holes, I transferr'd my tables and precepts to the ivory leaves of a memorandum book, on which the lines were drawn with red ink, that made a durable stain, and on those lines I mark'd my faults with a black-lead pencil, which marks I could easily wipe out with a wet sponge. After a while I went thro' one course only in a year, and after-

ward only one in several years, till at length
I omitted them entirely, being employ'd in
voyages and business abroad, with a multi-
plicity of affairs that interfered; but I always
carried my little book with me.

My scheme of ORDER gave me the most
trouble;[1] and I found that, tho' it might be
practicable where a man's business was such
as to leave him the disposition of his time, that
of a journeyman printer, for instance, it was
not possible to be exactly observed by a master,
who must mix with the world, and often receive people of business at their own hours.
Order, too, with regard to places for things,
papers, etc., I found extreamly difficult to
acquire. I had not been early accustomed to
it, and, having an exceeding good memory, I
was not so sensible of the inconvenience attending want of method. This article, therefore,
cost me so much painful attention, and my
faults in it vexed me so much, and I made so
little progress in amendment, and had such
frequent relapses, that I was almost ready
to give up the attempt, and content myself with

[1] Professor McMaster tells us that when Franklin was American Agent in France, his lack of business order was a source of
annoyance to his colleagues and friends. "Strangers who came to
see him were amazed to behold papers of the greatest importance
scattered in the most careless way over the table and floor."

a faulty character in that respect, like the
man who, in buying an ax of a smith, my neighbour, desired to have the whole of its surface
as bright as the edge. The smith consented
to grind it bright for him if he would turn the
wheel; he turn'd, while the smith press'd the
broad face of the ax hard and heavily on the

stone, which made the turning of it very fatigu-
ing. The man came every now and then from
the wheel to see how the work went on, and
at length would take his ax as it was, without
farther grinding. "No," said the smith, "turn
on, turn on; we shall have it bright by-and-by;
as yet, it is only speckled." "Yes," says the
man, *but I think I like a speckled ax best.*"
And I believe this may have been the case
with many, who, having, for want of some
such means as I employ'd, found the difficulty
of obtaining good and breaking bad habits in

other points of vice and virtue, have given up the struggle, and concluded that *" a speckled ax was best"*; for something, that pretended to be reason, was every now and then suggesting to me that such extream nicety as I exacted of myself might be a kind of foppery in morals, which, if it were known, would make me ridiculous; that a perfect character might be attended with the inconvenience of being envied and hated; and that a benevolent man should allow a few faults in himself, to keep his friends in countenance.

In truth, I found myself incorrigible with respect to Order; and now I am grown old, and my memory bad, I feel very sensibly the want of it. But, on the whole, tho' I never arrived at the perfection I had been so ambitious of obtaining, but fell far short of it, yet I was, by the endeavour, a better and a happier man than I otherwise should have been if I had not attempted it; as those who aim at perfect writing by imitating the engraved copies, tho' they never reach the wish'd-for excellence of those copies, their hand is mended by the endeavour, and is tolerable while it continues fair and legible.

It may be well my posterity should be informed that to this little artifice, with the blessing of God, their ancestor ow'd the constant felicity of his life, down to his 79th year, in which this is written. What reverses may attend the remainder is in the hand of Providence; but, if they arrive, the reflection on past happiness enjoy'd ought to help his bearing them with more resignation. To Temperance he ascribes his long-continued health, and what is still left to him of a good constitution; to Industry and Frugality, the early easiness of his circumstances and acquisition of his fortune, with all that knowledge that enabled him to be a useful citizen, and obtained for him some degree of reputation among the learned; to Sincerity and Justice, the confidence of his country, and the honorable employs it conferred upon him; and to the joint influence of the whole mass of the virtues,[1] even in the imperfect state he was able to acquire them, all that evenness of temper, and that cheerfulness in conversation, which makes his company still sought for, and agreeable

[1] While there can be no question that Franklin's moral improvement and happiness were due to the practice of these virtues, yet most people will agree that we shall have to go back of his plan for the impelling motive to a virtuous life. Franklin's own suggestion that the scheme smacks of "foppery in morals" seems justified. Woodrow Wilson well puts it: "Men do not take fire from such thoughts, unless something deeper, which is missing here, shine through them. What may have seemed to the

even to his younger acquaintance. I hope, therefore, that some of my descendants may follow the example and reap the benefit.

It will be remark'd that, tho' my scheme was not wholly without religion, there was in it no mark of any of the distinguishing tenets of any particular sect. I had purposely avoided them; for, being fully persuaded of the utility and excellency of my method, and that it might be serviceable to people in all religions, and intending some time or other to publish it, I would not have anything in it that should prejudice anyone, of any sect, against it. I purposed writing a little comment on each virtue, in which I would have shown the advantages of possessing it, and the mischiefs attending its opposite vice; and I should have called my book THE ART OF VIRTUE,[1] because it would have shown the means and manner of obtaining virtue, which would have distinguished it from the mere exhortation to be good, that does not instruct and indicate the means, but

eighteenth century a system of morals seems to us nothing more vital than a collection of the precepts of good sense and sound conduct. What redeems it from pettiness in this book is the scope of power and of usefulness to be seen in Franklin himself, who set these standards up in all seriousness and candor for his own life." See *Galatians,* chapter V, for the Christian plan of moral perfection.

[1] Nothing so likely to make a man's fortune as virtue.—*Marg. note.*

is like the apostle's man of verbal charity, who only without showing to the naked and hungry how or where they might get clothes or victuals, exhorted them to be fed and clothed. —James ii. 15, 16.

But it so happened that my intention of writing and publishing this comment was never fulfilled. I did, indeed, from time to time, put down short hints of the sentiments, reasonings, etc., to be made use of in it, some of which I have still by me; but the necessary close attention to private business in the earlier part of my life, and public business since, have occasioned my postponing it; for, it being connected in my mind with *a great and extensive project,* that required the whole man to execute, and which an unforeseen succession of employs prevented my attending to, it has hitherto remain'd unfinish'd.

In this piece it was my design to explain and enforce this doctrine, that vicious actions are not hurtful because they are forbidden, but forbidden because they are hurtful, the nature of man alone considered; that it was, therefore, everyone's interest to be virtuous who wish'd to be happy even in this world; and I should, from this circumstance (there being always in the world a number of rich merchants, nobility, states, and princes, who have need of honest instruments for the management of their affairs, and such being so rare), have endeavoured to convince young persons that no qualities were so likely to make a poor man's fortune as those of probity and integrity.

My list of virtues contain'd at first but twelve; but a Quaker friend having kindly informed me that I was generally thought proud; that my pride show'd itself frequently in conversation; that I was not content with being in the right when discussing any point, but was overbearing, and rather insolent, of which he convinc'd me by mentioning several instances; I determined endeavouring to cure myself, if I could, of this vice or folly among the rest, and I added *Humility* to my list, giving an extensive meaning to the word.

I cannot boast of much success in acquiring the *reality* of this virtue, but I had a good deal with regard to the *appearance* of it. I made it a rule to forbear all direct contradiction to the sentiments of others, and all positive assertion of my own. I even forbid myself, agreeably to the old laws of our Junto, the use of every word or expression in the language that imported a fix'd opinion, such as *certainly, undoubtedly,* etc., and I adopted,

instead of them, *I conceive, I apprehend,* or
I imagine a thing to be so or so; or it *so appears
to me at present.* When another asserted something that I thought an error, I deny'd myself
the pleasure of contradicting him abruptly, and
of showing immediately some absurdity in his
proposition; and in answering I began by observing that in certain cases or circumstances
his opinion would be right, but in the present
case there *appear'd* or *seem'd* to me some difference, etc. I soon found the advantage of
this change in my manner; the conversations
I engag'd in went on more pleasantly. The
modest way in which I propos'd my opinions
procur'd them a readier reception and less contradiction; I had less mortification when I was
found to be in the wrong, and I more easily
prevail'd with others to give up their mistakes
and join with me when I happened to be in
the right.

And this mode, which I at first put on with
some violence to natural inclination, became
at length so easy, and so habitual to me, that
perhaps for these fifty years past no one has
ever heard a dogmatical expression escape me.
And to this habit (after my character of integrity) I think it principally owing that I had
early so much weight with my fellow-citizens

when I proposed new institutions, or alterations in the old, and so much influence in public
councils when I became a member; for I was
but a bad speaker, never eloquent, subject to
much hesitation in my choice of words, hardly
correct in language, and yet I generally carried
my points.

In reality, there is, perhaps, no one of our
natural passions so hard to subdue as *pride*.
Disguise it, struggle with it, beat it down,
stifle it, mortify it as much as one pleases, it
is still alive, and will every now and then peep
out and show itself; you will see it, perhaps,
often in this history; for, even if I could conceive that I had compleatly overcome it, I
should probably be proud of my humility.

[Thus far written at Passy, 1784.]

[*"I am now about to write at home, August,*
1788, *but cannot have the help expected from
my papers, many of them being lost in the war.
I have, however, found the following."*] [1]

HAVING mentioned *a great and extensive
project* which I had conceiv'd, it seems proper
that some account should be here given of
that project and its object. Its first rise in

---

[1] This is a marginal memorandum.—B.

my mind appears in the following little paper, accidentally preserv'd, viz.:

Observations on my reading history, in Library, May 19th, 1731.

"That the great affairs of the world, the wars, revolutions, etc., are carried on and effected by parties.

"That the view of these parties is their present general interest, or what they take to be such.

"That the different views of these different parties occasion all confusion.

"That while a party is carrying on a general design, each man has his particular private interest in view.

"That as soon as a party has gain'd its general point, each member becomes intent upon his particular interest; which, thwarting others, breaks that party into divisions, and occasions more confusion.

"That few in public affairs act from a meer view of the good of their country, whatever they may pretend; and, tho' their actings bring real good to their country, yet men primarily considered that their own and their country's interest was united, and did not act from a principle of benevolence.

"That fewer still, in public affairs, act with a view to the good of mankind.

"There seems to me at present to be great occasion for raising a United Party for Virtue, by forming the virtuous and good men of all nations into a regular body, to be govern'd by suitable good and wise rules, which good and wise men may probably be more unanimous in their obedience to, than common people are to common laws.

"I at present think that whoever attempts this aright, and is well qualified, cannot fail of pleasing God, and of meeting with success.

B. F."

Revolving this project in my mind, as to be undertaken hereafter, when my circumstances should afford me the necessary leisure, I put down from time to time, on pieces of paper, such thoughts as occurr'd to me respecting it. Most of these are lost; but I find one purporting to be the substance of an intended creed, containing, as I thought, the essentials of every known religion, and being free of everything that might shock the professors of any religion. It is express'd in these words, viz.:

"That there is one God, who made all things.

"That he governs the world by his providence.

"That he ought to be worshiped by adoration, prayer, and thanksgiving.

"But that the most acceptable service of God is doing good to man.

"That the soul is immortal.

"And that God will certainly reward virtue and punish vice, either here or hereafter."

My ideas at that time were, that the sect should be begun and spread at first among young and single men only; that each person to be initiated should not only declare his assent to such creed, but should have exercised himself with the thirteen weeks' examination and practice of the virtues, as in the beforemention'd model; that the existence of such a society should be kept a secret, till it was become considerable, to prevent solicitations for the admission of improper persons, but that the members should each of them search among his acquaintance for ingenuous, well-disposed youths, to whom, with prudent caution, the scheme should be gradually communicated; that the members should engage to afford their advice, assistance, and support to each other in promoting one another's interests, business, and advancement in life; that, for distinction, we should be call'd *The Society of the Free and Easy:* free, as being, by the general practice and habit of the virtues, free from the dominion of vice; and particularly by the practice of industry and frugality, free from debt, which exposes a man to confinement, and a species of slavery to his creditors.

This is as much as I can now recollect of the project, except that I communicated it in part to two young men, who adopted it with some enthusiasm; but my then narrow circumstances, and the necessity I was under of sticking close to my business, occasion'd my postponing the further prosecution of it at that time; and my multifarious occupations, public and private, induc'd me to continue postponing, so that it has been omitted till I have no longer strength or activity left sufficient for such an enterprise; though I am still of opinion that it was a practicable scheme, and might have been very useful, by forming a great number of good citizens; and I was not discourag'd by the seeming magnitude of the undertaking, as I have always thought that one man of tolerable abilities may work great changes, and accomplish great affairs among mankind, if he first forms a good plan, and, cutting off all amusements or other employments that would divert his attention, makes the execution of that same plan his sole study and business.

X

POOR RICHARD'S ALMANAC AND OTHER ACTIVITIES

N 1732 I first publish'd my Almanack, under the name of *Richard Saunders;* it was continu'd by me about twenty-five years, commonly call'd *Poor Richard's Almanac.*[1] I endeavour'd to make it both entertaining and useful, and it accordingly came to be in such demand, that I reap'd considerable profit from it, vending annually near ten thousand. And observing that it was generally read, scarce any neighborhood in the province being without it, I consider'd it as a proper vehicle for conveying instruction among the common people, who bought scarcely any other books; I therefore filled all the little spaces that occurr'd between the remarkable days in the calendar with proverbial sentences, chiefly such as inculcated industry and frugality, as the means of pro-

---

[1] The almanac at that time was a kind of periodical as well as a guide to natural phenomena and the weather. Franklin took his title from *Poor Robin,* a famous English almanac, and from Richard Saunders, a well-known almanac publisher. For the maxims of Poor Richard, see pages 331-335.

curing wealth, and thereby securing virtue; it being more difficult for a man in want, to act always honestly, as, to use here one of those proverbs, *it is hard for an empty sack to stand upright.*

These proverbs, which contained the wisdom of many ages and nations, I assembled and form'd into a connected discourse prefix'd to the Almanack of 1757, as the harangue of a wise old man to the people attending an auction. The bringing all these scatter'd councils thus into a focus enabled them to make greater impression. The piece, being universally approved, was copied in all the newspapers of the Continent; reprinted in Britain on a broadside, to be stuck up in houses; two translations were made of it in French, and great numbers bought by the clergy and gentry, to distribute gratis among their poor parishioners and tenants. In Pennsylvania, as it discouraged useless expense in foreign superfluities, some thought it had its share of influence in producing that growing plenty of money which was observable for several years after its publication.

I considered my newspaper, also, as another means of communicating instruction, and in that view frequently reprinted in it extracts

Two pages from *Poor Richard's Almanac* for 1736. Size of original.
Reproduced from a copy at the New York Public Library.

IV Mon. June hath xxx days.

Things that are bitter, bitterrer than Gall
Phyſicians ſay are always phyſical :
Now Women's Tongues if into Powder beaten,
May in a Potion or a Pill be eaten,
And as there's nought more bitter, I do muſe,
That Women's Tongues in Phyſick they ne'er uſe.
My ſelf and others who lead reſtleſs Lives,
Would ſpare that bitter Member of our Wives.

1	3	*fine weather,*	4	♌	4	36	8	☽ ſet 10 12 aſt
2	4	Aſcenſion Day	5	19	4	35	8	*He that can have*
3	5	☌ ♄ ♀ *ſudden*	6	♍	4	35	8	*Patience, can*
4	6	*ſhowers*	6h	19	4	35	8	*have what he*
5	7	*of Rain.*	7	♎	4	35	8	Firſt Quarter.
6	C	Exaudi	8	19	4	35	8	*will.*
7	2	△ ♂ ☿ *thunder,*	9	♏	4	35	8	☊ 5 ♎
8	3	*perhaps hail.*	10	17	4	35	8	☉ent. ♋ 10 day
9	4	7* riſe 2 15	10	♐	4	34	8	making longeſt
10	5	*very hot,*	11	13	4	34	8	day 14 h. 51 m.
11	6	St. Barnabas.	12	26	4	34	8	Full ● 12 day,
12	7	*then rain.*	1	♑	4	34	8	at 1 morn.
13	C	Whitſunday.	2	20	4	35	8	☽ riſe 8 20 aſt.
14	2		2h	♒	4	35	8	*Now I've a ſheep*
15	3	K. Geo. II. procl	3	15	4	35	8	*and a cow, every*
16	4	ſſ. ☉ ♄ *wind, rain,*	4	27	4	35	8	*body bids me good*
17	5	✶ ♄ ☿ *hail and*	5	♓	4	35	8	*morrow.*
18	6	*thunder.*	6	21	4	35	8	☽ riſe 11 10 aſ.
19	7	Day ſhorter 2 m.	6h	♈	4	35	8	
20	C	Trinity Sund.	7	15	4	36	8	Laſt Quarter.
21	2	*If we have rain a-*	8	27	4	36	8	*God helps them*
22	3	*bout the Change,*	9	♉	4	36	8	*that help them-*
23	4	*Let not my reader*	10	22	4	36	8	*ſelves.*
24	5	St. John Bap.	10	♊	4	36	8	☽ riſe 2 morn.
25	6	7* riſe 1 8	11	18	4	37	8	*Why does the*
26	7	vc ☉ ♃ *think it*	12	♋	4	37	8	*blind man's wife*
27	C	*ſtrange.*	1	16	4	38	8	New ☽ 27 day,
28	2	✶ ♄ ♂ *hail and*	2	♌	4	38	8	near noon.
29	3	St. Peter & Paul	2h	15	4	39	8	*paint herſelf.*
30	4	□ ♂ ♀ *rain.*	3	♍	4	40	8	☽ ſets 9 30

Who can charge *Ebrio* with Thirſt of Wealth?
See he conſumes his Money, Time and Health,
In drunken Frolicks which will all confound,
Neglects his Farm, forgets to till his Ground,
His Stock grows leſs that might be kept with eaſe ;
In nought but Guts and Debts he finds Encreaſe.
In Town reels as if he'd ſhove down each Wall,
Yet Walls muſt ſtand, poor Soul, or he muſt fall.

1	5	Day ſhort. 11 mi.	14	15	4	40	8	*None preaches*
2	6	7* riſe 12 32	5	♎	4	41	8	*better than the*
3	7	windy weather.	6	15	4	41	8	*ant, and ſhe ſays*
4	☾	2 Sund. p Trinit.	6h		4	42	8	First Quarter.
5	2	Vc ♃ ♀ now	7	14	4	43	8	*nothing.*
6	3	pleaſant weather	8	27	4	44	8	☽ ſets 12 30 m
7	4	ſome days	9	♐	4	45	8	*The abſent are*
8	5	together,	10	23	4	46	8	*never without*
9	6	but inclines to	10	♑	4	47	8	*fault, nor the*
10	7	falling	11	18	4	48	8	*preſent without*
11	☾	3 Sund. p. Trin.	12	♒	4	49	8	Full ● 11 day,
12	2	* ♄ ☿ weather.	1	13	4	50	8	2 afternoon.
13	3	Dog-days begin	2	25	4	50	8	☉ in ♌
14	4	Days 14 h. 20 m	2h	♓	4	51	8	☽ riſe 8 35 aft.
15	5	St. Swithin.	3	19	4	52	8	*excuſe.*
16	6	☍ ☿ ♎	4	♈	4	53	8	
17	7	☌ ☉ ☿ rain	5	13	4	54	8	*Gifts burſt*
18	☾	7* riſe 11 40	6	25	4	55	8	*rocks*
19	2	hail or rain,	6h	♉	4	56	8	Last Quarter.
20	3	* ☉ ♄ thunder.	7	19	4	57	8	☽ riſe 11 52 at
21	4	7* riſe 11 18	8	♊	4	57	8	*If wind blows on*
22	5	then high	9	14	4	58	8	*you thro' a hole,*
23	6	wind.	10	27	4	59	8	*Make your will*
24	7	☍ ☉ ♃	10	♋	4	59	8	*and take care of*
25	☾	St. James.	11	25	5	0	7	*your ſoul.*
26	2	hail	12	♌	5	1	7	New ☽ 26 day,
27	3	☽ near cor ♌	1	24	5	2	7	near 8 aftern
28	4	☍ ♃ ♀ a clear	2	♍	5	3	7	☽ ſets 8 aftern.
29	5	air, and fine	2h	24	5	4	7	*The rotten Apple*
30	6	weather	3	♎	5	5	7	*ſpoils his Com-*
31	7	7* riſe 10 40	4	25	5	6	7	*panion.*

from the Spectator, and other moral writers; and sometimes publish'd little pieces of my own, which had been first compos'd for reading in our Junto. Of these are a Socratic dialogue, tending to prove that, whatever might be his parts and abilities, a vicious man could not properly be called a man of sense; and a discourse on self-denial, showing that virtue was not secure till its practice became a habitude, and was free from the opposition of contrary inclinations. These may be found in the papers about the beginning of 1735.[1]

In the conduct of my newspaper, I carefully excluded all libeling and personal abuse, which is of late years become so disgraceful to our country. Whenever I was solicited to insert anything of that kind, and the writers pleaded, as they generally did, the liberty of the press, and that a newspaper was like a stage-coach, in which anyone who would pay had a right to a place, my answer was, that I would print the piece separately if desired, and the author might have as many copies as he pleased to distribute himself, but that I would not take upon me to spread his detraction; and that, having contracted with my subscribers to furnish them with what might be either useful or enter-

[1] June 23 and July 7, 1730.—Smyth.

taining, I could not fill their papers with private altercation, in which they had no concern, without doing them manifest injustice. Now, many of our printers make no scruple of gratifying the malice of individuals by false accusations of the fairest characters among ourselves, augmenting animosity even to the producing of duels; and are, moreover, so indiscreet as to print scurrilous reflections on the government of neighboring states, and even on the conduct of our best national allies, which may be attended with the most pernicious consequences. These things I mention as a caution to young printers, and that they may be encouraged not to pollute their presses and disgrace their profession by such infamous practices, but refuse steadily, as they may see by my example that such a course of conduct will not, on the whole, be injurious to their interests.

In 1733 I sent one of my journeymen to Charleston, South Carolina, where a printer was wanting. I furnish'd him with a press and letters, on an agreement of partnership, by which I was to receive one-third of the profits of the business, paying one-third of the expense. He was a man of learning, and honest but ignorant in matters of account; and, tho' he sometimes made me remittances, I could get no account from him, nor any satisfactory state of our partnership while he lived. On his decease, the business was continued by his widow, who, being born and bred in Holland, where, as I have been inform'd, the knowledge of accounts makes a part of female education, she not only sent me as clear a state as she could find of the transactions past, but continued to account with the greatest regularity and exactness every quarter afterwards, and managed the business with such success, that she not only brought up reputably a family of children, but, at the expiration of the term, was able to purchase of me the printing-house, and establish her son in it.

I mention this affair chiefly for the sake of recommending that branch of education for our young females, as likely to be of more use to them and their children, in case of widowhood, than either music or dancing, by preserving them from losses by imposition of crafty men, and enabling them to continue, perhaps, a profitable mercantile house, with establish'd correspondence, till a son is grown up fit to undertake and go on with it, to the lasting advantage and enriching of the family.

About the year 1734 there arrived among us
from Ireland a young Presbyterian preacher,
named Hemphill, who delivered with a good
voice, and apparently extempore, most excellent
discourses, which drew together considerable
numbers of different persuasions, who join'd
in admiring them. Among the rest, I became
one of his constant hearers, his sermons pleasing me, as they had little of the dogmatical
kind, but inculcated strongly the practice of
virtue, or what in the religious stile are called
good works. Those, however, of our congregation, who considered themselves as orthodox
Presbyterians, disapprov'd his doctrine, and
were join'd by most of the old clergy, who
arraign'd him of heterodoxy before the synod,
in order to have him silenc'd. I became his
zealous partisan, and contributed all I could
to raise a party in his favour, and we com-
bated for him awhile with some hopes of success. There was much scribbling pro and con
upon the occasion; and finding that, tho' an
elegant preacher, he was but a poor writer, I
lent him my pen and wrote for him two or
three pamphlets, and one piece in the Gazette
of April, 1735. Those pamphlets, as is generally the case with controversial writings, tho'
eagerly read at the time, were soon out of

vogue, and I question whether a single copy of them now exists.[1]

During the contest an unlucky occurrence hurt his cause exceedingly. One of our adversaries having heard him preach a sermon that was much admired, thought he had somewhere read the sermon before, or at least a part of it. On search, he found that part quoted at length, in one of the British Reviews, from a discourse of Dr. Foster's.[2] This detection gave many of our party disgust, who accordingly abandoned his cause, and occasion'd our more speedy discomfiture in the synod. I stuck by him, however, as I rather approv'd his giving us good sermons composed by others, than bad ones of his own manufacture, tho' the latter was the practice of our common teachers. He afterward acknowledg'd to me that none of those he preach'd were his own; adding, that his memory was such as enabled him to retain and repeat any sermon after one reading only.

[1] See "A List of Books written by, or relating to Benjamin Franklin," by Paul Leicester Ford. 1889. p. 15.—Smyth.

[2] Dr. James Foster (1697-1753) :—
> "Let modest Foster, if he will excel
> Ten metropolitans in preaching well."
> —Pope (Epilogue to the Satires, I, 132).

"Those who had not heard Farinelli sing and Foster preach were not qualified to appear in genteel company," Hawkins. "History of Music."—Smyth.

On our defeat, he left us in search elsewhere
of better fortune, and I quitted the congregation, never joining it after, tho' I continu'd
many years my subscription for the support
of its ministers.

I had begun in 1733 to study languages; I
soon made myself so much a master of the
French as to be able to read the books with
ease. I then undertook the Italian. An acquaintance, who was also learning it, us'd often
to tempt me to play chess with him. Finding
this took up too much of the time I had to
spare for study, I at length refus'd to play
any more, unless on this condition, that the
victor in every game should have a right to
impose a task, either in parts of the grammar
to be got by heart, or in translations, etc.,
which tasks the vanquish'd was to perform
upon honour, before our next meeting. As we
play'd pretty equally, we thus beat one another
into that language. I afterwards with a little
painstaking, acquir'd as much of the Spanish
as to read their books also.

I have already mention'd that I had only one
year's instruction in a Latin school, and that
when very young, after which I neglected that
language entirely. But, when I had attained
an acquaintance with the French, Italian, and

Spanish, I was surpriz'd to find, on looking over a Latin Testament, that I understood so much more of that language than I had imagined, which encouraged me to apply myself again to the study of it, and I met with more success, as those preceding languages had greatly smooth'd my way.

From these circumstances, I have thought that there is some inconsistency in our common mode of teaching languages. We are told that it is proper to begin first with the Latin, and, having acquir'd that, it will be more easy to attain those modern languages which are deriv'd from it; and yet we do not begin with the Greek, in order more easily to acquire the Latin. It is true that, if you can clamber and get to the top of a staircase without using the steps, you will more easily gain them in descending; but certainly, if you begin with the lowest you will with more ease ascend to the top; and I would therefore offer it to the consideration of those who superintend the education of our youth, whether, since many of those who begin with the Latin quit the same after spending some years without having made any great proficiency, and what they have learnt becomes almost useless, so that their time has been lost, it would not have been better to have begun with the French, proceeding to the Italian, etc.; for, tho', after spending the same time, they should quit the study of languages and never arrive at the Latin, they would, however, have acquired another tongue or two, that, being in modern use, might be serviceable to them in common life.[1]

After ten years' absence from Boston, and having become easy in my circumstances, I made a journey thither to visit my relations, which I could not sooner well afford. In returning, I call'd at Newport to see my brother, then settled there with his printing-house. Our former differences were forgotten, and our meeting was very cordial and affectionate. He was fast declining in his health, and requested of me that, in case of his death, which he apprehended not far distant, I would take home his son, then but ten years of age, and bring

[1] "The authority of Franklin, the most eminently practical man of his age, in favor of reserving the study of the dead languages until the mind has reached a certain maturity, is confirmed by the confession of one of the most eminent scholars of any age.

"'Our seminaries of learning,' says Gibbon, 'do not exactly correspond with the precept of a Spartan king, that the child should be instructed in the arts which will be useful to the man; since a finished scholar may emerge from the head of Westminster or Eton, in total ignorance of the business and conversation of English gentlemen in the latter end of the eighteenth century. But these schools may assume the merit of teaching all that they pretend to teach, the Latin and Greek languages.'"—Bigelow.

him up to the printing business. This I accordingly perform'd, sending him a few years to school before I took him into the office. His mother carried on the business till he was grown up, when I assisted him with an assortment of new types, those of his father being in a manner worn out. Thus it was that I made

my brother ample amends for the service I had depriv'd him of by leaving him so early.

In 1736 I lost one of my sons, a fine boy of four years old, by the small-pox, taken in the common way. I long regretted bitterly, and still regret that I had not given it to him by inoculation. This I mention for the sake of parents who omit that operation, on the supposition that they should never forgive themselves if a child died under it; my example showing that the regret may be the same either way, and that, therefore, the safer should be chosen.

Our club, the Junto, was found so useful, and

afforded such satisfaction to the members, that several were desirous of introducing their friends, which could not well be done without exceeding what we had settled as a convenient number, viz., twelve. We had from the beginning made it a rule to keep our institution a secret, which was pretty well observ'd; the intention was to avoid applications of improper persons for admittance, some of whom, perhaps, we might find it difficult to refuse. I was one of those who were against any addition to our number, but, instead of it, made in writing a proposal, that every member separately should endeavour to form a subordinate club, with the same rules respecting queries, etc., and without informing them of the connection with the Junto. The advantages proposed were, the improvement of so many more young citizens by the use of our institutions; our better acquaintance with the general sentiments of the inhabitants on any occasion, as the Junto member might propose what queries we should desire, and was to report to the Junto what pass'd in his separate club; the promotion of our particular interests in business by more extensive recommendation, and the increase of our influence in public affairs, and our power of doing good by spreading thro' the several clubs the sentiments of the Junto.

The project was approv'd, and every member undertook to form his club, but they did not all succeed. Five or six only were compleated, which were called by different names, as the Vine, the Union, the Band, etc. They were useful to themselves, and afforded us a good deal of amusement, information, and instruction, besides answering, in some considerable degree, our views of influencing the public opinion on particular occasions, of which I shall give some instances in course of time as they happened.

My first promotion was my being chosen, in 1736, clerk of the General Assembly. The choice was made that year without opposition; but the year following, when I was again propos'd (the choice, like that of the members, being annual), a new member made a long speech against me, in order to favour some other candidate. I was, however, chosen, which was the more agreeable to me, as, besides the pay for the immediate service as clerk, the place gave me a better opportunity of keeping up an interest among the members, which secur'd to me the business of printing the votes, laws, paper money, and other occasional jobbs for the public, that, on the whole, were very profitable.

I therefore did not like the opposition of this new member, who was a gentleman of fortune and education, with talents that were likely to give him, in time, great influence in the House, which, indeed, afterwards happened. I did not, however, aim at gaining his favour by paying any servile respect to him, but, after some time, took this other method. Having heard that he had in his library a certain very scarce and curious book, I wrote a note to him, expressing my desire of perusing that book, and requesting he would do me the favour of lending it to me for a few days. He sent it immediately, and I return'd it in about a week with another note, expressing strongly my sense of the favour. When we next met in the House, he spoke to me (which he had never done before), and with great civility; and he ever after manifested a readiness to serve me on all occasions, so that we became great friends, and our friendship continued to his death. This is another instance of the truth of an old maxim I had learned, which says, *"He that has once done you a kindness will be more ready to do you another, than he whom you yourself have obliged."* And it shows how

much more profitable it is prudently to remove, than to resent, return, and continue
inimical proceedings.

In 1737, Colonel Spotswood, late governor
of Virginia, and then postmaster-general, being
dissatisfied with the conduct of his deputy at
Philadelphia, respecting some negligence in
rendering, and inexactitude of his accounts, took
from him the commission and offered it to
me. I accepted it readily, and found it of great
advantage; for, tho' the salary was small, it
facilitated the correspondence that improv'd
my newspaper, increas'd the number demanded,
as well as the advertisements to be inserted,
so that it came to afford me a considerable income. My old competitor's newspaper declin'd
proportionately, and I was satisfy'd without
retaliating his refusal, while postmaster, to permit my papers being carried by the riders.
Thus he suffer'd greatly from his neglect in
due accounting; and I mention it as a lesson
to those young men who may be employ'd in
managing affairs for others, that they should
always render accounts, and make remittances,
with great clearness and punctuality. The character of observing such a conduct is the most
powerful of all recommendations to new employments and increase of business.

XI

INTEREST IN PUBLIC AFFAIRS

BEGAN now to turn my thoughts a little to public affairs, beginning, however, with small matters. The city watch was one of the first things that I conceiv'd to want regulation. It was managed by the constables of the respective wards in turn; the constable warned a number of housekeepers to attend him for the night. Those who chose never to attend, paid him six shillings a year to be excus'd, which was suppos'd to be for hiring substitutes, but was, in reality, much more than was necessary for that purpose, and made the constableship a place of profit; and the constable, for a little drink, often got such ragamuffins about him as a watch, that respectable housekeepers did not choose to mix with. Walking the rounds, too, was often neglected, and most of the nights spent in tippling. I thereupon wrote a paper to be read in Junto, representing these irregularities, but insisting more particularly on the inequality of this six-shilling tax of the constables, respecting the circumstances of those who paid it, since a poor widow housekeeper, all whose property to be guarded by the watch did not perhaps exceed the value of fifty pounds, paid as much as the wealthiest merchant, who had thousands of pounds' worth of goods in his stores.

On the whole, I proposed as a more effectual watch, the hiring of proper men to serve constantly in that business; and as a more equitable way of supporting the charge, the levying a tax that should be proportion'd to the property. This idea, being approv'd by the Junto, was communicated to the other clubs, but as arising in each of them; and though the plan was not immediately carried into execution, yet, by preparing the minds of people for the change, it paved the way for the law obtained a few years after, when the members of our clubs were grown into more influence.

About this time I wrote a paper (first to be read in Junto, but it was afterward publish'd) on the different accidents and carelessnesses by which houses were set on fire, with cautions against them, and means proposed of avoiding them. This was much spoken of as a useful piece, and gave rise to a project, which soon followed it, of forming a company for the more ready extinguishing of fires, and mutual assistance in removing and securing of goods when in danger. Associates in this scheme were presently found, amounting to thirty. Our articles of agreement oblig'd every member to keep always in good order, and fit for use, a certain number of leather buckets, with strong bags and baskets (for packing and transporting of goods), which were to be brought to every fire; and we agreed to meet once a month and spend a social evening together, in discoursing and communicating such ideas as occurred to us upon the subjects of fires, as might be useful in our conduct on such occasions.

The utility of this institution soon appeared, and many more desiring to be admitted than we thought convenient for one company, they were advised to form another, which was accordingly done; and this went on, one new company being formed after another, till they became so numerous as to include most of the inhabitants who were men of property; and now, at the time of my writing this, tho' upward of fifty years since its establishment, that which I first formed, called the Union Fire Company, still subsists and flourishes, tho' the first members are all deceas'd but myself and one, who is older by a year than I am. The small fines that have been paid by members for absence at the monthly meetings have been apply'd to the purchase of fire-engines, ladders, fire-hooks, and other useful implements for each company, so that I question whether there

is a city in the world better provided with the means of putting a stop to beginning conflagrations; and, in fact, since these institutions, the city has never lost by fire more than one or two houses at a time, and the flames have often been extinguished before the house in which they began has been half consumed.

In 1739 arrived among us from Ireland the Reverend Mr. Whitefield,[1] who had made himself remarkable there as an itinerant preacher. He was at first permitted to preach in some

[1] George Whitefield, pronounced Hwit'field (1714-1770), a celebrated English clergyman and pulpit orator, one of the founders of Methodism.

of our churches; but the clergy, taking a dislike to him, soon refus'd him their pulpits, and he was oblig'd to preach in the fields. The multitudes of all sects and denominations that attended his sermons were enormous, and it was matter of speculation to me, who was one of the number, to observe the extraordinary influence of his oratory on his hearers, and how much they admir'd and respected him, notwithstanding his common abuse of them, by assuring them they were naturally *half beasts and half devils*. It was wonderful to see the change soon made in the manners of our inhabitants. From being thoughtless or indifferent about religion, it seem'd as if all the world were growing religious, so that one could not walk thro' the town in an evening without hearing psalms sung in different families of every street.

And it being found inconvenient to assemble in the open air, subject to its inclemencies, the building of a house to meet in was no sooner propos'd, and persons appointed to receive contributions, but sufficient sums were soon receiv'd to procure the ground and erect the building, which was one hundred feet long and seventy broad, about the size of Westminster Hall; [1]

[1] A part of the palace of Westminster, now forming the vestibule to the Houses of Parliament in London.

and the work was carried on with such spirit
as to be finished in a much shorter time than
could have been expected. Both house and
ground were vested in trustees, expressly for
the use of any preacher of any religious persuasion who might desire to say something to
the people at Philadelphia; the design in building not being to accommodate any particular
sect, but the inhabitants in general; so that
even if the Mufti of Constantinople were to
send a missionary to preach Mohammedanism
to us, he would find a pulpit at his service.

Mr. Whitefield, in leaving us, went preaching all the way thro' the colonies to Georgia.
The settlement of that province had lately been
begun, but, instead of being made with hardy,
industrious husbandmen, accustomed to labour,
the only people fit for such an enterprise, it
was with families of broken shop-keepers and
other insolvent debtors, many of indolent and
idle habits, taken out of the jails, who, being
set down in the woods, unqualified for clearing
land, and unable to endure the hardships of a
new settlement, perished in numbers, leaving
many helpless children unprovided for. The
sight of their miserable situation inspir'd the
benevolent heart of Mr. Whitefield with the
idea of building an Orphan House there, in

which they might be supported and educated. Returning northward, he preach'd up this charity, and made large collections, for his eloquence had a wonderful power over the hearts and purses of his hearers, of which I myself was an instance.

I did not disapprove of the design, but, as Georgia was then destitute of materials and workmen, and it was proposed to send them from Philadelphia at a great expense, I thought it would have been better to have built the house here, and brought the children to it. This I advis'd; but he was resolute in his first project, rejected my counsel, and I therefore refus'd to contribute. I happened soon after to attend one of his sermons, in the course of which I perceived he intended to finish with a collection, and I silently resolved he should get nothing from me. I had in my pocket a handful of copper money, three or four silver dollars, and five pistoles in gold. As he proceeded I began to soften, and concluded to give the coppers. Another stroke of his oratory made me asham'd of that, and determin'd me to give the silver; and he finish'd so admirably, that I empty'd my pocket wholly into the collector's dish, gold and all. At this sermon there was also one of our club, who, being of

my sentiments respecting the building in
Georgia, and suspecting a collection might be
intended, had, by precaution, emptied his pockets before he came from home. Towards the
conclusion of the discourse, however, he felt
a strong desire to give, and apply'd to a neighbour who stood near him, to borrow some
money for the purpose. The application was
unfortunately [made] to perhaps the only man
in the company who had the firmness not to
be affected by the preacher. His answer was,
"*At any other time, Friend Hopkinson, I would
lend to thee freely; but not now, for thee seems
to be out of thy right senses.*"

Some of Mr. Whitefield's enemies affected
to suppose that he would apply these collections to his own private emolument; but I, who
was intimately acquainted with him (being employed in printing his Sermons and Journals,
etc.), never had the least suspicion of his integrity, but am to this day decidedly of opinion
that he was in all his conduct a perfectly
honest man; and methinks my testimony in his
favour ought to have the more weight, as we
had no religious connection. He us'd, indeed,
sometimes to pray for my conversion, but
never had the satisfaction of believing that
his prayers were heard. Ours was a mere civil

friendship, sincere on both sides, and lasted to his death.

The following instance will show something of the terms on which we stood. Upon one of his arrivals from England at Boston, he wrote to me that he should come soon to Philadelphia, but knew not where he could lodge when there, as he understood his old friend and host, Mr. Benezet was removed to Germantown. My answer was, "You know my house; if you can make shift with its scanty accommodations, you will be most heartily welcome." He reply'd, that if I made that kind offer for Christ's sake, I should not miss of a reward. And I returned, *"Don't let me be mistaken; it was not for Christ's sake, but for your sake."* One of our common acquaintance jocosely remark'd, that, knowing it to be the custom of the saints, when they received any favour, to shift the burden of the obligation from off their own shoulders, and place it in heaven, I had contriv'd to fix it on earth.

The last time I saw Mr. Whitefield was in London, when he consulted me about his Orphan House concern, and his purpose of appropriating it to the establishment of a college.

He had a loud and clear voice, and articulated his words and sentences so perfectly, that

he might be heard and understood at a great
distance, especially as his auditories, however
numerous, observ'd the most exact silence. He
preach'd one evening from the top of the Court-
house steps, which are in the middle of Market-
street, and on the west side of Second-street,
which crosses it at right angles. Both streets
were fill'd with his hearers to a considerable
distance. Being among the hindmost in Market-street, I had the curiosity to learn how
far he could be heard, by retiring backwards
down the street towards the river; and I found
his voice distinct till I came near Front-street,
when some noise in that street obscur'd it.
Imagining then a semicircle, of which my distance should be the radius, and that it were
fill'd with auditors, to each of whom I allow'd
two square feet, I computed that he might
well be heard by more than thirty thousand.
This reconcil'd me to the newspaper accounts
of his having preach'd to twenty-five thousand
people in the fields, and to the antient histories
of generals haranguing whole armies, of which
I had sometimes doubted.

By hearing him often, I came to distinguish
easily between sermons newly compos'd, and
those which he had often preach'd in the course
of his travels. His delivery of the latter was

so improv'd by frequent repetitions that every accent, every emphasis, every modulation of voice, was so perfectly well turn'd and well plac'd, that, without being interested in the subject, one could not help being pleas'd with the discourse; a pleasure of much the same kind with that receiv'd from an excellent piece of musick. This is an advantage itinerant preachers have over those who are stationary, as the latter cannot well improve their delivery of a sermon by so many rehearsals.

His writing and printing from time to time gave great advantage to his enemies; unguarded expressions, and even erroneous opinions, delivered in preaching, might have been afterwards explain'd or qualifi'd by supposing others that might have accompani'd them, or they might have been deny'd; but *litera scripta manet*. Critics attack'd his writings violently, and with so much appearance of reason as to diminish the number of his votaries and prevent their increase; so that I am of opinion if he had never written anything, he would have left behind him a much more numerous and important sect, and his reputation might in that case have been still growing, even after his death, as there being nothing of his writing on which to found a censure and give him a lower character, his proselytes would be left at liberty to feign for him as great a variety of excellences as their enthusiastic admiration might wish him to have possessed.

My business was now continually augmenting, and my circumstances growing daily easier, my newspaper having become very profitable, as being for a time almost the only one in this and the neighbouring provinces. I experienced, too, the truth of the observation, *"that after getting the first hundred pound, it is more easy to get the second,"* money itself being of a prolific nature.

The partnership at Carolina having succeeded, I was encourag'd to engage in others, and to promote several of my workmen, who had behaved well, by establishing them with printing-houses in different colonies, on the same terms with that in Carolina. Most of them did well, being enabled at the end of our term, six years, to purchase the types of me and go on working for themselves, by which means several families were raised. Partnerships often finish in quarrels; but I was happy in this, that mine were all carried on and ended amicably, owing, I think, a good deal to the precaution of having very explicitly settled, in our articles, everything to be done by or expected from each partner, so that there was nothing to dispute, which precaution I would therefore recommend to all who enter into partnerships; for, whatever esteem partners may have for, and confidence in each other at the time of the contract, little jealousies and disgusts may arise, with ideas of inequality in the care and burden of the business, etc., which are attended often with breach of friendship and of the connection, perhaps with lawsuits and other disagreeable consequences.

XII

DEFENSE OF THE PROVINCE

HAD, on the whole, abundant reason to be satisfied with my being established in Pennsylvania. There were, however, two things that I regretted, there being no provision for defense, nor for a compleat education of youth; no militia, nor any college. I therefore, in 1743, drew up a proposal for establishing an academy; and at that time, thinking the Reverend Mr. Peters, who was out of employ, a fit person to superintend such an institution, I communicated the project to him; but he, having more profitable views in the service of the proprietaries, which succeeded, declin'd the undertaking; and, not knowing another at that time suitable for such a trust, I let the scheme lie awhile dormant. I succeeded better the next year, 1744, in proposing and establishing a Philosophical Society. The paper I wrote for that purpose will be found among my writings, when collected.

With respect to defense, Spain having been

several years at war against Great Britain, and
being at length join'd by France, which brought
us into great danger; and the laboured and
long-continued endeavour of our governor,
Thomas, to prevail with our Quaker Assembly
to pass a militia law, and make other provisions for the security of the province, having
proved abortive, I determined to try what might
be done by a voluntary association of the
people. To promote this, I first wrote and
published a pamphlet, entitled PLAIN TRUTH,
in which I stated our defenceless situation in
strong lights, with the necessity of union and
discipline for our defense, and promis'd to propose in a few days an association, to be generally
signed for that purpose. The pamphlet had a
sudden and surprising effect. I was call'd upon
for the instrument of association, and having
settled the draft of it with a few friends, I appointed a meeting of the citizens in the large
building before mentioned. The house was pretty
full; I had prepared a number of printed copies,
and provided pens and ink dispers'd all over
the room. I harangued them a little on the
subject, read the paper, and explained it, and
then distributed the copies, which were eagerly
signed, not the least objection being made.

When the company separated, and the papers

were collected, we found above twelve hundred hands; and, other copies being dispersed in the country, the subscribers amounted at length to upward of ten thousand. These all furnished themselves as soon as they could with arms, formed themselves into companies

One of the flags of the Pennsylvania Association, 1747. Designed by Franklin and made by the women of Philadelphia.

and regiments, chose their own officers, and met every week to be instructed in the manual exercise, and other parts of military discipline. The women, by subscriptions among themselves, provided silk colours, which they presented to the companies, painted with different devices and mottos, which I supplied.

The officers of the companies composing the Philadelphia regiment, being met, chose me for their colonel; but, conceiving myself unfit

I declin'd that station, and recommended Mr.
Lawrence, a fine person, and man of influence,
who was accordingly appointed. I then propos'd a lottery to defray the expense of building a battery below the town, and furnishing
it with cannon. It filled expeditiously, and the
battery was soon erected, the merlons being
fram'd of logs and fill'd with earth. We bought
some old cannon from Boston, but, these not
being sufficient, we wrote to England for more,
soliciting, at the same time, our proprietaries
for some assistance, tho' without much expectation of obtaining it.

Meanwhile, Colonel Lawrence, William Allen,
Abram Taylor, Esqr., and myself were sent to
New York by the associators, commission'd to
borrow some cannon of Governor Clinton. He
at first refus'd us peremptorily; but at dinner
with his council, where there was great drinking of Madeira wine, as the custom of that
place then was, he softened by degrees, and
said he would lend us six. After a few more
bumpers he advanc'd to ten; and at length
he very good-naturedly conceded eighteen.
They were fine cannon, eighteen-pounders, with
their carriages, which we soon transported and
mounted on our battery, where the associators
kept a nightly guard while the war lasted, and

among the rest I regularly took my turn of duty there as a common soldier.

My activity in these operations was agreeable to the governor and council; they took me into confidence, and I was consulted by them in every measure wherein their concurrence was thought useful to the association. Calling in the aid of religion, I propos'd to them the proclaiming a fast, to promote reformation, and implore the blessing of Heaven on our undertaking. They embrac'd the motion; but, as it was the first fast ever thought of in the province, the secretary had no precedent from which to draw the proclamation. My education in New England, where a fast is proclaimed every year, was here of some advantage: I drew it in the accustomed stile, it was translated into German,[1] printed in both languages, and divulg'd thro' the province. This gave the clergy of the different sects an opportunity of influencing their congregations to join in the association, and it would probably have been general among all but Quakers if the peace had not soon interven'd.

It was thought by some of my friends that,

[1] Wm. Penn's agents sought recruits for the colony of Pennsylvania in the low countries of Germany, and there are still in eastern Pennsylvania many Germans, inaccurately called Pennsylvania Dutch. Many of them use a Germanized English.

by my activity in these affairs, I should offend
that sect, and thereby lose my interest in the
Assembly of the province, where they formed
a great majority. A young gentleman who had
likewise some friends in the House, and wished
to succeed me as their clerk, acquainted me
that it was decided to displace me at the next
election; and he, therefore, in good will, advis'd me to resign, as more consistent with my
honour than being turn'd out. My answer to
him was, that I had read or heard of some
public man who made it a rule never to ask
for an office, and never to refuse one when
offer'd to him. "I approve," says I, "of his
rule, and will practice it with a small addition;
I shall never *ask*, never *refuse,* nor ever *resign*
an office. If they will have my office of clerk
to dispose of to another, they shall take it from
me. I will not, by giving it up, lose my right
of some time or other making reprisals on my
adversaries." I heard, however, no more of
this; I was chosen again unanimously as usual
at the next election. Possibly, as they dislik'd
my late intimacy with the members of council,
who had join'd the governors in all the disputes about military preparations, with which
the House had long been harass'd, they might
have been pleas'd if I would voluntarily have

left them; but they did not care to displace me on account merely of my zeal for the association, and they could not well give another reason.

Indeed I had some cause to believe that the defense of the country was not disagreeable to any of them, provided they were not requir'd to assist in it. And I found that a much greater number of them than I could have imagined, tho' against offensive war, were clearly for the defensive. Many pamphlets *pro and con* were publish'd on the subject, and some by good Quakers, in favour of defense, which I believe convinc'd most of their younger people.

A transaction in our fire company gave me some insight into their prevailing sentiments. It had been propos'd that we should encourage the scheme for building a battery by laying out the present stock, then about sixty pounds, in tickets of the lottery. By our rules, no money could be dispos'd of till the next meeting after the proposal. The company consisted of thirty members, of which twenty-two were Quakers, and eight only of other persuasions. We eight punctually attended the meeting; but, tho' we thought that some of the Quakers would join us, we were by no means

sure of a majority. Only one Quaker, Mr.
James Morris, appear'd to oppose the measure.
He expressed much sorrow that it had ever
been propos'd, as he said *Friends* were all
against it, and it would create such discord
as might break up the company. We told him
that we saw no reason for that; we were the
minority, and if *Friends* were against the measure, and outvoted us, we must and should,
agreeably to the usage of all societies, submit.
When the hour for business arriv'd it was
mov'd to put the vote; he allow'd we might
then do it by the rules, but, as he could assure
us that a number of members intended to be
present for the purpose of opposing it, it would
be but candid to allow a little time for their
appearing.

While we were disputing this, a waiter came
to tell me two gentlemen below desir'd to speak
with me. I went down, and found they were
two of our Quaker members. They told me
there were eight of them assembled at a tavern
just by; that they were determin'd to come
and vote with us if there should be occasion,
which they hop'd would not be the case, and
desir'd we would not call for their assistance
if we could do without it, as their voting for
such a measure might embroil them with their

elders and friends. Being thus secure of a
majority, I went up, and after a little seeming
hesitation, agreed to a delay of another hour.
This Mr. Morris allow'd to be extreamly fair.
Not one of his opposing friends appear'd, at
which he express'd great surprize; and, at the
expiration of the hour, we carri'd the resolution
eight to one; and as, of the twenty-two Quakers,
eight were ready to vote with us, and thirteen,
by their absence, manifested that they were
not inclin'd to oppose the measure, I afterward
estimated the proportion of Quakers sincerely
against defense as one to twenty-one only; for
these were all regular members of that society,
and in good reputation among them, and had
due notice of what was propos'd at that
meeting.

The honorable and learned Mr. Logan, who
had always been of that sect, was one who
wrote an address to them, declaring his approbation of defensive war, and supporting his
opinion by many strong arguments. He put
into my hands sixty pounds to be laid out in
lottery tickets for the battery, with directions
to apply what prizes might be drawn wholly
to that service. He told me the following
anecdote of his old master, William Penn, respecting defense. He came over from Eng-

land, when a young man, with that proprietary,
and as his secretary. It was war-time, and
their ship was chas'd by an armed vessel, suppos'd to be an enemy. Their captain prepar'd
for defense; but told William Penn, and his
company of Quakers, that he did not expect
their assistance, and they might retire into the
cabin, which they did, except James Logan,[1]
who chose to stay upon deck, and was quarter'd to a gun. The suppos'd enemy prov'd a
friend, so there was no fighting; but when the
secretary went down to communicate the intelligence, William Penn rebuk'd him severely
for staying upon deck, and undertaking to
assist in defending the vessel, contrary to the
principles of *Friends*, especially as it had not
been required by the captain. This reproof,
being before all the company, piqu'd the secretary, who answer'd, *"I being thy servant,
why did thee not order me to come down? But
thee was willing enough that I should stay and
help to fight the ship when thee thought there
was danger."*

My being many years in the Assembly, the
majority of which were constantly Quakers,

[1] James Logan (1674-1751) came to America with William Penn
in 1699, and was the business agent for the Penn family. He be-
queathed his valuable library, preserved at his country seat, " Sten-
ton," to the city of Philadelphia.—Smyth.

gave me frequent opportunities of seeing the embarrassment given them by their principle against war, whenever application was made to them, by order of the crown, to grant aids for military purposes. They were unwilling to offend government, on the one hand, by a direct refusal; and their friends, the body of the Quakers, on the other, by compliance contrary to their principles; hence a variety of evasions to avoid complying, and modes of disguising the compliance when it became unavoidable. The common mode at last was, to grant money under the phrase of its being "*for the king's use*," and never to inquire how it was applied.

But, if the demand was not directly from the crown, that phrase was found not so proper, and some other was to be invented. As, when powder was wanting (I think it was for the garrison at Louisburg), and the government of New England solicited a grant of some from Pennsilvania, which was much urg'd on the House by Governor Thomas, they could not grant money to buy powder, because that was an ingredient of war; but they voted an aid to New England of three thousand pounds, to be put into the hands of the governor, and appropriated it for the purchasing of bread, flour, wheat or *other grain*. Some of the council, desirous of giving the House still further embarrassment, advis'd the governor not to accept provision, as not being the thing he had demanded; but he repli'd, " I shall take the money, for I understand very well their meaning; other grain is gunpowder," which he accordingly bought, and they never objected to it.[1]

It was in allusion to this fact that, when in our fire company we feared the success of our proposal in favour of the lottery, and I had said to my friend Mr. Syng, one of our members, " If we fail, let us move the purchase of a fire-engine with the money; the Quakers can have no objection to that; and then, if you nominate me and I you as a committee for that purpose, we will buy a great gun, which is certainly a *fire-engine*." " I see," says he, " you have improv'd by being so long in the Assembly; your equivocal project would be just a match for their wheat or *other grain*."

These embarrassments that the Quakers suffer'd from having establish'd and published it as one of their principles that no kind of war was lawful, and which, being once published, they could not afterwards, however they might change their minds, easily get rid of, reminds

[1] See the votes.—*Marg. note.*

me of what I think a more prudent conduct in another sect among us, that of the Dunkers. I was acquainted with one of its founders, Michael Welfare, soon after it appear'd. He complain'd to me that they were grievously calumniated by the zealots of other persuasions, and charg'd with abominable principles and practices to which they were utter strangers. I told him this had always been the case with new sects, and that, to put a stop to such abuse, I imagin'd it might be well to publish the articles of their belief, and the rules of their discipline. He said that it had been pro-pos'd among them, but not agreed to, for this reason: "When we were first drawn together as a society," says he, "it had pleased God to enlighten our minds so far as to see that some doctrines, which we once esteemed truths, were errors; and that others, which we had esteemed errors, were real truths. From time to time He has been pleased to afford us farther light, and our principles have been improving, and our er-rors diminishing. Now we are not sure that we are arrived at the end of this progression, and at the perfection of spiritual or theological knowledge; and we fear that, if we should once print our confession of faith, we should feel ourselves as if bound and confin'd by it, and perhaps be unwilling to receive further improvement, and our successors still more so, as conceiving what we their elders and founders had done, to be something sacred, never to be departed from."

This modesty in a sect is perhaps a singular instance in the history of mankind, every other sect supposing itself in possession of all truth, and that those who differ are so far in the wrong; like a man traveling in foggy weather, those at some distance before him on the road he sees wrapped up in the fog, as well as those behind him, and also the people in the fields on each side, but near him all appears clear, tho' in truth he is as much in the fog as any of them. To avoid this kind of embarrassment, the Quakers have of late years been gradually declining the public service in the Assembly and in the magistracy, choosing rather to quit their power than their principle.

In order of time, I should have mentioned before, that having, in 1742, invented an open stove [1] for the better warming of rooms, and at the same time saving fuel, as the fresh air admitted was warmed in entering, I made a present of the model to Mr. Robert Grace, one of my early friends, who, having an iron-fur-

[1] The Franklin stove is still in use.

nace,[1] found the casting of the plates for these stoves a profitable thing, as they were growing in demand. To promote that demand, I wrote and published a pamphlet, entitled *"An Account of the new-invented Pennsylvania Fireplaces; wherein their Construction and Manner of Operation is particularly explained; their Advantages above every other Method of warming Rooms demonstrated; and all Objections that have been raised against the Use of them answered and obviated,"* etc. This pamphlet had a good effect. Gov'r. Thomas was so pleas'd with the construction of this stove, as described in it, that he offered to give me a patent for the sole vending of them for a term of years; but I declin'd it from a principle which has ever weighed with me on such occasions, viz., *That, as we enjoy great advantages from the inventions of others, we should be glad of an opportunity to serve others by any invention of ours; and this we should do freely and generously.*

An ironmonger in London however, assuming a good deal of my pamphlet, and working it up into his own, and making some small changes in the machine, which rather hurt its

---

[1] Warwick Furnace, Chester County, Pennsylvania, across the Schuylkill River from Pottstown.

operation, got a patent for it there, and made, as I was told, a little fortune by it. And this is not the only instance of patents taken out for my inventions by others, tho' not always with the same success, which I never contested, as having no desire of profiting by patents myself, and hating disputes. The use of these fireplaces in very many houses, both of this and the neighbouring colonies, has been, and is, a great saving of wood to the inhabitants.

XIII

PUBLIC SERVICES AND DUTIES
(1749-1753)

PEACE being concluded, and the association business therefore at an end, I turn'd my thoughts again to the affair of establishing an academy. The first step I took was to associate in the design a number of active friends, of whom the Junto furnished a good part; the next was to write and publish a pamphlet, entitled *Proposals Relating to the Education of Youth in Pennsylvania.* This I distributed among the principal inhabitants gratis; and as soon as I could suppose their minds a little prepared by the perusal of it, I set on foot a subscription for opening and supporting an academy; it was to be paid in quotas yearly for five years; by so dividing it, I judg'd the subscription might be larger, and I believe it was so, amounting to no less, if I remember right, than five thousand pounds.

In the introduction to these proposals, I stated their publication, not as an act of mine, but of some *publick-spirited gentlemen,* avoiding as much as I could, according to my usual rule, the presenting myself to the publick as the author of any scheme for their benefit.

The subscribers, to carry the project into immediate execution, chose out of their number twenty-four trustees, and appointed Mr. Francis,[1] then attorney-general, and myself to draw up constitutions for the government of the academy; which being done and signed, a house was hired, masters engag'd, and the schools opened, I think, in the same year, 1749.

The scholars increasing fast, the house was soon found too small, and we were looking out for a piece of ground, properly situated, with intention to build, when Providence threw into our way a large house ready built, which, with a few alterations, might well serve our purpose. This was the building before mentioned, erected by the hearers of Mr. Whitefield, and was obtained for us in the following manner.

It is to be noted that the contributions to this building being made by people of different sects, care was taken in the nomination of trustees, in whom the building and ground was

[1] Tench Francis, uncle of Sir Philip Francis, emigrated from England to Maryland, and became attorney for Lord Baltimore. He removed to Philadelphia and was attorney-general of Pennsylvania from 1741 to 1755. He died in Philadelphia August 16, 1758.—Smyth.

to be vested, that a predominancy should not be given to any sect, lest in time that predominancy might be a means of appropriating the whole to the use of such sect, contrary to the original intention. It was therefore that one of each sect was appointed, viz., one Church-of-England man, one Presbyterian, one Baptist, one Moravian, etc., those, in case of vacancy by death, were to fill it by election from among the contributors. The Moravian happen'd not to please his colleagues, and on his death they resolved to have no other of that sect. The difficulty then was, how to avoid having two of some other sect, by means of the new choice.

Several persons were named, and for that reason not agreed to. At length one mention'd me, with the observation that I was merely an honest man, and of no sect at all, which prevailed with them to chuse me. The enthusiasm which existed when the house was built had long since abat'd, and its trustees had not been able to procure fresh contributions for paying the ground-rent, and discharging some other debts the building had occasion'd, which embarrass'd them greatly. Being now a member of both sects of trustees, that for the building and that for the academy, I had a good opportunity of negotiating with both, and brought them finally to an agreement, by which the trustees for the building were to cede it to those of the academy, the latter undertaking to discharge the debt, to keep forever open in the building a large hall for occasional preachers, according to the original intention, and maintain a free-school for the instruction of poor children. Writings were accordingly drawn, and on paying the debts the trustees of the academy were put in possession of the premises; and by dividing the great and lofty hall into stories, and different rooms above and below for the several schools, and purchasing some additional ground, the whole was soon made fit for our purpose, and the scholars remov'd into the building. The care and trouble of agreeing with the workmen, purchasing materials, and superintending the work, fell upon me; and I went thro' it the more cheerfully, as it did not then interfere with my private business, having the year before taken a very able, industrious, and honest partner, Mr. David Hall, with whose character I was well acquainted, as he had work'd for me four years. He took off my hands all care of the printing-office, paying me punctually my share of the profits. The partnership continued eighteen years, successfully for us both.

The trustees of the academy, after a while, were incorporated by a charter from the governor; their funds were increas'd by contributions in Britain and grants of land from the proprietaries, to which the Assembly has since made considerable addition; and thus was established the present University of Philadelphia.[1] I have been continued one of its trustees from the beginning, now near forty years, and have had the very great pleasure of seeing a number of the youth who have receiv'd their education in it, distinguish'd by their improv'd abilities, serviceable in public stations, and ornaments to their country.

When I disengaged myself, as above mentioned, from private business, I flatter'd myself that, by the sufficient tho' moderate fortune I had acquir'd, I had secured leisure during the rest of my life for philosophical studies and amusements. I purchased all Dr. Spence's apparatus, who had come from England to lecture here, and I proceeded in my electrical experiments with great alacrity; but the publick, now considering me as a man of leisure, laid hold of me for their purposes, every part of our civil government, and almost at the same time, imposing some duty upon me. The governor

[1] Later called the University of Pennsylvania.

put me into the commission of the peace; the corporation of the city chose me of the common council, and soon after an alderman; and the citizens at large chose me a burgess to represent them in Assembly. This latter station was the more agreeable to me, as I was at length tired with sitting there to hear debates, in which, as clerk, I could take no part, and which were often so unentertaining that I was induc'd to amuse myself with making magic squares or circles, or anything to avoid weariness; and I conceiv'd my becoming a member would enlarge my power of doing good. I would not, however, insinuate that my ambition was not flatter'd by all these promotions; it certainly was; for, considering my low beginning, they were great things to me; and they were still more pleasing, as being so many spontaneous testimonies of the public good opinion, and by me entirely unsolicited.

The office of justice of the peace I try'd a little, by attending a few courts, and sitting on the bench to hear causes; but finding that more knowledge of the common law than I possess'd was necessary to act in that station with credit, I gradually withdrew from it, excusing myself by my being oblig'd to attend the higher duties of a legislator in the Assembly. My election to this trust was repeated every year for ten years, without my ever asking any elector for his vote, or signifying, either directly or indirectly, any desire of being chosen. On taking my seat in the House, my son was appointed their clerk.

The year following, a treaty being to be held with the Indians at Carlisle, the governor sent a message to the House, proposing that they should nominate some of their members, to be join'd with some members of council, as commissioners for that purpose.[1] The House named the speaker (Mr. Norris) and myself; and, being commission'd, we went to Carlisle, and met the Indians accordingly.

As those people are extreamly apt to get drunk, and, when so, are very quarrelsome and disorderly, we strictly forbad the selling any liquor to them; and when they complain'd of this restriction, we told them that if they would continue sober during the treaty, we would give them plenty of rum when business was over. They promis'd this, and they kept their promise, because they could get no liquor, and the treaty was conducted very orderly, and concluded to mutual satisfaction. They then claim'd and receiv'd the rum; this was in the

[1] See the votes to have this more correctly.—*Marg. note.*

afternoon: they were near one hundred men, women, and children, and were lodg'd in temporary cabins, built in the form of a square, just without the town. In the evening, hearing a great noise among them, the commissioners walk'd out to see what was the matter. We found they had made a great bonfire in the middle of the square; they were all drunk, men and women, quarreling and fighting. Their dark-colour'd bodies, half naked, seen only by the gloomy light of the bonfire, running after and beating one another with firebrands, accompanied by their horrid yellings, form'd a scene the most resembling our ideas of hell that could well be imagin'd; there was no appeasing the tumult, and we retired to our lodging. At midnight a number of them came thundering at our door, demanding more rum, of which we took no notice.

The next day, sensible they had misbehav'd in giving us that disturbance, they sent three of their old counselors to make their apology. The orator acknowledg'd the fault, but laid it upon the rum; and then endeavoured to excuse the rum by saying, " *The Great Spirit, who made all things, made everything for some use, and whatever use he design'd anything for, that use it should always be put to. Now, when he made rum, he said, ' Let this be for the Indians to get drunk with,' and it must be so."* And, indeed, if it be the design of Providence to extirpate these savages in order to make room for cultivators of the earth, it seems not improbable that rum may be the appointed means. It has already annihilated all the tribes who formerly inhabited the sea-coast.

In 1751, Dr. Thomas Bond, a particular friend of mine, conceived the idea of establishing a hospital in Philadelphia (a very beneficent design, which has been ascrib'd to me, but was originally his), for the reception and cure of poor sick persons, whether inhabitants of the province or strangers. He was zealous and active in endeavouring to procure subscriptions for it, but the proposal being a novelty in America, and at first not well understood, he met but with small success.

At length he came to me with the compliment that he found there was no such thing as carrying a public-spirited project through without my being concern'd in it. " For," says he, " I am often ask'd by those to whom I propose subscribing, Have you consulted Franklin upon this business? And what does he think of it? And when I tell them that I have not (supposing it rather out of your line), they do not subscribe, but say they will consider of it." I enquired into the nature and probable utility of his scheme, and receiving from him a very satisfactory explanation, I not only subscrib'd to it myself, but engag'd heartily in the design of procuring subscriptions from others. Previously, however, to the solicitation, I endeavoured to prepare the minds of the people by writing on the subject in the newspapers, which was my usual custom in such cases, but which he had omitted.

The subscriptions afterwards were more free and generous; but, beginning to flag, I saw they would be insufficient without some assistance from the Assembly, and therefore propos'd to petition for it, which was done. The country members did not at first relish the project; they objected that it could only be serviceable to the city, and therefore the citizens alone should be at the expense of it; and they doubted whether the citizens themselves generally approv'd of it. My allegation on the contrary, that it met with such approbation as to leave no doubt of our being able to raise two thousand pounds by voluntary donations, they considered as a most extravagant supposition, and utterly impossible.

On this I form'd my plan; and, asking leave

to bring in a bill for incorporating the contributors according to the prayer of their petition, and granting them a blank sum of money, which leave was obtained chiefly on the consideration that the House could throw the bill out if they did not like it, I drew it so as to make the important clause a conditional one, viz., " And be it enacted, by the authority aforesaid, that when the said contributors shall have met and chosen their managers and treasurer, *and shall have raised by their contributions a capital stock of* —— *value* (the yearly interest of which is to be applied to the accommodating of the sick poor in the said hospital, free of charge for diet, attendance, advice, and medicines), *and shall make the same appear to the satisfaction of the speaker of the Assembly for the time being,* that *then* it shall and may be lawful for the said speaker, and he is hereby required, to sign an order on the provincial treasurer for the payment of two thousand pounds, in two yearly payments, to the treasurer of the said hospital, to be applied to the founding, building, and finishing of the same."

This condition carried the bill through; for the members, who had oppos'd the grant, and now conceiv'd they might have the credit of being charitable without the expense, agreed to its passage; and then, in soliciting subscriptions among the people, we urg'd the conditional promise of the law as an additional motive to give, since every man's donation would be doubled; thus the clause work'd both ways. The subscriptions accordingly soon exceeded the requisite sum, and we claim'd and receiv'd the public gift, which enabled us to carry the design into execution. A convenient and handsome building was soon erected; the institution has by constant experience been found useful, and flourishes to this day; and I do not remember any of my political manœuvers, the success of which gave me at the time more pleasure, or wherein, after thinking of it, I more easily excus'd myself for having made some use of cunning.

It was about this time that another projector, the Rev. Gilbert Tennent,[1] came to me with a request that I would assist him in procuring a subscription for erecting a new meeting-house. It was to be for the use of a congregation he had gathered among the Presbyterians, who were originally disciples of Mr. Whitefield. Unwilling to make myself dis-

---

[1] Gilbert Tennent (1703-1764) came to America with his father, Rev. William Tennent, and taught for a time in the "Log College," from which sprang the College of New Jersey.—Smyth.

agreeable to my fellow-citizens by too frequently soliciting their contributions, I absolutely refus'd. He then desired I would furnish
him with a list of the names of persons I knew
by experience to be generous and public-spirited. I thought it would be unbecoming in
me, after their kind compliance with my solicitations, to mark them out to be worried by
other beggars, and therefore refus'd also to
give such a list. He then desir'd I would at
least give him my advice. " That I will readily
do," said I; " and, in the first place, I advise
you to apply to all those whom you know will
give something; next, to those whom you are
uncertain whether they will give anything or
not, and show them the list of those who have
given; and, lastly, do not neglect those who
you are sure will give nothing, for in some of
them you may be mistaken." He laugh'd and
thank'd me, and said he would take my advice.
He did so, for he ask'd of *everybody,* and he
obtain'd a much larger sum than he expected,
with which he erected the capacious and very
elegant meeting-house that stands in Arch-
street.

Our city, tho' laid out with a beautifull regularity, the streets large, straight, and crossing
each other at right angles, had the disgrace

of suffering those streets to remain long un-
pav'd, and in wet weather the wheels of heavy
carriages plough'd them into a quagmire, so
that it was difficult to cross them; and in dry
weather the dust was offensive. I had liv'd
near what was call'd the Jersey Market, and
saw with pain the inhabitants wading in mud
while purchasing their provisions. A strip of
ground down the middle of that market was at
length pav'd with brick, so that, being once in
the market, they had firm footing, but were
often over shoes in dirt to get there. By talking and writing on the subject, I was at length
instrumental in getting the street pav'd with
stone between the market and the brick'd foot-
pavement, that was on each side next the
houses. This, for some time, gave an easy
access to the market dry-shod; but, the rest of
the street not being pav'd, whenever a carriage
came out of the mud upon this pavement, it
shook off and left its dirt upon it, and it was
soon cover'd with mire, which was not remov'd, the city as yet having no scavengers.

After some inquiry, I found a poor, industrious man, who was willing to undertake keeping
the pavement clean, by sweeping it twice a
week, carrying off the dirt from before all the
neighbours' doors, for the sum of sixpence per

month, to be paid by each house. I then wrote and printed a paper setting forth the advantages to the neighbourhood that might be obtain'd by this small expense; the greater ease in keeping our houses clean, so much dirt not being brought in by people's feet; the benefit to the shops by more custom, etc., etc., as buyers could more easily get at them; and by not having, in windy weather, the dust blown in upon their goods, etc., etc. I sent one of these papers to each house, and in a day or two went round to see who would subscribe an agreement to pay these sixpences; it was unanimously sign'd, and for a time well executed. All the inhabitants of the city were delighted with the cleanliness of the pavement that surrounded the market, it being a convenience to all, and this rais'd a general desire to have all the streets paved, and made the people more willing to submit to a tax for that purpose.

After some time I drew a bill for paving the city, and brought it into the Assembly. It was just before I went to England, in 1757, and did not pass till I was gone,[1] and then with an alteration in the mode of assessment, which I thought not for the better, but with an addi-

[1] See votes.

tional provision for lighting as well as paving
the streets, which was a great improvement.
It was by a private person, the late Mr. John
Clifton, his giving a sample of the utility of
lamps, by placing one at his door, that the
people were first impress'd with the idea of en-
lighting all the city. The honour of this public
benefit has also been ascrib'd to me, but it
belongs truly to that gentleman. I did but
follow his example, and have only some merit
to claim respecting the form of our lamps, as
differing from the globe lamps we were at first
supply'd with from London. Those we found
inconvenient in these respects: they admitted
no air below; the smoke, therefore, did not
readily go out above, but circulated in the globe,
lodg'd on its inside, and soon obstructed the
light they were intended to afford; giving, besides, the daily trouble of wiping them clean;
and an accidental stroke on one of them would
demolish it, and render it totally useless. I
therefore suggested the composing them of four
flat panes, with a long funnel above to draw
up the smoke, and crevices admitting air below,
to facilitate the ascent of the smoke; by this
means they were kept clean, and did not grow
dark in a few hours, as the London lamps do,
but continu'd bright till morning, and an acci-

dental stroke would generally break but a single pane, easily repair'd.

I have sometimes wonder'd that the Londoners did not, from the effect holes in the bottom of the globe lamps us'd at Vauxhall [1] have in keeping them clean, learn to have such holes in their street lamps. But, these holes being made for another purpose, viz., to communicate flame more suddenly to the wick by a little flax hanging down thro' them, the other use, of letting in air, seems not to have been thought of; and therefore, after the lamps have been lit a few hours, the streets of London are very poorly illuminated.

The mention of these improvements puts me in mind of one I propos'd, when in London, to Dr. Fothergill, who was among the best men I have known, and a great promoter of useful projects. I had observ'd that the streets, when dry, were never swept, and the light dust carried away; but it was suffer'd to accumulate till wet weather reduc'd it to mud, and then, after lying some days so deep on the pavement that there

[1] Vauxhall Gardens, once a popular and fashionable London resort, situated on the Thames above Lambeth. The Gardens were closed in 1859, but they will always be remembered because of Sir Roger de Coverley's visit to them in the *Spectator* and from the descriptions in Smollett's *Humphry Clinker* and Thackeray's *Vanity Fair*.

was no crossing but in paths kept clean by poor
people with brooms, it was with great labour
rak'd together and thrown up into carts open
above, the sides of which suffer'd some of the
slush at every jolt on the pavement to shake
out and fall, sometimes to the annoyance of
foot-passengers. The reason given for not

sweeping the dusty streets was that the dust
would fly into the windows of shops and houses.

An accidental occurrence had instructed me
how much sweeping might be done in a little
time. I found at my door in Craven-street,[1]
one morning, a poor woman sweeping my pavement with a birch broom; she appeared very
pale and feeble, as just come out of a fit of
sickness. I ask'd who employ'd her to sweep
there; she said, "Nobody, but I am very poor

[1] A short street near Charing Cross, London.

and in distress, and I sweeps before gentle-
folkses doors, and hopes they will give me
something." I bid her sweep the whole street
clean, and I would give her a shilling; this was
at nine o'clock; at 12 she came for the shilling.
From the slowness I saw at first in her working, I could scarce believe that the work was
done so soon, and sent my servant to examine
it, who reported that the whole street was
swept perfectly clean, and all the dust plac'd
in the gutter, which was in the middle; and
the next rain wash'd it quite away, so that the
pavement and even the kennel were perfectly
clean.

I then judg'd that, if that feeble woman could
sweep such a street in three hours, a strong,
active man might have done it in half the time.
And here let me remark the convenience of having but one gutter in such a narrow street,
running down its middle, instead of two, one
on each side, near the footway; for where all
the rain that falls on a street runs from the
sides and meets in the middle, it forms there a
current strong enough to wash away all the
mud it meets with; but when divided into two
channels, it is often too weak to cleanse either,
and only makes the mud it finds more fluid, so
that the wheels of carriages and feet of horses

throw and dash it upon the foot-pavement, which is thereby rendered foul and slippery, and sometimes splash it upon those who are walking. My proposal, communicated to the good doctor, was as follows:

"For the more effectual cleaning and keeping clean the streets of London and Westminster, it is proposed that the several watchmen be contracted with to have the dust swept up in dry seasons, and the mud rak'd up at other times, each in the several streets and lanes of his round; that they be furnish'd with brooms and other proper instruments for these purposes, to be kept at their respective stands, ready to furnish the poor people they may employ in the service.

"That in the dry summer months the dust be all swept up into heaps at proper distances, before the shops and windows of houses are usually opened, when the scavengers, with close-covered carts, shall also carry it all away.

"That the mud, when rak'd up, be not left in heaps to be spread abroad again by the wheels of carriages and trampling of horses, but that the scavengers be provided with bodies of carts, not plac'd high upon wheels, but low upon sliders, with lattice bottoms, which, being cover'd with straw, will retain the mud thrown into them, and permit the water to drain from it, whereby it will become much lighter, water making the greatest part of its weight; these bodies of carts to be plac'd at convenient distances, and the mud brought to them in wheelbarrows; they remaining where plac'd till the mud is drain'd, and then horses brought to draw them away."

I have since had doubts of the practicability of the latter part of this proposal, on account of the narrowness of some streets, and the difficulty of placing the draining-sleds so as not to encumber too much the passage; but I am still of opinion that the former, requiring the dust to be swept up and carry'd away before the shops are open, is very practicable in the summer, when the days are long; for, in walking thro' the Strand and Fleet-street one morning at seven o'clock, I observ'd there was not one shop open, tho' it had been daylight and the sun up above three hours; the inhabitants of London chusing voluntarily to live much by candle-light, and sleep by sunshine, and yet often complain, a little absurdly, of the duty on candles, and the high price of tallow.

Some may think these trifling matters not worth minding or relating; but when they consider that tho' dust blown into the eyes of a single person, or into a single shop on a windy day, is but of small importance, yet the great number of the instances in a populous city, and its frequent repetitions give it weight and consequence, perhaps they will not censure very severely those who bestow some attention to affairs of this seemingly low nature. Human felicity is produc'd not so much by great pieces of good fortune that seldom happen, as by little advantages that occur every day. Thus, if you teach a poor young man to shave himself, and keep his razor in order, you may contribute more to the happiness of his life than in giving him a thousand guineas. The money may be soon spent, the regret only remaining of having foolishly consumed it; but in the other case, he escapes the frequent vexation of waiting for barbers, and of their sometimes dirty fingers, offensive breaths, and dull razors; he shaves when most convenient to him, and enjoys daily the pleasure of its being done with a good instrument. With these sentiments I have hazarded the few preceding pages, hoping they may afford hints which some time or other may be useful to a city I love, having lived many years in it very happily, and perhaps to some of our towns in America.

Having been for some time employed by the

postmaster-general of America as his comptroller in regulating several offices, and bringing the officers to account, I was, upon his death in 1753, appointed, jointly with Mr. William Hunter, to succeed him, by a commission from the postmaster-general in England. The American office never had hitherto paid anything to that of Britain. We were to have six hundred pounds a year between us, if we could make that sum out of the profits of the office. To do this, a variety of improvements were necessary; some of these were inevitably at first expensive, so that in the first four years the office became above nine hundred pounds in debt to us. But it soon after began to repay us; and before I was displac'd by a freak of the ministers, of which I shall speak hereafter, we had brought it to yield *three times* as much clear revenue to the crown as the post-office of Ireland. Since that imprudent transaction, they have receiv'd from it—not one farthing!

The business of the postoffice occasion'd my taking a journey this year to New England, where the College of Cambridge, of their own motion, presented me with the degree of Master of Arts. Yale College, in Connecticut, had before made me a similar compliment. Thus, without studying in any college, I came to partake of their honours. They were conferr'd in consideration of my improvements and discoveries in the electric branch of natural philosophy.

XIV

ALBANY PLAN OF UNION

N 1754, war with France being again apprehended, a congress of commissioners from the different colonies was, by an order of the Lords of Trade, to be assembled at Albany, there to confer with the chiefs of the Six Nations concerning the means of defending both their country and ours. Governor Hamilton, having receiv'd this order, acquainted the House with it, requesting they would furnish proper presents for the Indians, to be given on this occasion; and naming the speaker (Mr. Norris) and myself to join Mr. Thomas Penn and Mr. Secretary Peters as commissioners to act for Pennsylvania. The House approv'd the nomination, and provided the goods for the present, and tho' they did not much like treating out of the provinces; and we met the other commissioners at Albany about the middle of June.

In our way thither, I projected and drew a plan for the union of all the colonies under one government, so far as might be necessary for defense, and other important general purposes. As we pass'd thro' New York, I had there shown my project to Mr. James Alexander and Mr. Kennedy, two gentlemen of great knowledge in public affairs, and, being fortified by their approbation, I ventur'd to lay it before the Congress. It then appeared that several of the commissioners had form'd plans of the same

JOIN, or DIE.

kind. A previous question was first taken, whether a union should be established, which pass'd in the affirmative unanimously. A committee was then appointed, one member from each colony, to consider the several plans and report. Mine happen'd to be preferr'd, and, with a few amendments, was accordingly reported.

By this plan the general government was to be administered by a president-general, appointed and supported by the crown, and a grand council was to be chosen by the repre-

sentatives of the people of the several colonies,
met in their respective assemblies. The debates
upon it in Congress went on daily, hand in
hand with the Indian business. Many objections and difficulties were started, but at length
they were all overcome, and the plan was unanimously agreed to, and copies ordered to be
transmitted to the Board of Trade and to the
assemblies of the several provinces. Its fate
was singular; the assemblies did not adopt it,
as they all thought there was too much *pre-
rogative* in it, and in England it was judg'd
to have too much of the *democratic*. The Board
of Trade therefore did not approve of it, nor
recommend it for the approbation of his
majesty; but another scheme was form'd, supposed to answer the same purpose better,
whereby the governors of the provinces, with
some members of their respective councils, were
to meet and order the raising of troops, building of forts, etc., and to draw on the treasury
of Great Britain for the expense, which was
afterwards to be refunded by an act of Parliament laying a tax on America. My plan, with
my reasons in support of it, is to be found
among my political papers that are printed.

Being the winter following in Boston, I had
much conversation with Governor Shirley upon

both the plans. Part of what passed between us on the occasion may also be seen among those papers. The different and contrary reasons of dislike to my plan makes me suspect that it was really the true medium; and I am still of opinion it would have been happy for both sides the water if it had been adopted. The colonies, so united, would have been sufficiently strong to have defended themselves; there would then have been no need of troops from England; of course, the subsequent pretence for taxing America, and the bloody contest it occasioned, would have been avoided. But such mistakes are not new; history is full of the errors of states and princes.

> " Look round the habitable world, how few
> Know their own good, or, knowing it, pursue ! "

Those who govern, having much business on their hands, do not generally like to take the trouble of considering and carrying into execution new projects. The best public measures are therefore seldom *adopted from previous wisdom, but forc'd by the occasion.*

The Governor of Pennsylvania, in sending it down to the Assembly, express'd his approbation of the plan, " as appearing to him to be drawn up with great clearness and strength of judgment, and therefore recommended it as well worthy of their closest and most serious attention." The House, however, by the management of a certain member, took it up when I happen'd to be absent, which I thought not very fair, and reprobated it without paying any attention to it at all, to my no small mortification.

XV

QUARRELS WITH THE PROPRIETARY GOVERNORS

N my journey to Boston this year, I met at New York with our new governor, Mr. Morris, just arriv'd there from England, with whom I had been before intimately acquainted. He brought a commission to supersede Mr. Hamilton, who, tir'd with the disputes his proprietary instructions subjected him to, had resign'd. Mr. Morris ask'd me if I thought he must expect as uncomfortable an administration. I said, "No; you may, on the contrary, have a very comfortable one, if you will only take care not to enter into any dispute with the Assembly." "My dear friend," says he, pleasantly, "how can you advise my avoiding disputes? You know I love disputing; it is one of my greatest pleasures; however, to show the regard I have for your counsel, I promise you I will, if possible, avoid them." He had some reason for loving to dispute, being eloquent, an acute sophister, and, therefore, generally suc-

cessful in argumentative conversation. He had
been brought up to it from a boy, his father,
as I have heard, accustoming his children to
dispute with one another for his diversion, while
sitting at table after dinner; but I think the
practice was not wise; for, in the course of my
observation, these disputing, contradicting, and
confuting people are generally unfortunate in
their affairs. They get victory sometimes, but
they never get good will, which would be of
more use to them. We parted, he going to
Philadelphia, and I to Boston.

In returning, I met at New York with the
votes of the Assembly, by which it appear'd
that, notwithstanding his promise to me, he
and the House were already in high contention;
and it was a continual battle between them as
long as he retain'd the government. I had my
share of it; for, as soon as I got back to my
seat in the Assembly, I was put on every committee for answering his speeches and messages,
and by the committees always desired to make
the drafts. Our answers, as well as his messages, were often tart, and sometimes indecently
abusive; and, as he knew I wrote for the Assembly, one might have imagined that, when
we met, we could hardly avoid cutting throats;
but he was so good-natur'd a man that no per-

sonal difference between him and me was occasion'd by the contest, and we often din'd together.

One afternoon, in the height of this public
quarrel, we met in the street. "Franklin," says
he, "you must go home with me and spend the

evening; I am to have some company that you
will like;" and, taking me by the arm, he led
me to his house. In gay conversation over our
wine, after supper, he told us, jokingly, that
he much admir'd the idea of Sancho Panza,[1]
who, when it was proposed to give him a government, requested it might be a government
of *blacks,* as then, if he could not agree with
his people, he might sell them. One of his
friends, who sat next to me, says, "Franklin,
why do you continue to side with these damn'd

[1] The "round, selfish, and self-important" squire of Don Quixote
in Cervantes' romance of that name.

Quakers? Had not you better sell them? The proprietor would give you a good price." "The governor," says I, "has not yet *blacked* them enough." He, indeed, had laboured hard to blacken the Assembly in all his messages, but they wip'd off his colouring as fast as he laid it on, and plac'd it, in return, thick upon his own face; so that, finding he was likely to be negrofied himself, he, as well as Mr. Hamilton, grew tir'd of the contest, and quitted the government.

These public quarrels[1] were all at bottom owing to the proprietaries, our hereditary governors, who, when any expense was to be incurred for the defense of their province, with incredible meanness instructed their deputies to pass no act for levying the necessary taxes, unless their vast estates were in the same act expressly excused; and they had even taken bonds of these deputies to observe such instructions. The Assemblies for three years held out against this injustice, tho' constrained to bend at last. At length Captain Denny, who was Governor Morris's successor, ventured to disobey those instructions; how that was brought about I shall show hereafter.

But I am got forward too fast with my story:

[1] My acts in Morris's time, military, etc.—*Marg. note.*

there are still some transactions to be mention'd that happened during the administration of Governor Morris.

War being in a manner commenced with France, the government of Massachusetts Bay projected an attack upon Crown Point,[1] and sent Mr. Quincy to Pennsylvania, and Mr. Pownall, afterward Governor Pownall, to New York, to solicit assistance. As I was in the Assembly, knew its temper, and was Mr. Quincy's countryman, he appli'd to me for my influence and assistance. I dictated his address to them, which was well received. They voted an aid of ten thousand pounds, to be laid out in provisions. But the governor refusing his assent to their bill (which included this with other sums granted for the use of the crown), unless a clause were inserted exempting the proprietary estate from bearing any part of the tax that would be necessary, the Assembly, tho' very desirous of making their grant to New England effectual, were at a loss how to accomplish it. Mr. Quincy labored hard with the governor to obtain his assent, but he was obstinate.

[1] On Lake Champlain, ninety miles north of Albany. It was captured by the French in 1731, attacked by the English in 1755 and 1756, and abandoned by the French in 1759. It was finally captured from the English by the Americans in 1775.

I then suggested a method of doing the business without the governor, by orders on the trustees of the Loan office, which, by law, the Assembly had the right of drawing. There was, indeed, little or no money at that time in the office, and therefore I propos'd that the orders should be payable in a year, and to bear an interest of five per cent. With these orders I suppos'd the provisions might easily be purchas'd. The Assembly, with very little hesitation, adopted the proposal. The orders were immediately printed, and I was one of the committee directed to sign and dispose of them. The fund for paying them was the interest of all the paper currency then extant in the province upon loan, together with the revenue arising from the excise, which being known to be more than sufficient, they obtain'd instant credit, and were not only receiv'd in payment for the provisions, but many money'd people, who had cash lying by them, vested it in those orders, which they found advantageous, as they bore interest while upon hand, and might on any occasion be used as money; so that they were eagerly all bought up, and in a few weeks none of them were to be seen. Thus this important affair was by my means completed. Mr. Quincy return'd thanks to the Assembly in a

handsome memorial, went home highly pleas'd
with this success of his embassy, and ever after
bore for me the most cordial and affectionate
friendship.

XVI

BRADDOCK'S EXPEDITION

THE British government, not chusing to permit the union of the colonies as propos'd at Albany, and to trust that union with their defense, lest they should thereby grow too military, and feel their own strength, suspicions and jealousies at this time being entertain'd of them, sent over General Braddock with two regiments of regular English troops for that purpose. He landed at Alexandria, in Virginia, and thence march'd to Frederictown, in Maryland, where he halted for carriages. Our Assembly apprehending, from some information, that he had conceived violent prejudices against them, as averse to the service, wish'd me to wait upon him, not as from them, but as postmaster-general, under the guise of proposing to settle with him the mode of conducting with most celerity and certainty the despatches between him and the governors of the several provinces, with whom he must necessarily have continual correspondence, and of which they propos'd to pay the expense. My son accompanied me on this journey.

We found the general at Frederictown, waiting impatiently for the return of those he had sent thro' the back parts of Maryland and Virginia to collect waggons. I stayed with him several days, din'd with him daily, and had full opportunity of removing all his prejudices, by the information of what the Assembly had before his arrival actually done, and were still willing to do, to facilitate his operations. When I was about to depart, the returns of waggons to be obtained were brought in, by which it appear'd that they amounted only to twenty-five, and not all of those were in serviceable condition. The general and all the officers were surpris'd, declar'd the expedition was then at an end, being impossible, and exclaim'd against the ministers for ignorantly landing them in a country destitute of the means of conveying their stores, baggage, etc., not less than one hundred and fifty waggons being necessary.

I happen'd to say I thought it was pity they had not been landed rather in Pennsylvania, as in that country almost every farmer had his waggon. The general eagerly laid hold of my words, and said, "Then you, sir, who are a man of interest there, can probably procure them for us; and I beg you will undertake it." I ask'd what terms were to be offer'd the owners of the waggons, and I was desir'd to put on paper the terms that appeared to me necessary. This I did, and they were agreed to, and a commission and instructions accordingly prepar'd immediately. What those terms were will appear in the advertisement I publish'd as soon as I arriv'd at Lancaster, which being, from the great and sudden effect it produc'd, a piece of some curiosity, I shall insert it at length, as follows:

" ADVERTISEMENT.

" LANCASTER, *April* 26, 1755.
"Whereas, one hundred and fifty waggons, with four horses to each waggon, and fifteen hundred saddle or pack horses, are wanted for the service of his majesty's forces now about to rendezvous at Will's Creek, and his excellency General Braddock having been pleased to empower me to contract for the hire of the same, I hereby give notice that I shall attend for that purpose at Lancaster from this day to next Wednesday evening, and at York from next Thursday morning till Friday evening, where I shall be ready to agree for waggons and

teams, or single horses, on the following terms, viz.: 1. That there shall be paid for each waggon, with four good horses and a driver, fifteen shillings per diem; and for each able horse with a pack-saddle, or other saddle and furniture, two shillings per diem; and for each able horse without a saddle, eighteen pence per diem. 2. That the pay commence from the time of their joining the forces at Will's Creek, which must be on or before the 20th of May ensuing, and that a reasonable allowance be paid over and above for the time necessary for their travelling to Will's Creek and home again after their discharge. 3. Each waggon and team, and every saddle or pack horse, is to be valued by indifferent persons chosen between me and the owner; and in case of the loss of any waggon, team, or other horse in the service, the price according to such valuation is to be allowed and paid. 4. Seven days' pay is to be advanced and paid in hand by me to the owner of each waggon and team, or horse, at the time of contracting, if required, and the remainder to be paid by General Braddock, or by the paymaster of the army, at the time of their discharge, or from time to time, as it shall be demanded. 5. No drivers of waggons, or persons taking care of the hired horses, are on any account to be called upon to do the duty of soldiers, or be otherwise employed than in conducting or taking care of their carriages or horses. 6. All oats, Indian corn, or other forage that waggons or horses bring to the camp, more than is necessary for the subsistence of the horses, is to be taken for the use of the army, and a reasonable price paid for the same.

"Note.—My son, William Franklin, is empowered to enter into like contracts with any person in Cumberland county.

"B. FRANKLIN."

"To the inhabitants of the Counties of Lancaster, York, and Cumberland.

"Friends and Countrymen,

"Being occasionally [1] at the camp at Frederic a few days since, I found the general and officers extremely exasperated on account of their not being supplied with horses and carriages, which had been expected from this province, as most able to furnish them; but, through the dissensions between our governor and Assembly, money had not been provided, nor any steps taken for that purpose.

"It was proposed to send an armed force immediately into these counties, to seize as

[1] By chance.

many of the best carriages and horses as should be wanted, and compel as many persons into the service as would be necessary to drive and take care of them.

"I apprehended that the progress of British soldiers through these counties on such an occasion, especially considering the temper they are in, and their resentment against us, would be attended with many and great inconveniences to the inhabitants, and therefore more willingly took the trouble of trying first what might be done by fair and equitable means. The people of these back counties have lately complained to the Assembly that a sufficient currency was wanting; you have an opportunity of receiving and dividing among you a very considerable sum; for, if the service of this expedition should continue, as it is more than probable it will, for one hundred and twenty days, the hire of these waggons and horses will amount to upward of thirty thousand pounds, which will be paid you in silver and gold of the king's money.

"The service will be light and easy, for the army will scarce march above twelve miles per day, and the waggons and baggage-horses, as they carry those things that are absolutely necessary to the welfare of the army, must march with the army, and no faster; and are, for the army's sake, always placed where they can be most secure, whether in a march or in a camp.

"If you are really, as I believe you are, good and loyal subjects to his majesty, you may now do a most acceptable service, and make it easy to yourselves; for three or four of such as cannot separately spare from the business of their plantations a waggon and four horses and a driver, may do it together, one furnishing the waggon, another one or two horses, and another the driver, and divide the pay proportionately between you, but if you do not this service to your king and country voluntarily, when such good pay and reasonable terms are offered to you, your loyalty will be strongly suspected. The king's business must be done; so many brave troops, come so far for your defense, must not stand idle through your backwardness to do what may be reasonably expected from you; waggons and horses must be had; violent measures will probably be used, and you will be left to seek for a recompense where you can find it, and your case, perhaps, be little pitied or regarded.

"I have no particular interest in this affair, as, except the satisfaction of endeavouring to do good, I shall have only my labour for my pains. If this method of obtaining the waggons and horses is not likely to succeed, I am obliged to send word to the general in fourteen days; and I suppose Sir John St. Clair, the hussar, with a body of soldiers, will immediately enter the province for the purpose, which I shall be sorry to hear, because I am very sincerely and truly your friend and well-wisher,

"B. FRANKLIN."

I received of the general about eight hundred pounds, to be disbursed in advance-money to the waggon owners, etc.; but that sum being insufficient, I advanc'd upward of two hundred pounds more, and in two weeks the one hundred and fifty waggons, with two hundred and fifty-nine carrying horses, were on their march for the camp. The advertisement promised payment according to the valuation, in case any waggon or horse should be lost. The owners, however, alleging they did not know General Braddock, or what dependence might be had on his promise, insisted on my bond for the performance, which I accordingly gave them.

While I was at the camp, supping one evening with the officers of Colonel Dunbar's regiment, he represented to me his concern for the subalterns, who, he said, were generally not in affluence, and could ill afford, in this dear country, to lay in the stores that might be necessary in so long a march, thro' a wilderness, where nothing was to be purchas'd. I commiserated their case, and resolved to endeavour procuring them some relief. I said nothing, however, to him of my intention, but wrote the next morning to the committee of the Assembly, who had the disposition of some public money, warmly recommending the case of these officers to their consideration, and proposing that a present should be sent them of necessaries and refreshments. My son, who had some experience of a camp life, and of its wants, drew up a list for me, which I enclos'd in my letter. The committee approv'd, and used such diligence that, conducted by my son, the stores arrived at the camp as soon as the waggons. They consisted of twenty parcels, each containing

6 lbs. loaf sugar.
6 lbs. good Muscovado do.
1 lb. good green tea.
1 lb. good bohea do.
6 lbs. good ground coffee.
6 lbs. chocolate.
1-2 cwt. best white biscuit.
1-2 lb. pepper.
1 quart best white wine vinegar.
1 Gloucester cheese.
1 kegg containing 20 lbs. good butter.
2 doz. old Madeira wine.
2 gallons Jamaica spirits.
1 bottle flour of mustard.
2 well-cur'd hams.
1-2 dozen dry'd tongues.
6 lbs. rice.
6 lbs. raisins.

These twenty parcels, well pack'd, were placed on as many horses, each parcel, with the horse, being intended as a present for one officer. They were very thankfully receiv'd, and the kindness acknowledg'd by letters to me from the colonels of both regiments, in the most grateful terms. The general, too, was highly satisfied with my conduct in procuring him the waggons, etc., and readily paid my account of disbursements, thanking me repeatedly, and requesting my farther assistance in sending provisions after him. I undertook this also, and was busily employ'd in it till we heard of his defeat, advancing for the service of my own money, upwards of one thousand pounds sterling, of which I sent him an account. It came to his hands, luckily for me, a few days before the battle, and he return'd me immediately an order on the paymaster for the round sum of one thousand pounds, leaving the remainder to the next account. I consider this payment as good luck, having never been able to obtain that remainder, of which more hereafter.

This general was, I think, a brave man, and might probably have made a figure as a good officer in some European war. But he had too much self-confidence, too high an opinion of the validity of regular troops, and too mean a one of both Americans and Indians. George Croghan, our Indian interpreter, join'd him on his march with one hundred of those people, who might have been of great use to his army as guides, scouts, etc., if he had treated them kindly; but he slighted and neglected them, and they gradually left him.

In conversation with him one day, he was giving me some account of his intended progress. "After taking Fort Duquesne," [1] says he, "I am to proceed to Niagara; and, having taken that, to Frontenac, [2] if the season will allow time; and I suppose it will, for Duquesne can hardly detain me above three or four days; and then I see nothing that can obstruct my march to Niagara." Having before revolv'd in my mind the long line his army must make in their march by a very narrow road, to be cut for them thro' the woods and bushes, and also what I had read of a former defeat of fifteen hundred French, who invaded the Iroquois country, I had conceiv'd some doubts and some fears for the event of the campaign. But I ventur'd only to say, "To be sure, sir, if you arrive well before Duquesne, with these

[1] Pittsburg.
[2] Kingston, at the eastern end of Lake Ontario.

fine troops, so well provided with artillery, that place not yet completely fortified, and as we hear with no very strong garrison, can probably make but a short resistance. The only danger I apprehend of obstruction to your march is from ambuscades of Indians, who, by constant practice, are dexterous in laying and executing them; and the slender line, near four miles long, which your army must make, may expose it to be attack'd by surprise in its flanks, and to be cut like a thread into several pieces, which, from their distance, cannot come up in time to support each other."

He smil'd at my ignorance, and reply'd, "These savages may, indeed, be a formidable enemy to your raw American militia, but upon the king's regular and disciplin'd troops, sir, it is impossible they should make any impression." I was conscious of an impropriety in my disputing with a military man in matters of his profession, and said no more. The enemy, however, did not take the advantage of his army which I apprehended its long line of march expos'd it to, but let it advance without interruption till within nine miles of the place; and then, when more in a body (for it had just passed a river, where the front had halted till all were come over), and in a more

open part of the woods than any it had pass'd,
attack'd its advanced guard by heavy fire from
behind trees and bushes, which was the first
intelligence the general had of an enemy's being near him. This guard being disordered, the
general hurried the troops up to their assistance, which was done in great confusion, thro'
waggons, baggage, and cattle; and presently

the fire came upon their flank: the officers, being on horseback, were more easily distinguish'd, pick'd out as marks, and fell very fast;
and the soldiers were crowded together in a
huddle, having or hearing no orders, and standing to be shot at till two-thirds of them were
killed; and then, being seiz'd with a panick,
the whole fled with precipitation.

The waggoners took each a horse out of his

team and scamper'd; their example was immediately followed by others; so that all the waggons, provisions, artillery, and stores were left to the enemy. The general, being wounded, was brought off with difficulty; his secretary, Mr. Shirley, was killed by his side; and out of eighty-six officers, sixty-three were killed or wounded, and seven hundred and fourteen men killed out of eleven hundred. These eleven hundred had been picked men from the whole army; the rest had been left behind with Colonel Dunbar, who was to follow with the heavier part of the stores, provisions, and baggage. The flyers, not being pursu'd, arriv'd at Dunbar's camp, and the panick they brought with them instantly seiz'd him and all his people; and, tho' he had now above one thousand men, and the enemy who had beaten Braddock did not at most exceed four hundred Indians and French together, instead of proceeding, and endeavouring to recover some of the lost honour, he ordered all the stores, ammunition, etc., to be destroy'd, that he might have more horses to assist his flight towards the settlements, and less lumber to remove. He was there met with requests from the governors of Virginia, Maryland, and Pennsylvania, that he would post his troops on the frontier, so as to afford some protection to the inhabitants; but he continu'd his hasty march thro' all the country, not thinking himself safe till he arriv'd at Philadelphia, where the inhabitants could protect him. This whole transaction gave us Americans the first suspicion that our exalted ideas of the prowess of British regulars had not been well founded.[1]

In their first march, too, from their landing till they got beyond the settlements, they had plundered and stripped the inhabitants, totally ruining some poor families, besides insulting, abusing, and confining the people if they remonstrated. This was enough to put us out of conceit of such defenders, if we had really wanted any. How different was the conduct of our French friends in 1781, who, during a march thro' the most inhabited part of our country from Rhode Island to Virginia, near seven hundred miles, occasioned not the smallest complaint for the loss of a pig, a chicken, or even an apple.

Captain Orme, who was one of the general's aids-de-camp, and, being grievously wounded, was brought off with him, and continu'd with

---

[1] Other accounts of this expedition and defeat may be found in Fiske's *Washington and his Country,* or Lodge's *George Washington,* Vol. I.

him to his death, which happen'd in a few days, told me that he was totally silent all the first day, and at night only said, *"Who would have thought it?"* That he was silent again the following day, saying only at last, *"We shall better know how to deal with them another time";* and dy'd in a few minutes after.

The secretary's papers, with all the general's orders, instructions, and correspondence, falling into the enemy's hands, they selected and translated into French a number of the articles, which they printed, to prove the hostile intentions of the British court before the declaration of war. Among these I saw some letters of the general to the ministry, speaking highly of the great service I had rendered the army, and recommending me to their notice. David Hume,[1] too, who was some years after secretary to Lord Hertford, when minister in France, and afterward to General Conway, when secretary of state, told me he had seen among the papers in that office, letters from Braddock highly recommending me. But, the expedition having been unfortunate, my service, it seems, was not thought of much value, for those recommendations were never of any use to me.

[1] A famous Scotch philosopher and historian (1711-1776).

As to rewards from himself, I ask'd only one, which was, that he would give orders to his officers not to enlist any more of our bought servants, and that he would discharge such as had been already enlisted. This he readily granted, and several were accordingly return'd to their masters, on my application. Dunbar, when the command devolv'd on him, was not so generous. He being at Philadelphia, on his retreat, or rather flight, I apply'd to him for the discharge of the servants of three poor farmers of Lancaster county that he had enlisted, reminding him of the late general's orders on that head. He promised me that, if the masters would come to him at Trenton, where he should be in a few days on his march to New York, he would there deliver their men to them. They accordingly were at the expense and trouble of going to Trenton, and there he refus'd to perform his promise, to their great loss and disappointment.

As soon as the loss of the waggons and horses was generally known, all the owners came upon me for the valuation which I had given bond to pay. Their demands gave me a great deal of trouble, my acquainting them that the money was ready in the paymaster's hands, but that orders for paying it must first be obtained from General Shirley,[1] and my assuring them that I had apply'd to that general by letter; but, he being at a distance, an answer could not soon be receiv'd, and they must have patience, all this was not sufficient to satisfy, and some began to sue me. General Shirley at length relieved me from this terrible situation by appointing commissioners to examine the claims, and ordering payment. They amounted to near twenty thousand pound, which to pay would have ruined me.

Before we had the news of this defeat, the two Doctors Bond came to me with a subscription paper for raising money to defray the expense of a grand firework, which it was intended to exhibit at a rejoicing on receipt of the news of our taking Fort Duquesne. I looked grave, and said it would, I thought, be time enough to prepare for the rejoicing when we knew we should have occasion to rejoice. They seem'd surpris'd that I did not immediately comply with their proposal. "Why the d—l!" says one of them, "you surely don't suppose that the fort will not be taken?"

---

[1] Governor of Massachusetts and commander of the British forces in America.

"I don't know that it will not be taken, but I know that the events of war are subject to great uncertainty." I gave them the reasons of my doubting; the subscription was dropt, and the projectors thereby missed the mortification they would have undergone if the firework had been prepared. Dr. Bond, on some other occasion afterward, said that he did not like Franklin's forebodings.

Governor Morris, who had continually worried the Assembly with message after message before the defeat of Braddock, to beat them into the making of acts to raise money for the defense of the province, without taxing, among others, the proprietary estates, and had rejected all their bills for not having such an exempting clause, now redoubled his attacks with more hope of success, the danger and necessity being greater. The Assembly, however, continu'd firm, believing they had justice on their side, and that it would be giving up an essential right if they suffered the governor to amend their money-bills. In one of the last, indeed, which was for granting fifty thousand pounds, his propos'd amendment was only of a single word. The bill express'd "that all estates, real and personal, were to be taxed, those of the proprietaries *not* excepted."

His amendment was, for *not* read *only:* a small, but very material alteration. However, when the news of this disaster reached England, our friends there whom we had taken care to furnish with all the Assembly's answers to the governor's messages, rais'd a clamor against the proprietaries for their meanness and injustice in giving their governor such instructions; some going so far as to say that, by obstructing the defense of their province, they forfeited their right to it. They were intimidated by this, and sent orders to their receiver-general to add five thousand pounds of their money to whatever sum might be given by the Assembly for such purpose.

This, being notified to the House, was accepted in lieu of their share of a general tax, and a new bill was form'd, with an exempting clause, which passed accordingly. By this act I was appointed one of the commissioners for disposing of the money, sixty thousand pounds. I had been active in modelling the bill and procuring its passage, and had, at the same time, drawn a bill for establishing and disciplining a voluntary militia, which I carried thro' the House without much difficulty, as care was taken in it to leave the Quakers at their liberty. To promote the association necessary to form the militia, I wrote a dialogue,[1] stating and answering all the objections I could think of to such a militia, which was printed, and had, as I thought, great effect.

[1] This dialogue and the militia act are in the Gentleman's Magazine for February and March, 1756.—*Marg. note.*

XVII

FRANKLIN'S DEFENSE OF THE FRONTIER

HILE the several companies in the city and country were forming, and learning their exercise, the governor prevail'd with me to take charge of our North-western frontier, which was infested by the enemy, and provide for the defense of the inhabitants by raising troops and building a line of forts. I undertook this military business, tho' I did not conceive myself well qualified for it. He gave me a commission with full powers, and a parcel of blank commissions for officers, to be given to whom I thought fit. I had but little difficulty in raising men, having soon five hundred and sixty under my command. My son, who had in the preceding war been an officer in the army rais'd against Canada, was my aid-de-camp, and of great use to me. The Indians had burned Gnadenhut,[1] a village settled by the Moravians, and massacred the in-

[1] Pronounced Gna'-den-hoot.

habitants; but the place was thought a good situation for one of the forts.

In order to march thither, I assembled the companies at Bethlehem, the chief establishment of those people. I was surprised to find it in so good a posture of defense; the destruction of Gnadenhut had made them apprehend danger. The principal buildings were defended by a stockade; they had purchased a quantity of arms and ammunition from New York, and had even plac'd quantities of small paving stones between the windows of their high stone houses, for their women to throw down upon the heads of any Indians that should attempt to force into them. The armed brethren, too, kept watch, and reliev'd as methodically as in any garrison town. In conversation with the bishop, Spangenberg, I mention'd this my surprise; for, knowing they had obtained an act of Parliament exempting them from military duties in the colonies, I had suppos'd they were conscientiously scrupulous of bearing arms. He answer'd me that it was not one of their established principles, but that, at the time of their obtaining that act, it was thought to be a principle with many of their people. On this occasion, however, they, to their surprise, found it adopted

by but a few. It seems they were either deceiv'd in themselves, or deceiv'd the Parliament; but common sense, aided by present danger, will sometimes be too strong for whimsi-
cal opinions.

It was the beginning of January when we
set out upon this business of building forts.
I sent one detachment toward the Minisink,
with instructions to erect one for the security
of that upper part of the country, and another
to the lower part, with similar instructions;
and I concluded to go myself with the rest of
my force to Gnadenhut, where a fort was tho't
more immediately necessary. The Moravians
procur'd me five waggons for our tools, stores,
baggage, etc.

Just before we left Bethlehem, eleven farmers, who had been driven from their plantations by the Indians, came to me requesting a
supply of firearms, that they might go back
and fetch off their cattle. I gave them each a
gun with suitable ammunition. We had not
march'd many miles before it began to rain,
and it continued raining all day; there were
no habitations on the road to shelter us, till
we arriv'd near night at the house of a German, where, and in his barn, we were all hud-
dled together, as wet as water could make us.

It was well we were not attack'd in our march,
for our arms were of the most ordinary sort,
and our men could not keep their gun locks [1]
dry. The Indians are dexterous in contri-
vances for that purpose, which we had not.
They met that day the eleven poor farmers
above mentioned, and killed ten of them. The

one who escap'd inform'd that his and his
companions' guns would not go off, the priming being wet with the rain.

The next day being fair, we continu'd our
march, and arriv'd at the desolated Gnadenhut.
There was a saw-mill near, round which were
left several piles of boards, with which we soon
hutted ourselves; an operation the more necessary at that inclement season, as we had no

[1] Flint-lock guns, discharged by means of a spark struck from
flint and steel into powder (priming) in an open pan.

tents. Our first work was to bury more effectually the dead we found there, who had been half interr'd by the country people.

The next morning our fort was plann'd and mark'd out, the circumference measuring four hundred and fifty-five feet, which would require as many palisades to be made of trees, one with another, of a foot diameter each. Our axes, of which we had seventy, were immediately set to work to cut down trees, and, our men being dexterous in the use of them, great despatch was made. Seeing the trees fall so fast, I had the curiosity to look at my watch when two men began to cut at a pine; in six minutes they had it upon the ground, and I found it of fourteen inches diameter. Each pine made three palisades of eighteen feet long, pointed at one end. While these were preparing, our other men dug a trench all round, of three feet deep, in which the palisades were to be planted; and, our waggons, the bodys being taken off, and the fore and hind wheels separated by taking out the pin which united the two parts of the perch,[1] we had ten carriages, with two horses each, to bring the palisades from the woods to the spot. When they were set up, our carpenters built a stage

[1] Here the pole connecting the front and rear wheels of a wagon.

of boards all round within, about six feet high, for the men to stand on when to fire thro' the loopholes. We had one swivel gun, which we mounted on one of the angles, and fir'd it as soon as fix'd, to let the Indians know, if any were within hearing, that we had such pieces; and thus our fort, if such a magnificent name may be given to so miserable a stockade, was finish'd in a week, though it rain'd so hard every other day that the men could not work.

This gave me occasion to observe, that, when men are employ'd, they are best content'd; for on the days they worked they were good-natur'd and cheerful, and, with the consciousness of having done a good day's work, they spent the evening jollily; but on our idle days they were mutinous and quarrelsome, finding fault with their pork, the bread, etc., and in continual ill-humour, which put me in mind of a sea-captain, whose rule it was to keep his men constantly at work; and, when his mate once told him that they had done everything, and there was nothing further to employ them about, *" Oh," says he, " make them scour the anchor."*

This kind of fort, however contemptible, is a sufficient defense against Indians, who have no cannon. Finding ourselves now posted securely, and having a place to retreat to on occasion, we ventur'd out in parties to scour the adjacent country. We met with no Indians, but we found the places on the neighbouring hills where they had lain to watch our proceedings. There was an art in their contrivance of those places that seems worth mention. It being winter, a fire was necessary for them; but a common fire on the surface of the ground would by its light have discover'd their position at a distance. They had therefore dug holes in the ground about three feet diameter, and somewhat deeper; we saw where they had with their hatchets cut off the charcoal from the sides of burnt logs lying in the woods. With these coals they had made small fires in the bottom of the holes, and we observ'd among the weeds and grass the prints of their bodies, made by their laying all round, with their legs hanging down in the holes to keep their feet warm, which, with them, is an essential point. This kind of fire, so manag'd, could not discover them, either by its light, flame, sparks, or even smoke: it appear'd that their number was not great, and it seems they saw we were too many to be attacked by them with prospect of advantage.

We had for our chaplain a zealous Presby-

terian minister, Mr. Beatty, who complained
to me that the men did not generally attend
his prayers and exhortations. When they enlisted, they were promised, besides pay and
provisions, a gill of rum a day, which was
punctually serv'd out to them, half in the
morning, and the other half in the evening;
and I observ'd they were as punctual in attending to receive it; upon which I said to Mr.
Beatty, "It is, perhaps, below the dignity of
your profession to act as steward of the rum,
but if you were to deal it out and only just
after prayers, you would have them all about
you." He liked the tho't, undertook the office,
and, with the help of a few hands to measure out the liquor, executed it to satisfaction,
and never were prayers more generally and
more punctually attended; so that I thought
this method preferable to the punishment in-
flicted by some military laws for non-attend-
ance on divine service.

I had hardly finish'd this business, and got
my fort well stor'd with provisions, when I
receiv'd a letter from the governor, acquainting me that he had call'd the Assembly, and
wished my attendance there, if the posture of
affairs on the frontiers was such that my remaining there was no longer necessary. My

friends, too, of the Assembly, pressing me by
their letters to be, if possible, at the meeting,
and my three intended forts being now compleated, and the inhabitants contented to remain on their farms under that protection, I
resolved to return; the more willingly, as a
New England officer, Colonel Clapham, experienced in Indian war, being on a visit to
our establishment, consented to accept the
command. I gave him a commission, and, pa-
rading the garrison, had it read before them,
and introduc'd him to them as an officer who,
from his skill in military affairs, was much
more fit to command them than myself; and,
giving them a little exhortation, took my
leave. I was escorted as far as Bethlehem,
where I rested a few days to recover from the
fatigue I had undergone. The first night, being in a good bed, I could hardly sleep, it was
so different from my hard lodging on the
floor of our hut at Gnaden wrapt only in a
blanket or two.

While at Bethlehem, I inquir'd a little into
the practice of the Moravians: some of them
had accompanied me, and all were very kind
to me. I found they work'd for a common
stock, ete at common tables, and slept in common dormitories, great numbers together. In

the dormitories I observed loopholes, at certain distances all along just under the ceiling, which I thought judiciously placed for change of air. I was at their church, where I was entertain'd with good musick, the organ being accompanied with violins, hautboys, flutes, clarinets, etc. I understood that their sermons were not usually preached to mixed congregations of men, women, and children, as is our common practice, but that they assembled sometimes the married men, at other times their wives, then the young men, the young women, and the little children, each division by itself. The sermon I heard was to the latter, who came in and were plac'd in rows on benches; the boys under the conduct of a young man, their tutor, and the girls conducted by a young woman. The discourse seem'd well adapted to their capacities, and was deliver'd in a pleasing, familiar manner, coaxing them, as it were, to be good. They behav'd very orderly, but looked pale and unhealthy, which made me suspect they were kept too much within doors, or not allow'd sufficient exercise.

I inquir'd concerning the Moravian marriages, whether the report was true that they were by lot. I was told that lots were us'd only in particular cases; that generally, when a young man found himself dispos'd to marry, he inform'd the elders of his class, who consulted the elder ladies that govern'd the young women. As these elders of the different sexes were well acquainted with the tempers and dispositions of their respective pupils, they could best judge what matches were suitable, and their judgments were generally acquiesc'd in; but if, for example, it should happen that two or three young women were found to be equally proper for the young man, the lot was then recurred to. I objected, if the matches are not made by the mutual choice of the parties, some of them may chance to be very unhappy. "And so they may," answer'd my informer, "if you let the parties chuse for themselves;" which, indeed, I could not deny.

Being returned to Philadelphia, I found the association went on swimmingly, the inhabitants that were not Quakers having pretty generally come into it, formed themselves into companies, and chose their captains, lieutenants, and ensigns, according to the new law. Dr. B. visited me, and gave me an account of the pains he had taken to spread a general good liking to the law, and ascribed much to those endeavours. I had had the vanity to asscribe all to my *Dialogue;* however, not knowing but that he might be in the right, I let him enjoy his opinion, which I take to be generally the best way in such cases. The officers, meeting, chose me to be colonel of the regiment, which I this time accepted. I forget how many companies we had, but we paraded about twelve hundred well-looking men, with a company of artillery, who had been furnished with six brass field-pieces, which they had become so expert in the use of as to fire twelve times in a minute. The first time I reviewed my regiment they accompanied me to my house, and would salute me with some rounds fired before my door, which shook down and broke several glasses of my electrical apparatus. And my new honour proved not much less brittle; for all our commissions were soon after broken by a repeal of the law in England.

During this short time of my colonelship, being about to set out on a journey to Virginia, the officers of my regiment took it into their heads that it would be proper for them to escort me out of town, as far as the Lower Ferry. Just as I was getting on horseback they came to my door, between thirty and forty, mounted, and all in their uniforms. I had not been previously acquainted with the

project, or I should have prevented it, being
naturally averse to the assuming of state on
any occasion; and I was a good deal chagrin'd
at their appearance, as I could not avoid their
accompanying me. What made it worse was,
that, as soon as we began to move, they drew
their swords and rode with them naked all the
way. Somebody wrote an account of this to
the proprietor, and it gave him great offense.
No such honour had been paid him when in
the province, nor to any of his governors; and
he said it was only proper to princes of the
blood royal, which may be true for aught I
know, who was, and still am, ignorant of the
etiquette in such cases.

This silly affair, however, greatly increased
his rancour against me, which was before not
a little, on account of my conduct in the Assembly respecting the exemption of his estate
from taxation, which I had always oppos'd
very warmly, and not without severe reflections on his meanness and injustice of contending for it. He accused me to the ministry as
being the great obstacle to the King's service,
preventing, by my influence in the House, the
proper form of the bills for raising money, and
he instanced this parade with my officers as a
proof of my having an intention to take the

government of the province out of his hands
by force. He also applied to Sir Everard
Fawkener, the postmaster-general, to deprive
me of my office; but it had no other effect
than to procure from Sir Everard a gentle ad-
monition.

Notwithstanding the continual wrangle between the governor and the House, in which
I, as a member, had so large a share, there
still subsisted a civil intercourse between that
gentleman and myself, and we never had any
personal difference. I have sometimes since
thought that his little or no resentment
against me, for the answers it was known I
drew up to his messages, might be the effect
of professional habit, and that, being bred a
lawyer, he might consider us both as merely
advocates for contending clients in a suit, he
for the proprietaries and I for the Assembly.
He would, therefore, sometimes call in a
friendly way to advise with me on difficult
points, and sometimes, tho' not often, take my
advice.

We acted in concert to supply Braddock's
army with provisions; and, when the shock-
ing news arrived of his defeat, the governor
sent in haste for me, to consult with him on
measures for preventing the desertion of the

back counties. I forget now the advice I gave; but I think it was, that Dunbar should be written to, and prevail'd with, if possible, to post his troops on the frontiers for their protection, till, by reënforcements from the colonies, he might be able to proceed on the expedition. And, after my return from the frontier, he would have had me undertake the conduct of such an expedition with provincial troops, for the reduction of Fort Duquesne, Dunbar and his men being otherwise employed; and he proposed to commission me as general. I had not so good an opinion of my military abilities as he profess'd to have, and I believe his professions must have exceeded his real sentiments; but probably he might think that my popularity would facilitate the raising of the men, and my influence in Assembly, the grant of money to pay them, and that, perhaps, without taxing the proprietary estate. Finding me not so forward to engage as he expected, the project was dropt, and he soon after left the government, being superseded by Captain Denny.

XVIII

SCIENTIFIC EXPERIMENTS

EFORE I proceed in relating the part I had in public affairs under this new governor's administration, it may not be amiss here to give some account of the rise and progress of my philosophical reputation.

In 1746, being at Boston, I met there with a Dr. Spence, who was lately arrived from Scotland, and show'd me some electric experiments. They were imperfectly perform'd, as he was not very expert; but, being on a subject quite new to me, they equally surpris'd and pleased me. Soon after my return to Philadelphia, our library company receiv'd from Mr. P. Collinson, Fellow of the Royal Society [1] of London, a present of a glass tube, with some account of the use of it in making such experiments. I eagerly seized the opportunity of repeating what I had seen at Boston; and, by much practice, acquir'd great

---

[1] The Royal Society of London for Improving Natural Knowledge was founded in 1660 and holds the foremost place among English societies for the advancement of science.

readiness in performing those, also, which we had an account of from England, adding a number of new ones. I say much practice, for my house was continually full, for some time, with people who came to see these new wonders.

To divide a little this incumbrance among my friends, I caused a number of similar tubes to be blown at our glass-house, with which they furnish'd themselves, so that we had at length several performers. Among these, the principal was Mr. Kinnersley, an ingenious neighbour, who, being out of business, I encouraged to undertake showing the experiments for money, and drew up for him two lectures, in which the experiments were rang'd in such order, and accompanied with such explanations in such method, as that the foregoing should assist in comprehending the following. He procur'd an elegant apparatus for the purpose, in which all the little machines that I had roughly made for myself were nicely form'd by instrument-makers. His lectures were well attended, and gave great satisfaction; and after some time he went thro' the colonies, exhibiting them in every capital town, and pick'd up some money. In the West India islands, indeed, it was with difficulty the experiments could be made, from the general moisture of the air.

Oblig'd as we were to Mr. Collinson for his present of the tube, etc., I thought it right he should be inform'd of our success in using it, and wrote him several letters containing accounts of our experiments. He got them read in the Royal Society, where they were not at first thought worth so much notice as to be printed in their Transactions. One paper, which I wrote for Mr. Kinnersley, on the sameness of lightning with electricity,[1] I sent to Dr. Mitchel, an acquaintance of mine, and one of the members also of that society, who wrote me word that it had been read, but was laughed at by the connoisseurs. The papers, however, being shown to Dr. Fothergill, he thought them of too much value to be stifled, and advis'd the printing of them. Mr. Collinson then gave them to *Cave* for publication in his Gentleman's Magazine; but he chose to print them separately in a pamphlet, and Dr. Fothergill wrote the preface. Cave, it seems, judged rightly for his profit, for by the additions that arrived afterward, they swell'd to a quarto volume, which has had five editions, and cost him nothing for copy-money.

It was, however, some time before those papers were much taken notice of in England.

[1] See page 327.

A copy of them happening to fall into the
hands of the Count de Buffon,[1] a philosopher
deservedly of great reputation in France, and,
indeed, all over Europe, he prevailed with M.
Dalibard[2] to translate them into French, and
they were printed at Paris. The publication
offended the Abbé Nollet, preceptor in Natural
Philosophy to the royal family, and an able
experimenter, who had form'd and publish'd a
theory of electricity, which then had the general
vogue. He could not at first believe that such
a work came from America, and said it must
have been fabricated by his enemies at Paris,
to decry his system. Afterwards, having been
assur'd that there really existed such a person
as Franklin at Philadelphia, which he had
doubted, he wrote and published a volume of
Letters, chiefly address'd to me, defending his
theory, and denying the verity of my experiments, and of the positions deduc'd from them.

I once purpos'd answering the abbé, and actually began the answer; but, on consideration
that my writings contain'd a description of ex-

[1] A celebrated French naturalist (1707-1788).

[2] Dalibard, who had translated Franklin's letters to Collinson
into French, was the first to demonstrate, in a practical application
of Franklin's experiment, that lightning and electricity are the
same. "This was May 10th, 1752, one month before Franklin
flew his famous kite at Philadelphia and proved the fact himself."—
McMaster.

periments which anyone might repeat and
verify, and if not to be verifi'd, could not be
defended; or of observations offer'd as conjectures, and not delivered dogmatically, therefore not laying me under any obligation to
defend them; and reflecting that a dispute
between two persons, writing in different languages, might be lengthened greatly by mis-
translations, and thence misconceptions of one
another's meaning, much of one of the abbé's
letters being founded on an error in the trans-
lation, I concluded to let my papers shift for
themselves, believing it was better to spend
what time I could spare from public business
in making new experiments, than in disputing
about those already made. I therefore never
answered M. Nollet, and the event gave me no
cause to repent my silence; for my friend M.
le Roy, of the Royal Academy of Sciences,
took up my cause and refuted him; my book
was translated into the Italian, German, and
Latin languages; and the doctrine it contain'd
was by degrees universally adopted by the
philosophers of Europe, in preference to that
of the abbé; so that he lived to see himself the
last of his sect, except Monsieur B———, of
Paris, his *élève* and immediate disciple.

What gave my book the more sudden and

general celebrity, was the success of one of its
proposed experiments, made by Messrs. Dalibard and De Lor at Marly, for drawing lightning from the clouds. This engag'd the public attention everywhere. M. de Lor, who had
an apparatus for experimental philosophy, and
lectur'd in that branch of science, undertook to
repeat what he called the *Philadelphia Experiments;* and, after they were performed before
the king and court, all the curious of Paris
flocked to see them. I will not swell this narrative with an account of that capital experiment, nor of the infinite pleasure I receiv'd in
the success of a similar one I made soon after
with a kite at Philadelphia, as both are to be
found in the histories of electricity.

Dr. Wright, an English physician, when at
Paris, wrote to a friend, who was of the Royal
Society, an account of the high esteem my experiments were in among the learned abroad,
and of their wonder that my writings had
been so little noticed in England. The society,
on this, resum'd the consideration of the letters that had been read to them; and the celebrated Dr. Watson drew up a summary account of them, and of all I had afterwards sent
to England on the subject, which he accompanied with some praise of the writer. This

summary was then printed in their Transactions; and some members of the society in London, particularly the very ingenious Mr. Canton, having verified the experiment of procuring lightning from the clouds by a pointed rod, and acquainting them with the success, they soon made me more than amends for the slight with which they had before treated me. Without my having made any application for that honour, they chose me a member, and voted that I should be excus'd the customary payments, which would have amounted to twenty-five guineas; and ever since have given me their Transactions gratis. They also presented me with the gold medal of Sir Godfrey Copley [1] for the year 1753, the delivery of which was accompanied by a very handsome speech of the president, Lord Macclesfield, wherein I was highly honoured.

[1] An English baronet (died in 1709), donator of a fund of £100, "in trust for the Royal Society of London for improving natural knowledge."

XIX

AGENT OF PENNSYLVANIA IN
LONDON

OUR new governor, Captain Denny, brought over for me the before-mentioned medal from the Royal Society, which he presented to me at an entertainment given him by the city. He accompanied it with very polite expressions of his esteem for me, having, as he said, been long acquainted with my character. After dinner, when the company, as was customary at that time, were engag'd in drinking, he took me aside into another room, and acquainted me that he had been advis'd by his friends in England to cultivate a friendship with me, as one who was capable of giving him the best advice, and of contributing most effectually to the making his administration easy; that he therefore desired of all things to have a good understanding with me, and he begged me to be assured of his readiness on all occasions to render me every service that might be in his power. He said much to me,

also, of the proprietor's good disposition towards the province, and of the advantage it
might be to us all, and to me in particular, if
the opposition that had been so long continu'd
to his measures was dropt, and harmony re-
stor'd between him and the people; in effect-
ing which, it was thought no one could be
more serviceable than myself; and I might depend on adequate acknowledgments and recom-
penses, etc., etc. The drinkers, finding we did
not return immediately to the table, sent us a
decanter of Madeira, which the governor
made liberal use of, and in proportion became
more profuse of his solicitations and promises.

My answers were to this purpose: that my
circumstances, thanks to God, were such as to
make proprietary favours unnecessary to me;
and that, being a member of the Assembly, I
could not possibly accept of any; that, however, I had no personal enmity to the proprietary, and that, whenever the public measures
he propos'd should appear to be for the good
of the people, no one should espouse and forward them more zealously than myself; my
past opposition having been founded on this,
that the measures which had been urged were
evidently intended to serve the proprietary interest, with great prejudice to that of the peo-

ple; that I was much obliged to him (the governor) for his professions of regard to me, and that he might rely on everything in my power to make his administration as easy as possible, hoping at the same time that he had not brought with him the same unfortunate instruction his predecessor had been hampered with.

On this he did not then explain himself; but when he afterwards came to do business with the Assembly, they appear'd again, the disputes were renewed, and I was as active as ever in the opposition, being the penman, first, of the request to have a communication of the instructions, and then of the remarks upon them, which may be found in the votes of the time, and in the Historical Review I afterward publish'd. But between us personally no enmity arose; we were often together; he was a man of letters, had seen much of the world, and was very entertaining and pleasing in conversation. He gave me the first information that my old friend Jas. Ralph was still alive; that he was esteem'd one of the best political writers in England; had been employed in the dispute [1] between Prince Frederic and the king, and had

[1] Quarrel between George II and his son, Frederick, Prince of Wales, who died before his father.

obtain'd a pension of three hundred a year; that his reputation was indeed small as a poet, Pope having damned his poetry in the *Dunciad*,[1] but his prose was thought as good as any man's.

The Assembly finally finding the proprietary obstinately persisted in manacling their deputies with instructions inconsistent not only with the privileges of the people, but with the service of the crown, resolv'd to petition the king against them, and appointed me their agent to go over to England, to present and support the petition. The House had sent up a bill to the governor, granting a sum of sixty thousand pounds for the king's use (ten thousand pounds of which was subjected to the orders of the then general, Lord Loudoun), which the governor absolutely refus'd to pass, in compliance with his instructions.

I had agreed with Captain Morris, of the packet at New York, for my passage, and my stores were put on board, when Lord Loudoun arriv'd at Philadelphia, expressly, as he told me, to endeavour an accommodation between the governor and Assembly, that his majesty's service might not be obstructed by their dis-

---

[1] A satirical poem by Alexander Pope directed against various contemporary writers.

sensions. Accordingly, he desir'd the governor and myself to meet him, that he might hear what was to be said on both sides. We met and discussed the business. In behalf of the Assembly, I urged all the various arguments that may be found in the public papers of that time, which were of my writing, and are printed with the minutes of the Assembly; and the governor pleaded his instructions, the bond he had given to observe them, and his ruin if he disobey'd, yet seemed not unwilling to hazard himself if Lord Loudoun would advise it. This his lordship did not chuse to do, though I once thought I had nearly prevail'd with him to do it; but finally he rather chose to urge the compliance of the Assembly; and he entreated me to use my endeavours with them for that purpose, declaring that he would spare none of the king's troops for the defense of our frontiers, and that, if we did not continue to provide for that defense ourselves, they must remain expos'd to the enemy.

I acquainted the House with what had pass'd, and, presenting them with a set of resolutions I had drawn up, declaring our rights, and that we did not relinquish our claim to those rights, but only suspended the exercise of them on this occasion thro' *force,* against which we protested, they at length agreed to drop that bill, and frame another conformable to the proprietary instructions. This of course the governor pass'd, and I was then at liberty to proceed on my voyage. But, in the meantime, the packet had sailed with my sea-stores, which was some loss to me, and my only recompense was his lordship's thanks for my service, all the credit of obtaining the accommodation falling to his share.

He set out for New York before me; and, as the time for dispatching the packet-boats was at his disposition, and there were two then remaining there, one of which, he said, was to sail very soon, I requested to know the precise time, that I might not miss her by any delay of mine. His answer was, "I have given out that she is to sail on Saturday next; but I may let you know, *entre nous,* that if you are there by Monday morning, you will be in time, but do not delay longer." By some accidental hindrance at a ferry, it was Monday noon before I arrived, and I was much afraid she might have sailed, as the wind was fair; but I was soon made easy by the information that she was still in the harbor, and would not move till the next day. One would imagine that I was now on the very point of departing for Europe. I thought so; but I was not then so well acquainted with his lordship's character, of which *indecision* was one of the strongest features. I shall give some instances. It was about the beginning of April that I came to New York, and I think it was near the end of June before we sail'd. There were then two of the packet-boats, which had been long in port, but were detained for the general's letters, which were always to be ready to-morrow. Another packet arriv'd; she too was detain'd; and, before we sail'd, a fourth was expected. Ours was the first to be dispatch'd, as having been there longest. Passengers were engaged in all, and some extremely impatient to be gone, and the merchants uneasy about their letters, and the orders they had given for insurance (it being war time) for fall goods; but their anxiety avail'd nothing; his lordship's letters were not ready; and yet whoever waited on him found him always at his desk, pen in hand, and concluded he must needs write abundantly.

Going myself one morning to pay my respects, I found in his antechamber one Innis, a messenger of Philadelphia, who had come

from thence express with a packet from
Governor Denny for the general. He delivered to me some letters from my friends
there, which occasion'd my inquiring when he
was to return, and where he lodg'd, that I
might send some letters by him. He told
me he was order'd to call to-morrow at nine
for the general's answer to the governor, and
should set off immediately. I put my letters
into his hands the same day. A fortnight
after I met him again in the same place. "So,
you are soon return'd, Innis?" "*Return'd!*
no, I am not *gone* yet.*" "How so?" "I
have called here by order every morning these
two weeks past for his lordship's letter, and
it is not yet ready." "Is it possible, when he
is so great a writer? for I see him constantly
at his escritoire." "Yes," says Innis, "but
he is like St. George on the signs, *always on
horseback, and never rides on.*" This observation of the messenger was, it seems, well
founded; for, when in England, I understood
that Mr. Pitt[1] gave it as one reason for removing this general, and sending Generals
Amherst and Wolfe, *that the minister never*

[1] William Pitt, first Earl of Chatham (1708-1778), a great English
statesman and orator. Under his able administration, England won
Canada from France. He was a friend of America at the time of
our Revolution.

heard from him, and could not know what he was doing.

This daily expectation of sailing, and all the three packets going down to Sandy Hook, to join the fleet there, the passengers thought it best to be on board, lest by a sudden order the ships should sail, and they be left behind. There, if I remember right, we were about six weeks, consuming our sea-stores, and oblig'd to procure more. At length the fleet sail'd, the general and all his army on board, bound to Louisburg, with the intent to besiege and take that fortress; all the packet-boats in company ordered to attend the general's ship, ready to receive his dispatches when they should be ready. We were out five days before we got a letter with leave to part, and then our ship quitted the fleet and steered for England. The other two packets he still detained, carried them with him to Halifax, where he stayed some time to exercise the men in sham attacks upon sham forts, then altered his mind as to besieging Louisburg, and returned to New York, with all his troops, together with the two packets above mentioned, and all their passengers! During his absence the French and savages had taken Fort George, on the frontier of that province, and the savages had massacred many of the garrison after capitulation.

I saw afterwards in London Captain Bonnell, who commanded one of those packets. He told me that, when he had been detain'd a month, he acquainted his lordship that his ship was grown foul, to a degree that must necessarily hinder her fast sailing, a point of consequence for a packet-boat, and requested an allowance of time to heave her down and clean her bottom. He was asked how long time that would require. He answered, three days. The general replied, "If you can do it in one day, I give leave; otherwise not; for you must certainly sail the day after to-morrow." So he never obtain'd leave, though detained afterwards from day to day during full three months.

I saw also in London one of Bonnell's passengers, who was so enrag'd against his lordship for deceiving and detaining him so long at New York, and then carrying him to Halifax and back again, that he swore he would sue him for damages. Whether he did or not, I never heard; but, as he represented the injury to his affairs, it was very considerable.

On the whole, I wonder'd much how such

a man came to be intrusted [1] with so important a business as the conduct of a great army; but, having since seen more of the great world, and the means of obtaining, and motives for giving places, my wonder is diminished. General Shirley, on whom the command of the army devolved upon the death of Braddock, would, in my opinion, if continued in place, have made a much better campaign than that of Loudoun in 1757, which was frivolous, expensive, and disgraceful to our nation beyond conception; for, tho' Shirley was not a bred soldier, he was sensible and sagacious in himself, and attentive to good advice from others, capable of forming judicious plans, and quick and active in carrying them into execution. Loudoun, instead of defending the colonies with his great army, left them totally expos'd while he paraded idly at Halifax, by which means Fort George was lost, besides, he derang'd all our mercantile operations, and distress'd our trade, by a long embargo on the exportation of provisions, on pretence of keeping supplies from being obtain'd by the enemy, but in reality for beat-

---

[1] This relation illustrates the corruption that characterized English public life in the eighteenth century. (See page 308). It was gradually overcome in the early part of the next century.

ing down their price in favour of the con-
tractors, in whose profits, it was said, perhaps
from suspicion only, he had a share. And,
when at length the embargo was taken off, by
neglecting to send notice of it to Charlestown,
the Carolina fleet was detain'd near three
months longer, whereby their bottoms were
so much damaged by the worm that a great
part of them foundered in their passage home.

Shirley was, I believe, sincerely glad of being relieved from so burdensome a charge as
the conduct of an army must be to a man unacquainted with military business. I was at
the entertainment given by the city of New
York to Lord Loudoun, on his taking upon
him the command. Shirley, tho' thereby superseded, was present also. There was a great
company of officers, citizens, and strangers, and,
some chairs having been borrowed in the
neighborhood, there was one among them
very low, which fell to the lot of Mr. Shirley.
Perceiving it as I sat by him, I said, "They
have given you, sir, too low a seat." "No
matter," says he, "Mr. Franklin, I find *a low
seat* the easiest."

While I was, as afore mention'd, detain'd at
New York, I receiv'd all the accounts of the
provisions, etc., that I had furnish'd to Brad-

dock, some of which accounts could not sooner be obtain'd from the different persons I had employ'd to assist in the business. I presented them to Lord Loudoun, desiring to be paid the ballance. He caus'd them to be regularly examined by the proper officer, who, after comparing every article with its voucher, certified them to be right; and the balance due for which his lordship promis'd to give me an order on the paymaster. This was, however, put off from time to time; and tho' I call'd often for it by appointment, I did not get it. At length, just before my departure, he told me he had, on better consideration, concluded not to mix his accounts with those of his predecessors. "And you," says he, "when in England, have only to exhibit your accounts at the treasury, and you will be paid immediately."

I mention'd, but without effect, the great and unexpected expense I had been put to by being detain'd so long at New York, as a reason for my desiring to be presently paid; and on my observing that it was not right I should be put to any further trouble or delay in obtaining the money I had advanc'd, as I charged no commission for my service, "O, Sir," says he, "you must not think of persuading us that you are no gainer; we understand better those affairs, and know that every one concerned in supplying the army finds means, in the doing it, to fill his own pockets." I assur'd him that was not my case, and that I had not pocketed a farthing; but he appear'd clearly not to believe me; and, indeed, I have since learnt that immense fortunes are often made in such employments. As to my ballance, I am not paid it to this day, of which more hereafter.

Our captain of the paquet had boasted much, before we sailed, of the swiftness of his ship; unfortunately, when we came to sea, she proved the dullest of ninety-six sail, to his no small mortification. After many conjectures respecting the cause, when we were near another ship almost as dull as ours, which, however, gain'd upon us, the captain ordered all hands to come aft, and stand as near the ensign staff as possible. We were, passengers included, about forty persons. While we stood there, the ship mended her pace, and soon left her neighbour far behind, which prov'd clearly what our captain suspected, that she was loaded too much by the head. The casks of water, it seems, had been all plac'd forward; these he therefore order'd to be mov'd further aft, on which the ship recover'd her character, and proved the best sailer in the fleet.

The captain said she had once gone at the rate of thirteen knots, which is accounted thirteen miles per hour. We had on board, as a passenger, Captain Kennedy, of the Navy, who contended that it was impossible, and that no ship ever sailed so fast, and that there must have been some error in the division of the log-line, or some mistake in heaving the log.[1] A wager ensu'd between the two captains, to be decided when there should be sufficient wind. Kennedy thereupon examin'd rigorously the log-line, and, being satisfi'd with that, he determin'd to throw the log himself. Accordingly some days after, when the wind blew very fair and fresh, and the captain of the paquet, Lutwidge, said he believ'd she then went at the rate of thirteen knots, Kennedy made the experiment, and own'd his wager lost.

The above fact I give for the sake of the following observation. It has been remark'd, as an imperfection in the art of ship-building, that it can never be known, till she is tried,

---

[1] A piece of wood shaped and weighted so as to keep it stable when in the water. To this is attached a line knotted at regular distances. By these devices it is possible to tell the speed of a ship.

whether a new ship will or will not be a
good sailer; for that the model of a good-sailing
ship has been exactly follow'd in a new one,
which has prov'd, on the contrary, remarka-
bly dull. I apprehend that this may partly be
occasion'd by the different opinions of seamen
respecting the modes of lading, rigging, and
sailing of a ship; each has his system; and the
same vessel, laden by the judgment and orders
of one captain, shall sail better or worse than
when by the orders of another. Besides, it
scarce ever happens that a ship is form'd, fitted for the sea, and sail'd by the same person.
One man builds the hull, another rigs her, a
third lades and sails her. No one of these has
the advantage of knowing all the ideas and experience of the others, and, therefore, cannot
draw just conclusions from a combination of the
whole.

Even in the simple operation of sailing when
at sea, I have often observ'd different judgments in the officers who commanded the suc-
cessive watches, the wind being the same.
One would have the sails trimm'd sharper or
flatter than another, so that they seem'd to
have no certain rule to govern by. Yet I
think a set of experiments might be instituted;
first, to determine the most proper form of

the hull for swift sailing; next, the best dimensions and properest place for the masts; then the form and quantity of sails, and their position, as the wind may be; and, lastly, the disposition of the lading. This is an age of experiments, and I think a set accurately made and combin'd would be of great use. I am persuaded, therefore, that ere long some ingenious philosopher will undertake it, to whom I wish success.

We were several times chas'd in our passage, but out-sail'd every thing, and in thirty days had soundings. We had a good observation, and the captain judg'd himself so near our port, Falmouth, that, if we made a good run in the night, we might be off the mouth of that harbor in the morning, and by running in the night might escape the notice of the enemy's privateers, who often cruis'd near the entrance of the channel. Accordingly, all the sail was set that we could possibly make, and the wind being very fresh and fair, we went right before it, and made great way. The captain, after his observation, shap'd his course, as he thought, so as to pass wide of the Scilly Isles; but it seems there is sometimes a strong indraught setting up St. George's Channel, which deceives seamen and caused the loss of Sir Cloudesley Shovel's squadron. This indraught was probably the cause of what happened to us.

We had a watchman plac'd in the bow, to whom they often called, *"Look well out before there,"* and he as often answered, *"Ay, ay"*; but perhaps had his eyes shut, and was half asleep at the time, they sometimes answering, as is said, mechanically; for he did not see a light just before us, which had been hid by the studding-sails from the man at the helm, and from the rest of the watch, but by an accidental yaw of the ship was discover'd, and occasion'd a great alarm, we being very near it, the light appearing to me as big as a cartwheel. It was midnight, and our captain fast asleep; but Captain Kennedy, jumping upon deck, and seeing the danger, ordered the ship to wear round, all sails standing; an operation dangerous to the masts, but it carried us clear, and we escaped shipwreck, for we were running right upon the rocks on which the lighthouse was erected. This deliverance impressed me strongly with the utility of lighthouses, and made me resolve to encourage the building more of them in America if I should live to return there.

In the morning it was found by the soundings, etc., that we were near our port, but a thick fog hid the land from our sight. About nine o'clock the fog began to rise, and seem'd to be lifted up from the water like the curtain at a play-house, discovering underneath, the town of Falmouth, the vessels in its harbor, and the fields that surrounded it. This was a most pleasing spectacle to those who had been so long without any other prospects than the uniform view of a vacant ocean, and it gave us the more pleasure as we were now free from the anxieties which the state of war occasion'd.

I set out immediately, with my son, for London, and we only stopt a little by the way to view Stonehenge [1] on Salisbury Plain, and

[1] A celebrated prehistoric ruin, probably of a temple built by the early Britons, near Salisbury, England. It consists of inner

Lord Pembroke's house and gardens, with his very curious antiquities at Wilton. We arrived in London the 27th of July, 1757.[1]

As soon as I was settled in a lodging Mr. Charles had provided for me, I went to visit Dr. Fothergill, to whom I was strongly recommended, and whose counsel respecting my proceedings I was advis'd to obtain. He was against an immediate complaint to government, and thought the proprietaries should first be personally appli'd to, who might possibly be induc'd by the interposition and persuasion of some private friends, to accommodate matters amicably. I then waited on my old friend and correspondent, Mr. Peter Collinson, who told me that John Hanbury, the great Virginia merchant, had requested to be informed when I should arrive, that he might carry me to Lord Granville's,[2] who was then President of the Council and wished to see me as soon as possible. I agreed to go with him

and outer circles of enormous stones, some of which are connected by stone slabs.

[1] "Here terminates the *Autobiography,* as published by Wm. Temple Franklin and his successors. What follows was written in the last year of Dr. Franklin's life, and was never before printed in English."—Mr. Bigelow's note in his edition of 1868.

[2] George Granville or Grenville (1712-1770). As English premier from 1763 to 1765, he introduced the direct taxation of the American Colonies and has sometimes been called the immediate cause of the Revolution.

the next morning. Accordingly Mr. Hanbury
called for me and took me in his carriage to
that nobleman's, who receiv'd me with great
civility; and after some questions respecting
the present state of affairs in America and discourse thereupon, he said to me: " You Americans have wrong ideas of the nature of your
constitution; you contend that the king's instructions to his governors are not laws, and
think yourselves at liberty to regard or disre-
gard them at your own discretion. But those
instructions are not like the pocket instructions given to a minister going abroad, for
regulating his conduct in some trifling point
of ceremony. They are first drawn up by
judges learned in the laws; they are then considered, debated, and perhaps amended in
Council, after which they are signed by the
king. They are then, so far as they relate to
you, the *law of the land,* for the king is the
LEGISLATOR OF THE COLONIES," [1]   I told his
lordship this was new doctrine to me. I had
always understood from our charters that our

[1] This whole passage shows how hopelessly divergent were the
English and American views on the relations between the mother
country and her colonies. Grenville here made clear that the Americans were to have no voice in making or amending their laws.
Parliament and the king were to have absolute power over the
colonies. No wonder Franklin was alarmed by this new doctrine.

laws were to be made by our Assemblies, to be presented indeed to the king for his royal assent, but that being once given the king could not repeal or alter them. And as the Assemblies could not make permanent laws without his assent, so neither could he make a law for them without theirs. He assur'd me I was totally mistaken. I did not think so, however, and his lordship's conversation having a little alarm'd me as to what might be the sentiments of the court concerning us, I wrote it down as soon as I return'd to my lodgings. I recollected that about 20 years before, a clause in a bill brought into Parliament by the ministry had propos'd to make the king's instructions laws in the colonies, but the clause was thrown out by the Commons, for which we adored them as our friends and friends of liberty, till by their conduct towards us in 1765 it seem'd that they had refus'd that point of sovereignty to the king only that they might reserve it for themselves.

After some days, Dr. Fothergill having

With his keen insight into human nature and his consequent knowledge of American character, he foresaw the inevitable result of such an attitude on the part of England. This conversation with Grenville makes these last pages of the *Autobiography* one of its most important parts.

spoken to the proprietaries, they agreed to a
meeting with me at Mr. T. Penn's house in
Spring Garden. The conversation at first consisted of mutual declarations of disposition to
reasonable accommodations, but I suppose each
party had its own ideas of what should be
meant by *reasonable*. We then went into consideration of our several points of complaint,
which I enumerated. The proprietaries justify'd their conduct as well as they could, and
I the Assembly's. We now appeared very
wide, and so far from each other in our opinions as to discourage all hope of agreement.
However, it was concluded that I should give
them the heads of our complaints in writing,
and they promis'd then to consider them. I
did so soon after, but they put the paper into
the hands of their solicitor, Ferdinand John
Paris, who managed for them all their law
business in their great suit with the neighbouring proprietary of Maryland, Lord Baltimore,
which had subsisted 70 years, and wrote for
them all their papers and messages in their
dispute with the Assembly. He was a proud,
angry man, and as I had occasionally in the
answers of the Assembly treated his papers
with some severity, they being really weak in
point of argument and haughty in expression,

he had conceived a mortal enmity to me, which discovering itself whenever we met, I declin'd the proprietary's proposal that he and I should discuss the heads of complaint between our two selves, and refus'd treating with anyone but them. They then by his advice put the paper into the hands of the Attorney and Solicitor-General for their opinion and counsel upon it, where it lay unanswered a year wanting eight days, during which time I made frequent demands of an answer from the proprietaries, but without obtaining any other than that they had not yet received the opinion of the Attorney and Solicitor-General. What it was when they did receive it I never learnt, for they did not communicate it to me, but sent a long message to the Assembly drawn and signed by Paris, reciting my paper, complaining of its want of formality, as a rudeness on my part, and giving a flimsy justification of their conduct, adding that they should be willing to accommodate matters if the Assembly would send out *some person of candour* to treat with them for that purpose, intimating thereby that I was not such.

The want of formality or rudeness was, probably, my not having address'd the paper to them with their assum'd titles of True and

Absolute Proprietaries of the Province of Pennsylvania, which I omitted as not thinking it necessary in a paper, the intention of which was only to reduce to a certainty by writing, what in conversation I had delivered *viva voce*.

But during this delay, the Assembly having prevailed with Gov'r Denny to pass an act taxing the proprietary estate in common with the estates of the people, which was the grand point in dispute, they omitted answering the message.

When this act however came over, the proprietaries, counselled by Paris, determined to oppose its receiving the royal assent. Accordingly they petition'd the king in Council, and a hearing was appointed in which two lawyers were employ'd by them against the act, and two by me in support of it. They alledg'd that the act was intended to load the proprietary estate in order to spare those of the people, and that if it were suffer'd to continue in force, and the proprietaries, who were in odium with the people, left to their mercy in proportioning the taxes, they would inevitably be ruined. We reply'd that the act had no such intention, and would have no such effect. That the assessors were honest and discreet men under an oath to assess fairly and equitably, and that any advantage each of them might expect in lessening his own tax by augmenting that of the proprietaries was too trifling to induce them to perjure themselves. This is the purport of what I remember as urged by both sides, except that we insisted strongly on the mischievous consequences that must attend a repeal, for that the money, £100,000, being printed and given to the king's use, expended in his service, and now spread among the people, the repeal would strike it dead in their hands to the ruin of many, and the total discouragement of future grants, and the selfishness of the proprietors in soliciting such a general catastrophe, merely from a groundless fear of their estate being taxed too highly, was insisted on in the strongest terms. On this, Lord Mansfield, one of the counsel, rose, and beckoning me took me into the clerk's chamber, while the lawyers were pleading, and asked me if I was really of opinion that no injury would be done the proprietary estate in the execution of the act. I said certainly. " Then," says he, " you can have little objection to enter into an engagement to assure that point." I answer'd, " None at all." He then call'd in Paris, and after some discourse, his lordship's

proposition was accepted on both sides; a
paper to the purpose was drawn up by the
Clerk of the Council, which I sign'd with Mr.
Charles, who was also an Agent of the Province for their ordinary affairs, when Lord
Mansfield returned to the Council Chamber,
where finally the law was allowed to pass.
Some changes were however recommended
and we also engaged they should be made by
a subsequent law, but the Assembly did not
think them necessary; for one year's tax having been levied by the act before the order of
Council arrived, they appointed a committee
to examine the proceedings of the assessors,
and on this committee they put several particular friends of the proprietaries. After a
full enquiry, they unanimously sign'd a report
that they found the tax had been assess'd with
perfect equity.

The Assembly looked into my entering into
the first part of the engagement, as an essential service to the Province, since it secured
the credit of the paper money then spread
over all the country. They gave me their
thanks in form when I return'd. But the proprietaries were enraged at Governor Denny
for having pass'd the act, and turn'd him out
with threats of suing him for breach of in-

structions which he had given bond to observe. He, however, having done it at the instance of the General, and for His Majesty's service, and having some powerful interest at court, despis'd the threats and they were never put in execution. . . . [unfinished]

APPENDIX

ELECTRICAL KITE

To Peter Collinson

[Philadelphia], Oct. 19, 1752.

Sir,

As frequent mention is made in public papers from Europe of the success of the *Philadelphia* experiment for drawing the electric fire from clouds by means of pointed rods of iron erected on high buildings, &c., it may be agreeable to the curious to be informed, that the same experiment has succeeded in *Philadelphia,* though made in a different and more easy manner, which is as follows:

Make a small cross of two light strips of cedar, the arms so long as to reach to the four corners of a large, thin silk handkerchief when extended; tie the corners of the handkerchief to the extremities of the cross, so you have the body of a kite; which being properly accommodated with a tail, loop, and string, will rise in the air, like those made of paper; but this being of silk, is fitter to bear the wet and wind of a thundergust without tearing. To the top of the upright stick of the cross is to be fixed a very sharp-pointed wire, rising a foot or more above the wood. To the end of the twine, next the hand, is to be tied a silk ribbon, and where the silk and twine join, a key may be fastened. This kite is to be raised when a thunder-gust appears to be coming on, and the person who holds the string must stand within a door or window, or under some cover, so that the silk ribbon may not be wet; and care must be taken that the twine does not touch the frame of the door or window. As soon as any of the thunder clouds come over the kite, the pointed wire will draw the electric fire from them, and the kite, with all the twine, will be electrified, and the loose filaments of the twine will stand out every way and be attracted by an approaching finger. And when the rain has wet the kite and twine, so that it can conduct the electric fire freely, you will find it stream out plentifully from the key on the approach of your knuckle. At this key the phial may be charged; and from electric fire thus obtained, spirits may be kindled, and all the electric experiments be performed, which are usually done by the help of a rubbed glass globe or tube, and thereby the sameness of the electric matter with that of lightning completely demonstrated.

B. FRANKLIN.

Father *Abraham* in his STUDY.

He's rarely warm in { Good-Nature, Wit, and Judgment round him wait ;
Censure or in Praise: { And thus he sits inthron'd in Classick-State :

To Failings mild, but zealous for Desert ;
The clearest Head, and the sincerest Heart.

{ Few Men deserve our
Praise either Ways.

THE SHADE of Him who Counsel can bestow,
Still pleas'd to teach, and yet not proud to know ;
Unbias'd or by Favour or by Spite ;
Nor dully prepossess'd, nor blindly right ;
Thô learn'd, well-bred ; and, thô well-bred, sincere ;
Modestly bold, and humanely severe ;
Who to a Friend his Faults can sweetly show,
And gladly praise the Merit of a Foe.
Here, there he sits, his chearful Aid to lend ;
A firm, unshaken, uncorrupted Friend,
Averse alike to flatter or offend.

Printed by Benjamin Mecom, *at the* New
Printing-Office, *(near the* TOWN-HOUSE, *in* Boston) *where*
BOOKS *are Sold, and* PRINTING-WORK *done, Cheap.*

From "Father Abraham's Speech," 1760. Reproduced from
a copy at the New York Public Library.

THE WAY TO WEALTH

(From "Father Abraham's Speech," forming the preface to *Poor Richard's Almanac* for 1758.)

It would be thought a hard Government that should tax its People one-tenth Part of their *Time,* to be employed in its Service. But *Idleness* taxes many of us much more, if we reckon all that is spent in absolute *Sloth,* or doing of nothing, with that which is spent in idle Employments or Amusements, that amount to nothing. *Sloth,* by bringing on Diseases, absolutely shortens Life. *Sloth, like Rust, consumes faster than Labor wears; while the used key is always bright, as Poor Richard says. But dost thou love Life, then do not squander Time, for that's the stuff Life is made of,* as *Poor Richard* says. How much more than is necessary do we spend in sleep, forgetting that *The sleeping Fox catches no Poultry,* and that *There will be sleeping enough in the Grave,* as Poor Richard says.

If Time be of all Things the most precious, wasting Time must be, as *Poor Richard* says, *the greatest Prodigality;* since, as he elsewhere tells us, *Lost Time is never found again; and what we call Time enough, always proves little enough:* Let us then up and be doing, and doing to the Purpose; so by Diligence shall we do more with less Perplexity. *Sloth makes all Things difficult, but Industry all easy,* as *Poor Richard* says; and *He that riseth late must trot all Day, and shall scarce overtake his Business at Night; while Laziness travels so slowly, that Poverty soon overtakes him,* as we read in *Poor Richard,* who adds, *Drive thy Business, let not that drive thee;* and *Early to Bed, and early to rise, makes a Man healthy, wealthy, and wise.*

Industry need not wish, and he that lives upon Hope will die fasting.

There are no Gains without Pains.

He that hath a Trade hath an Estate; and he that hath a Calling, hath an Office of Profit and Honor; but then the *Trade* must be worked at, and the *Calling* well followed, or neither the *Estate* nor the *Office* will enable us to pay our Taxes.

What though you have found no Treasure, nor has any rich Relation left you a Legacy, *Diligence is the Mother of Good-luck,* as *Poor Richard* says, *and God gives all Things to Industry.*

One To-day is worth two To-morrows, and farther, *Have you somewhat to do To-morrow, do it To-day.*

If you were a Servant, would you not be ashamed that a good Master should catch you idle? Are you then your own Master, *be ashamed to catch yourself idle.*

Stick to it steadily; and you will see great Effects, for *Constant Dropping wears away Stones,* and by *Diligence and Patience the Mouse ate in two the Cable;* and *Little Strokes fell great Oaks.*

Methinks I hear some of you say, *Must a Man afford himself no Leisure?* I will tell thee, my friend, what *Poor Richard* says, *Employ thy Time well, if thou meanest to gain Leisure; and, since thou art not sure of a Minute, throw not away an Hour.* Leisure, is Time for doing something useful; this Leisure the diligent Man will obtain, but the lazy Man never; so that, as *Poor Richard* says, *A Life of Leisure and a Life of Laziness are two things.*

Keep thy Shop, and thy Shop will keep thee; and again, *If you would have your business done, go; if not, send.*

If you would have a faithful Servant, and one that you like, serve yourself.

A little Neglect may breed great Mischief;

adding, *for want of a Nail the Shoe was lost; for want of a Shoe the Horse was lost; and for want of a Horse the Rider was lost, being overtaken and slain by the Enemy; all for the want of Care about a Horse-shoe Nail.*

So much for Industry, my Friends, and Attention to one's own Business; but to these we must add *Frugality.*

What maintains one Vice, would bring up two Children. You may think perhaps, that a *little* Tea, or a *little* Punch now and then, Diet a *little* more costly, Clothes a *little* finer, and a *little* Entertainment now and then, can be no *great* Matter; but remember what *Poor Richard* says, *Many a Little makes a Mickle.*

Beware of little expenses; A small Leak will sink a great Ship; and again, *Who Dainties love, shall Beggars prove;* and moreover, *Fools make Feasts, and wise Men eat them.*

Buy what thou hast no Need of, and ere long thou shalt sell thy Necessaries.

If you would know the Value of Money, go and try to borrow some; for, he that goes a borrowing goes a sorrowing.

The second Vice is Lying, the first is running in Debt.

Lying rides upon Debt's Back.

Poverty often deprives a Man of all Spirit and

Virtue: *'Tis hard for an empty Bag to stand up-right.*

And now to conclude, *Experience keeps a dear School, but Fools will learn in no other, and scarce in that;* for it is true, *we may give Advice, but we cannot give Conduct,* as *Poor Richard* says: However, remember this, *They that won't be counseled, can't be helped,* as *Poor Richard* says: and farther, That *if you will not hear Reason, she'll surely rap your Knuckles.*

THE WHISTLE

To Madame Brillon

Passy, November 10, 1779.

I am charmed with your description of Paradise, and with your plan of living there; and I approve much of your conclusion, that, in the meantime, we should draw all the good we can from this world. In my opinion, we might all draw more good from it than we do, and suffer less evil, if we would take care not to give too much for whistles. For to me it seems, that most of the unhappy people we meet with, are become so by neglect of that caution.

You ask what I mean? You love stories, and will excuse my telling one of myself.

When I was a child of seven year old, my friends, on a holiday, filled my pocket with coppers. I went directly to a shop where they sold toys for children; and being charmed with the sound of a *whistle,* that I met by the way in the hands of another boy, I voluntarily offered and gave all my money for one. I then came home, and went whistling all over the house, much pleased with my *whistle,* but disturbing all the family. My brothers, and sisters, and cousins, understanding the bargain I had made, told me I had given four times as much for it as it was worth; put me in mind what good things I might have bought with the rest of the money; and laughed at me so much for my folly, that I cried with vexation; and the reflection gave me more chagrin than the *whistle* gave me pleasure.

This, however, was afterwards of use to me, the impression continuing on my mind; so that often, when I was tempted to buy some unnecessary thing, I said to myself, *Don't give too much for the whistle;* and I saved my money.

As I grew up, came into the world, and observed the actions of men, I thought I met with many, very many, who *gave too much for the whistle.*

When I saw one too ambitious of court favor, sacrificing his time in attendance on levees, his repose, his liberty, his virtue, and perhaps his friends, to attain it, I have said to myself, *This man gives too much for his whistle.*

When I saw another fond of popularity, constantly employing himself in political bustles, neglecting his own affairs, and ruining them by neglect, *He pays, indeed,* said I, *too much for his whistle.*

If I knew a miser who gave up every kind of

comfortable living, all the pleasure of doing good to others, all the esteem of his fellow citizens, and the joys of benevolent friendship, for the sake of accumulating wealth, *Poor man,* said I, *you pay too much for your whistle.*

When I met with a man of pleasure, sacrificing every laudable improvement of the mind, or of his fortune, to mere corporeal sensations, and ruining his health in their pursuit, *Mistaken man,* said I, *you are providing pain for yourself, instead of pleasure; you give too much for your whistle.*

If I see one fond of appearance, or fine clothes, fine houses, fine furniture, fine equipages, all above his fortune, for which he contracts debts, and ends his career in a prison, *Alas!* say I, *he has paid dear, very dear, for his whistle.*

When I see a beautiful, sweet-tempered girl married to an ill-natured brute of a husband, *What a pity,* say I, *that she should pay so much for a whistle!*

In short, I conceive that great part of the miseries of mankind are brought upon them by the false estimates they have made of the value of things, and by their *giving too much for their whistles.*

Yet I ought to have charity for these unhappy people, when I consider, that, with all this wisdom of which I am boasting, there are certain

things in the world so tempting, for example,
the apples of King John, which happily are not
to be bought; for if they were put to sale by
auction, I might very easily be led to ruin myself in the purchase, and find that I had once
more given too much for the *whistle*.

Adieu, my dear friend, and believe me ever
yours very sincerely and with unalterable affection,

B. FRANKLIN.

A LETTER TO SAMUEL MATHER

REVD SIR,

It is now more than 60 years since I left Boston, but I remember well both your father and grandfather, having heard them both in the pulpit, and seen them in their houses. The last time I saw your father was in the beginning of 1724, when I visited him after my first trip to Pennsylvania. He received me in his library, and on my taking leave showed me a shorter way out of the house through a narrow passage, which was crossed by a beam overhead. We were still talking as I withdrew, he accompanying me behind, and I turning partly towards him, when he said hastily, "*Stoop, stoop!*" I did not understand him, till I felt my head hit against the beam. He was a man that never missed any occasion of giving instruction, and upon this he said to me, "*You are young, and have the world before you; stoop as you go through it, and you will miss many hard thumps.*" This advice, thus beat into my head, has frequently been of use to me; and I often think of it, when I see pride mortified, and misfortunes brought upon people by their carrying their heads too high.

B. FRANKLIN.

THE END.

BIBLIOGRAPHY

THE last and most complete edition of Franklin's works is that by the late Professor Albert H. Smyth, published in ten volumes by the Macmillan Company, New York, under the title, *The Writings of Benjamin Franklin.* The other standard edition is the *Works of Benjamin Franklin* by John Bigelow (New York, 1887). Mr. Bigelow's first edition of the *Autobiography* in one volume was published by the J. B. Lippincott Company of Philadelphia in 1868. The life of Franklin as a writer is well treated by J. B. McMaster in a volume of *The American Men of Letters Series;* his life as a statesman and diplomat, by J. T. Morse, *American Statesmen Series,* one volume; Houghton, Mifflin Company publish both books. A more exhaustive account of the life and times of Franklin may be found in James Parton's *Life and Times of Benjamin Franklin* (2 vols., New York, 1864). Paul Leicester Ford's *The Many-Sided Franklin* is a most chatty and readable book, replete with anecdotes and excellently and fully illustrated. An excellent criticism by Woodrow Wilson introduces an edition of the *Autobiography* in *The Century Classics* (Century Co., New York, 1901). Interesting magazine articles are those of E. E. Hale, *Christian Examiner,* lxxi, 447; W. P. Trent, *McClure's Magazine,* viii, 273; John Hay, *The Century Magazine,* lxxi, 447.

See also the histories of American literature by C. F.

Richardson, Moses Coit Tyler, Brander Matthews, John Nichol, and Barrett Wendell, as well as the various encyclopedias. An excellent bibliography of Franklin is that of Paul Leicester Ford, entitled *A List of Books Written by, or Relating to Benjamin Franklin* (New York, 1889).

The following list of Franklin's works contains the more interesting publications, together with the dates of first issue.

1722. *Dogood Papers.*
Letters in the style of Addison's *Spectator*, contributed to James Franklin's newspaper and signed "Silence Dogood."

1729. *The Busybody.*
A series of essays published in Bradford's Philadelphia *Weekly Mercury*, six of which only are ascribed to Franklin. They are essays on morality, philosophy and politics, similar to the *Dogood Papers*.

1729. *A Modest Enquiry into the Nature and Necessity of a Paper Currency.*

1732. *Prefaces to Poor Richard's Almanac.*
to   Among these are *Hints for those that would be Rich*, 1737;
1757.   and *Plan for saving one hundred thousand pounds to New Jersey*, 1756.

1743. *A Proposal for Promoting Useful Knowledge Among the British Plantations in America.*
"This paper appears to contain the first suggestion, in any public form, for an *American Philosophical Society*." Sparks.

1744. *An Account of the New Invented Pennsylvania Fire-Places.*

1749. *Proposals Relating to the Education of Youth in Pennsylvania.*
Contains the plan for the school which later became the University of Pennsylvania.

1752. *Electrical Kite.*
A description of the famous kite experiment, first written in a letter to Peter Collinson, dated Oct. 19, 1752, which was published later in the same year in *The Gentleman's Magazine*.

1754. *Plan of Union.*
A plan for the union of the colonies presented to the colonial convention at Albany.

1755. *A Dialogue Between X, Y and Z.*
An appeal to enlist in the provincial army for the defense of Pennsylvania.

1758. *Father Abraham's Speech.*
Published as a preface to Poor Richard's Almanac and gathering into one writing the maxims of Poor Richard, which had already appeared in previous numbers of the Almanac. The *Speech* was afterwards published in pamphlet form as the *Way to Wealth.*

1760. *Of the Means of disposing the Enemy to Peace.*
A satirical plea for the prosecution of the war against France.

1760. *The Interest of Great Britain Considered, with regard to her Colonies, and the Acquisitions of Canada and Guadaloupe.*

1764. *Cool Thoughts on the Present Situation of our Public Affairs.*
A pamphlet favoring a Royal Government for Pennsylvania in exchange for that of the Proprietors.

1766. *The Examination of Doctor Benjamin Franklin, etc., in The British House of Commons, Relative to The Repeal of The American Stamp Act.*

1773. *Rules by which A Great Empire May Be Reduced to a Small One.*
Some twenty satirical rules embodying the line of conduct England was pursuing with America.

1773. *An Edict of The King of Prussia.*
A satire in which the King of Prussia was made to treat England as England was treating America because England was originally settled by Germans.

1777. *Comparison of Great Britain and the United States in Regard to the Basis of Credit in The Two Countries.*
One of several similar pamphlets written to effect loans for the American cause.

1782. *On the Theory of the Earth.*
The best of Franklin's papers on geology.

1782. *Letter purporting to emanate from a petty German Prince and to be addressed to his officer in Command in America.*

1785. *On the Causes and Cure of Smoky Chimneys.*

1786. *Retort Courteous.*
Sending Felons to America.
Answers to the British clamor for the payment of American debts.

1789. *Address to the Public from the Pennsylvania Society for Promoting Abolition of Slavery.*

1789. *An Account of the Supremest Court of Judicature in Pennsylvania, viz. The Court of the Press.*

1790. *Martin's Account of his Consulship.*
   A parody of a pro-slavery speech in Congress.

1791. *Autobiography.*
   The first edition.

1818. *Bagatelles.*
   The Bagatelles were first published in 1818 in William Temple Franklin's edition of his grandfather's works. The following are the most famous of these essays and the dates when they were written:
   1774? *A Parable Against Persecution.*
      Franklin called this the LI Chapter of *Genesis.*
   1774? *A Parable on Brotherly Love.*
   1778. *The Ephemera, an Emblem of Human Life.*
      A new rendition of an earlier essay on Human Vanity.
   1779. *The Story of the Whistle.*
   1779? *The Levee.*
   1779? *Proposed New Version of the Bible.*
      Part of the first chapter of *Job* modernized.
   (1779. Published) *The Morals of Chess.*
   1780? *The Handsome and Deformed Leg.*
   1780. *Dialogue between Franklin and the Gout.*
      (Published in 1802.)

1802. *A Petition of the Left Hand.*

1806. *The Art of Procuring Pleasant Dreams*

MAY WE HELP?

THE PUBLISHERS of *Star* books have tried to maintain a high standard in the selection of titles for their list, and to offer a consistent quality of workmanship and material. They trust that the book you have just read has, in part at least, earned your esteem for other titles in their list.

They are trying to make the *Star Library* comprehend the best in the literary fields of biography, science, history, true adventure, travel, art, philosophy, psychology, etc.

Believing that you will be interested in other books of a nature similar to that which you have just finished reading, the publishers have reproduced on the following pages a few extracts from other *Star* books. These are pages picked at random. Although there is no continuity, we hope that they will give you some idea of the style in which the books are written and perhaps the character of the subject from which you may form an opinion as to its place on your personal book shelf.

CHAPTER XII

1884—1885

AMIDST the various researches undertaken in his laboratory, one study was placed by Pasteur above every other, one mystery constantly haunted his mind—that of hydrophobia. When he was received at the Académie Française, Renan, hoping to prove himself a prophet for once, said to him: "Humanity will owe to you deliverance from a horrible disease and also from a sad anomaly: I mean the distrust which we cannot help mingling with the caresses of the animal in whom we see most of nature's smiling benevolence."

The two first mad dogs brought into the laboratory were given to Pasteur, in 1880, by M. Bourrel, an old army veterinary surgeon who had long been trying to find a remedy for hydrophobia. He had invented a preventive measure which consisted in filing down the teeth of dogs, so that they should not bite into the skin; in 1874, he had written that vivisection threw no light on that disease, the laws of which were "impenetrable to science until now." It now occurred to him that, perhaps, the investigators in the laboratory of the Ecole Normale might be more successful than he had been in his kennels in the Rue Fontaine-au-Roi.

One of the two dogs he sent was suffering from what is called *dumb madness:* his jaw hung, half opened and paralyzed, his tongue was covered with foam, and his eyes full of wistful anguish; the other made ferocious darts at anything held out to him, with a rabid fury in his bloodshot eyes, and, in the hallucinations of his delirium, gave vent to haunting, despairing howls.

Much confusion prevailed at that time regarding this disease, its seat, its causes, and its remedy. Three things seemed positive: firstly, that the rabic virus was contained in the saliva of the mad animals; secondly, that it was communicated through

390

bites; and thirdly, that the period of incubation might vary from a few days to several months. Clinical observation was reduced to complete impotence; perhaps experiments might throw some light on the subject.

Bouley had affirmed in April, 1870, that the germ of the evil was localized in the saliva, and a new fact had seemed to support this theory. On December 10, 1880, Pasteur was advised by Professor Lannelongue that a five-year-old child, bitten on the face a month before, had just been admitted into the Hôpital Trousseau. The unfortunate little patient presented all the characteristics of hydrophobia: spasms, restlessness, shudders at the least breath of air, an ardent thirst, accompanied with an absolute impossibility of swallowing, convulsive movements, fits of furious rage—not one symptom was absent. The child died after twenty-four hours of horrible suffering—suffocated by the mucus which filled the mouth. Pasteur gathered some of that mucus four hours after the child's death, and mixed it with water; he then inoculated this into some rabbits, which died in less than thirty-six hours, and whose saliva, injected into other rabbits, provoked an almost equally rapid death. Dr. Maurice Raynaud, who had already declared that hydrophobia could be transmitted to rabbits through the human saliva, and who had also caused the death of some rabbits with the saliva of that same child, thought himself justified in saying that those rabbits had died of hydrophobia.

Pasteur was slower in drawing conclusions. He had examined with a microscope the blood of those rabbits which had died in the laboratory, and had found in it a micro-organism; he had cultivated this organism in veal broth, inoculated it into rabbits and dogs, and, its virulence having manifested itself in these animals, their blood had been found to contain that same microbe. "But," added Pasteur at the meeting of the Academy of Medicine (January 18, 1881), "I am absolutely ignorant of the connection there may be between this new disease and hydrophobia." It was indeed a singular thing that the deadly issue of this disease should occur so early, when the incubation period of hydrophobia is usually so long. Was there not some unknown microbe associated with the rabic saliva? This query was followed by experiments made with the saliva of children who had died of ordinary diseases, and even with that of healthy adults. Thuillier, following up and studying this saliva microbe and its special virulence with his usual patience, soon applied to it with success the method of attenuation by the oxygen in air. "What did we want with a new disease?" said a good many people, and yet it was making a step forward to clear up this preliminary confusion. Pasteur, in the course of a long and minute study of the saliva of mad dogs—in which it was so generally admitted that the virulent principle of rabies had its seat, that precautions against saliva were the only ones taken at post-mortem examinations—discovered many other mistakes. If a healthy dog's saliva contains many microbes, licked up by the dog in various kinds of dirt, what must be the condition of the mouth of a rabid dog, springing upon everything he meets, to tear it and bite it? The rabic virus is therefore associated with many other micro-organisms, ready to play their part and puzzle experimentalists; abscesses, morbid complications of all sorts, may intervene before the development of the rabic virus. Hydrophobia might evidently be developed by the inoculation of saliva, but it could not be confidently asserted that it would. Pasteur had made endless efforts to inoculate rabies to rabbits solely through the saliva of a mad dog; as soon as a case of hydrophobia occurred in Bourrel's kennels, a telegram informed the laboratory, and a few rabbits were immediately taken round in a cab.

One day, Pasteur having wished to collect a little saliva from the jaws of a rabid dog, so as to obtain it directly, two of Bourrel's assistants undertook to drag a mad bulldog, foaming at the mouth, from its cage; they seized it by means of a lasso, and stretched it on a table. These two men, thus associated with Pasteur in the same danger, with the same calm heroism, held the struggling, ferocious animal down with their powerful hands, whilst the scientist drew, by means of a glass tube held between his lips, a few drops of the deadly saliva.

But the same uncertainty followed the inoculation of the saliva; the incubation was so slow that weeks and months often elapsed whilst the result of an experiment was being anxiously awaited. Evidently the saliva was not a sure agent for experiments, and if more knowledge was to be obtained, some other means had to be found of obtaining it.

Magendie and Renault had both tried experimenting with rabic blood, but with no results, and Paul Bert had been equally unsuccessful. Pasteur tried in his turn, but also in vain. "We must try other experiments," he said, with his usual indefatigable perseverance.

As the number of cases observed became larger, he felt a growing conviction that hydrophobia has its seat in the nervous system, and particularly in the medulla oblongata. "The propagation of the virus in a rabid dog's nervous system can almost be observed in its every stage," writes M. Roux, Pasteur's daily associate in these researches, which he afterwards made the subject of his thesis. "The anguish and fury due to the excitation of the grey cortex of the brain are followed by an alteration of the voice and a difficulty in deglutition. The medulla oblongata and the nerves starting from it are attacked in their turn; finally, the spinal cord itself becomes invaded and paralysis closes the scene."

As long as the virus has not reached the nervous centres, it may sojourn for weeks or months in some point of the body; this explains the slowness of certain incubations, and the fortunate escapes after some bites from rabid dogs. The *a priori* supposition that the virus attacks the nervous centres went very far back; it had served as a basis to a theory enunciated by Dr. Duboué (of Pau), who had, however, not supported it by any experiments. On the contrary, when M. Galtier, a professor at the Lyons Veterinary School, had attempted experiments in that direction, he had to inform the Academy of Medicine, in January, 1881, that he had only ascertained the existence of virus in rabid dogs in the lingual glands and in the buccopharyngeal mucous membrane. "More than ten times, and always unsuccessfully, have I inoculated the product obtained by pressure of the cerebral substances of the cerebellum or of the medulla oblongata of rabid dogs."

Pasteur was about to prove that it was possible to succeed by operating in a special manner, according to a rigorous technique, unknown in other laboratories. When the post-mortem examination of a mad dog had revealed no characteristic lesion, the brain was uncovered, and the surface of the medulla oblongata scalded with a glass stick, so as to destroy any external dust or dirt. Then, with a long tube, previously put through a flame, a particle of the substance was drawn and deposited in a glass just taken from a stove heated up to 200° C., and mixed with a little water or sterilized broth by means of a glass agitator, also previously put through a flame. The syringe used for inoculation on the rabbit or dog (lying ready on the operating board) had been purified in boiling water.

Most of the animals who received this inoculation under the

skin succumbed to hydrophobia; that virulent matter was therefore more successful than the saliva, which was a great result
obtained.

"The seat of the rabic virus," wrote Pasteur, "is therefore
not in the saliva only: the brain contains it in a degree of
virulence at least equal to that of the saliva of rabid animals."
But, to Pasteur's eyes, this was but a preliminary step on the
long road which stretched before him; it was necessary that
all the inoculated animals should contract hydrophobia, and
the period of incubation had to be shortened.

It was then that it occurred to Pasteur to inoculate the rabic
virus directly on the surface of a dog's brain. He thought
that, by placing the virus from the beginning in its true medium,
hydrophobia would more surely supervene and the incubation
might be shorter. The experiment was attempted: a dog
under chloroform was fixed to the operating board, and a small,
round portion of the cranium removed by means of a trephine
(a surgical instrument somewhat similar to a fret-saw); the
tough fibrous membrane called the dura-mater, being thus
exposed, was then injected with a small quantity of the prepared virus, which lay in readiness in a Pravaz syringe. The
wound was washed with carbolic and the skin stitched together, the whole thing lasting but a few minutes. The
dog, on returning to consciousness, seemed quite the same
as usual. But, after fourteen days, hydrophobia appeared:
rabid fury, characteristic howls, the tearing up and devour-
ing of his bed, delirious hallucination, and finally, paralysis
and death.

A method was therefore found by which rabies was contracted surely and swiftly. Trephinings were again performed
on chloroformed animals—Pasteur had a great horror of useless
sufferings, and always insisted on anæsthesia. In every case,
characteristic hydrophobia occurred after inoculation on the
brain. The main lines of this complicated question were beginning to be traceable; but other obstacles were in the way.
Pasteur could not apply the method he had hitherto used, i.e.
to isolate, and then to cultivate in an artificial medium,
the microbe of hydrophobia, for he failed in detecting this microbe.
Yet its existence admitted of no doubt; perhaps it was beyond
the limits of human sight. "Since this unknown being is
living," thought Pasteur, "we must cultivate it; failing an

artificial medium, let us try the brain of living rabbits; it would indeed be an experimental feat!"

As soon as a trephined and inoculated rabbit died paralyzed, a little of his rabic medulla was inoculated to another; each inoculation succeeded another, and the time of incubation became shorter and shorter, until, after a hundred uninterrupted inoculations, it came to be reduced to seven days. But the virus, having reached this degree, the virulence of which was found to be greater than that of the virus of dogs made rabid by an accidental bite, now became fixed; Pasteur had mastered it. He could now predict the exact time when death should occur in each of the inoculated animals; his predictions were verified with surprising accuracy.

Pasteur was not yet satisfied with the immense progress marked by infallible inoculation and the shortened incubation; he now wished to decrease the degrees of virulence—when the attenuation of the virus was once conquered, it might be hoped that dogs could be made refractory to rabies. Pasteur abstracted a fragment of the medulla from a rabbit which had just died of rabies after an inoculation of the fixed virus; this fragment was suspended by a thread in a sterilized phial, the air in which was kept dry by some pieces of caustic potash lying at the bottom of the vessel and which was closed by a cotton-wool plug to prevent the entrance of atmospheric dusts. The temperature of the room where this desiccation took place was maintained at 23° C. As the medulla gradually became dry, its virulence decreased, until, at the end of fourteen days, it had become absolutely extinguished. This now inactive medulla was crushed and mixed with pure water, and injected under the skin of some dogs. The next day they were inoculated with medulla which had been desiccating for thirteen days, and so on, using increased virulence until the medulla was used of a rabbit dead the same day. These dogs might now be bitten by rabid dogs given them as companions for a few minutes, or submitted to the intracranial inoculations of the deadly virus: they resisted both.

Having at last obtained this refractory condition, Pasteur was anxious that his results should be verified by a Commission. The Minister of Public Instruction acceded to this desire, and a Commission was constituted in May, 1884, composed of Messrs. Béclard, Dean of the Faculty of Medicine, Paul Bert, Bouley, Villemin, Vulpian, and Tisserand, Director of the

Reprinted from Lord Charnwood's
ABRAHAM LINCOLN
by permission.

resolved to take over the forts and other property in the seceded States that had belonged to the Union, and the first Confederate general, Beauregard, was sent to Charleston to hover over Fort Sumter.

3. *The Inauguration of Lincoln.*

The first necessary business of the President-elect, while he watched the gathering of what Emerson named " the hurricane in which he was called to the helm," was to construct a strong Cabinet, to which may be added the seemingly unnecessary business forced upon him of dealing with a horde of pilgrims who at once began visiting him to solicit some office or, in rarer cases, to press their disinterested opinions. His Cabinet, designed in principle, as has been said, while he was waiting in the telegraph office for election returns, was actually constructed with some delay and hesitation. Lincoln could not know personally all the men he invited to join him, but he proceeded with the view of conjoining in his administration representatives of the chief shades of opinion which in this critical time it would be his supreme duty to hold together. Not only different shades of opinion, but the local sentiment of different districts had to be considered; he once complained that if the twelve Apostles had to be chosen nowadays the principle of locality would have to be regarded; but at this time there was very solid reason why different States should be contented and why he should be advised as to their feelings. His own chief rivals for the Presidency offered a good choice from both these points of view. They were Seward of New York, Chase of Ohio, Bates of Missouri, Cameron of Pennsylvania. Seward and Chase were both able and outstanding men: the former was in a sense the old Republican leader, but was more and more coming to be regarded as the typical " Conservative," or cautious Republican; Chase on the other hand was a leader of the " Radicals," who were " stern and unbending " in their attitude towards slavery and towards the South.

These two must be got and kept together if possible. Bates was a good and capable man who moreover came from Missouri, a border slave State, where his influence was much to be desired. He became Attorney-General. Cameron, an unfortunate choice as it turned out, was a very wealthy business man of Pennsylvania, representative of the weighty Protectionist influence there. After he had been offered office, which had been without Lincoln's authority promised him in the Republican Convention, Lincoln was dismayed by representations that he was "a bad, corrupted man"; he wrote a curious letter asking Cameron to refuse his offer; Cameron instead produced evidence of the desire of Pennsylvania for him; Lincoln stuck to his offer; the old Whig element among Republicans, the Protectionist element, and above all, the friends of the indispensable Seward, would otherwise have been outweighted in the Cabinet. Cameron eventually became for a time Secretary of War. To these Lincoln, upon somebody's strong representations, tried, without much hope, to add some distinctly Southern politician. The effort, of course, failed. Ultimately the Cabinet was completed by the addition of Caleb Smith of Indiana as Secretary of the Interior, Gideon Welles of Connecticut as Secretary of the Navy, and Montgomery Blair of Maryland as Postmaster-General. Welles, with the guidance of a brilliant subordinate, Fox, served usefully, was very loyal to Lincoln, had an antipathy to England which was dangerous, and kept very diligently a diary for which we may be grateful now. Blair was a vehement, irresponsible person with an influential connection, and, which was important, his influence and that of his family lay in Maryland and other border slave States. Of all these men, Seward, Secretary of State—that is, Foreign Minister and something more—and Chase, Secretary of the Treasury, most concern us. Lincoln's offer to Seward was made and accepted in terms that did credit to both men, and Seward, still smarting at his own defeat, was admirably loyal. But his friends, though they had secured the appointment of

Cameron to support them, thought increasingly ill of the prospects of a Cabinet which included the Radical Chase. On the very night before his inauguration Lincoln received from Seward, who had just been helping to revise his Inaugural Address, a letter withdrawing his acceptance of office. By some not clearly recorded exercise of that great power over men, which, if with some failures, was generally at his command, he forced Seward to see that the unconditional withdrawal of this letter was his public duty. It must throughout what follows be remembered that Lincoln's first and most constant duty was to hold together the jarring elements in the North which these jarring elements in his own Cabinet represented; and it was one of his great achievements that he kept together, for as long as was needful, able but discordant public servants who could never have combined together without him.

On February 11, 1861, Lincoln, standing on the gallery at the end of a railway car, upon the instant of departure from the home to which he never returned, said to his old neighbours (according to the version of his speech which his private secretary got him to dictate immediately after) : " My friends, no one, not in my situation, can appreciate my feeling of sadness at this parting. To this place, and the kindness of these people, I owe everything. Here I have lived for a quarter of a century, and have passed from a young to an old man. Here my children have been born and one is buried. I now leave, not knowing when or whether ever I may return, with a task before me greater than that which rested upon Washington. Without the assistance of that Divine Being who ever attended him, I cannot succeed. With that assistance, I cannot fail. Trusting in Him who can go with me, and remain with you, and be everywhere for good, let us confidently hope that all will yet be well. To His care commending you, as I hope in your prayers you will commend me, I bid you an affectionate farewell."

He was, indeed, going to a task not less great than Washington's, but he was going to it with a preparation in many respects far inferior to his. For the last eight years he had laboured as a public speaker, and in a measure as a party leader, and had displayed and developed comprehension, perhaps unequalled, of some of the larger causes which mould public affairs. But, except in sheer moral discipline, those years had done nothing to supply the special training which he had previously lacked, for high executive office. In such office at such a time ready decision in an obscure and passing situation may often be a not less requisite than philosophic grasp either of the popular mind or of eternal laws. The powers which he had hitherto shown would still be needful to him, but so too would other powers which he had never practised in any comparable position, and which nature does not in a moment supply. Any attempt to judge of Lincoln's Presidency—and it can only be judged at all when it has gone on some way—must take account, not perhaps so much of his inexperience, as of his own reasonable consciousness of it and his great anxiety to use the advice of men who were in any way presumably more competent.

He deliberately delayed his arrival in Washington and availed himself of official invitations to stay at four great towns and five State capitals which he could conveniently pass on his way. The journey abounded in small incidents and speeches, some of which exposed him to a little ridicule in the press, though they probably created an undercurrent of sympathy for him. Near one station where the train stopped lived a little girl he knew, who had recently urged upon him to wear a beard or whiskers. To this dreadful young person, and to that persistent good nature of his which was now and then fatuous, was due the ill-designed hairy ornamentation which during his Presidency hid the really beautiful modelling of his jaw and chin. He enquired for her at the station, had her fetched from the crowd, claimed her praise for this supposed improvement, and kissed her in presence of the press. In New York he was guilty of a more sinister and tragic misfeasance. In that city, where, if it may be said with respect, there has existed from of old a fashionable circle not convinced of its own gentility and insisting the more rigorously on minor decorum, Lincoln went to the opera, and history still deplores that this misguided man went there and sat there with his large hands in black kid gloves. Here perhaps it is well to say that the educated world of the Eastern States, including those who privately deplored Lincoln's supposed unfitness, treated its untried chief magistrate with that engrained good breeding to which it was utterly indifferent how plain a man he might be. His lesser speeches as he went were unstudied appeals to loyalty, with very simple avowals of inadequacy to his task, and expressions of reliance on the people's support when he tried to do his duty. To a man who can sometimes speak from the heart and to the heart as Lincoln did it is perhaps not given to be uniformly felicitous. Among these speeches was that delivered at Philadelphia, which has already been quoted, but most of them were not considered felicitous at the time. They were too unpretentious. Moreover, they contained sentences which seemed to understate the gravity of the crisis in a way which threw doubt on his own serious statesmanship. Whether they were felicitous or not, the intention of these much-criticised utterances was the best proof of his statesmanship. He would appeal to the steady loyalty of the North, but he was not going to arouse its passion. He assumed to the last that calm reflection might prevail in the South, which was menaced by nothing but "an artificial crisis." He referred to war as a possibility, but left no doubt of his own wish by all means to avoid it. "There will," he said, "be no bloodshed unless it be forced on the Government. The Government will not use force unless force is used against it."

Before he passed through Baltimore he received earnest communications from Seward and from General Scott. Each had received trustworthy information of a plot, which existed, to murder him in that city. Owing to their warnings he went through Baltimore secretly at night, so that his arrival in Washington, on February 23, was unexpected. This was his obvious duty, and nobody who knew him was ever in doubt of his personal intrepidity; but of course it helped to damp the effect of what many people would have been glad to regard as a triumphal progress.

On March 4, 1861, old Buchanan came in his carriage to escort his successor to the inaugural ceremony, where it was the ironical fate of Chief Justice Taney to administer the oath to a President who had already gone far to undo his great work. Yet a third notable Democrat was there to do a pleasant little act. Douglas, Lincoln's defeated rival, placed himself with a fine ostentation by his side, and, observing that he was embarrassed as to where to put his new tall hat and preposterous gold-knobbed cane, took charge of these encumbrances before the moment arrived for the most eagerly awaited of all his speeches. Lincoln had submitted his draft of his "First Inaugural" to Seward, and this draft with Seward's abundant suggestions of amendment has been preserved. It has considerable literary interest, and, by the readiness with which most of Seward's suggestions were adopted, and the decision with which some, and those not the least important, were set aside by Lincoln, it illustrates well the working relation which, after one short struggle, was to be established between these two men. By Seward's advice Lincoln added to an otherwise dry speech some concluding paragraphs of emotional appeal. The last sentence of the speech, which alone is much remembered, is Seward's in the first conception of it, Seward's in the slightly hackneyed phrase with which it ends, Lincoln's alone in the touch of haunting beauty which is on it.

His "First Inaugural" was by general confession an able state paper, setting forth simply and well a situation with which we are now familiar. It sets out dispassionately the state of the controversy on slavery, lays down with brief argument the position that the Union is indissoluble, and proceeds to define the duty of the Gov-